GERONIMO

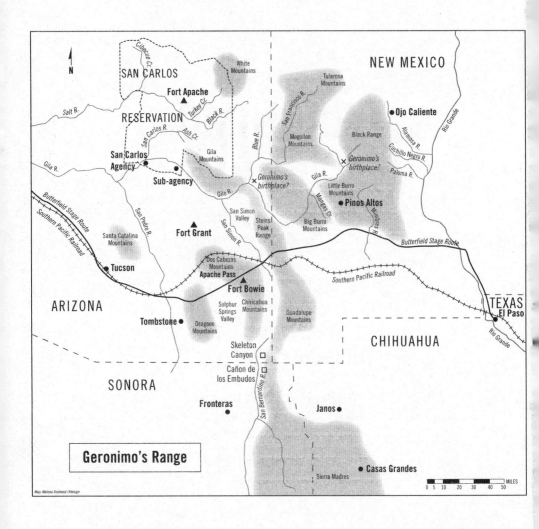

Geronimo's Range

N

SAN CARLOS

Cibecue Cr.

White Mountains

NEW MEXICO

Fort Apache ▲

Turkey Cr.

Tularosa Mountains

RESERVATION

Salt R.

Black R.

Ojo Caliente ●

San Carlos R.

Ash Cr.

Blue R.

San Francisco R.

Mogollon Mountains

Black Range

Alamosa R.

Rio Grande

Gila R.

San Carlos Agency

Gila Mountains

✕ Geronimo's birthplace?

Cuchillo Negro R.

Sub-agency

Gila R.

✕ Geronimo's birthplace?

Gila R.

Little Burro Mountains

Paloma R.

Mangas Cr.

Pinos Altos ●

San Pedro R.

San Simon Valley

Steins Peak Range

Big Burro Mountains

Mimbres R.

Butterfield Stage Route

Southern Pacific Railroad

Santa Catalina Mountains

Fort Grant ▲

San Simon R.

Butterfield Stage Route

Southern Pacific Railroad

Tucson ●

Dos Cabezas Mountains

Apache Pass

Fort Bowie ▲

ARIZONA

Sulphur Springs Valley

Chiricahua Mountains

Guadalupe Mountains

TEXAS
El Paso ●

Tombstone ●

Dragoon Mountains

CHIHUAHUA

Rio Grande

Skeleton Canyon ▢

Cañon de los Embudos ▢

SONORA

San Bernardino R.

Fronteras ●

Janos ●

Casas Grandes ●

Sierra Madres

MILES
0 5 10   20   30   40   50

Map: Melissa Rockwood / Rdesign

GERONIMO

Leadership Strategies of an American Warrior

Mike Leach
and Buddy Levy

GALLERY BOOKS

NEW YORK   LONDON   TORONTO   SYDNEY   NEW DELHI

G

Gallery Books
A Division of Simon & Schuster, Inc.
1230 Avenue of the Americas
New York, NY 10020

First Gallery Books hardcover edition May 2014

GALLERY BOOKS and colophon are registered trademarks of Simon & Schuster, Inc.

For information about special discounts for bulk purchases,
please contact Simon & Schuster Special Sales at 1-866-506-1949
or business@simonandschuster.com.

The Simon & Schuster Speakers Bureau can bring authors to your live event. For more information or to book an event, contact the Simon & Schuster Speakers Bureau at 1-866-248-3049 or visit our website at www.simonspeakers.com.

All photographs except the portrait of Geronimo on page 219 are courtesy of the Arizona Historical Society. The portrait on page 219 is courtesy of the Bridgeman Art Library.

Map courtesy Melissa Rockwood of Rdesign

Interior design by Davina Mock-Maniscalco
Jacket design by Christopher Sergio
Jacket photograph by A. F. Randall. Copyrighted 1886/Hulton Archive/Getty Images

Manufactured in the United States of America

10 9 8 7 6 5 4 3 2 1

Library of Congress Cataloging-in-Publication Data
Leach, Mike, 1961–
Geronimo : leadership strategies of an American warrior / Mike Leach, Buddy Levy.
   pages   cm
Includes bibliographical references and index.
   1. Geronimo, 1829–1909. 2. Apache Indians—Kings and rulers—Biography. 3. Apache Indians—History. 4. Leadership—United States—Case studies. I. Levy, Buddy, 1960–
II. Title.
E99.A6L38 2014
979.004'97250092—dc23   2013040851
[B]

ISBN 978-1-4767-3493-4
ISBN 978-1-4767-3498-9 (ebook)

Tough terrain breeds tough men.

—HERODOTUS

CONTENTS

FOREWORD

IN THE SPRING OF 2009, I traveled to Lubbock, Texas, to interview Mike Leach for a cover story I was writing about him for *Texas Monthly*. The preceding fall, he and his Texas Tech football team had electrified the nation with their dramatic run at a national championship. Though they had fallen short, for a few dazzling weeks the attention of America's football fans had been riveted on the high plains of West Texas. I was going there to try to figure out how a team with players few or no other elite football programs wanted could possibly have pulled off such a season. How Leach's scrappy, underdog Red Raiders could conceivably have knocked off the Nos. 1 and 8 teams in the country on successive weekends. If this had been his only such exploit, he might not have merited the cover story. But he had been working this sort of dark magic for twenty years at five different schools in three collegiate athletic divisions. His teams came as close to unstoppable as anything the college football world had seen. It was hard to find anyone who did not think Mike Leach was a certified football genius.

Which was why it was odd, half an hour after I landed in his office at Texas Tech, that Mike and I found ourselves deep in conversation about Native Americans. I was working on a book at the time about the Comanches that would become a national bestseller a year or so later as *Empire of the Summer Moon*, so I was very current on Indian history. So, as it turned out, was Mike. I had heard that he was smart and had eclectic interests—that included the history of piracy, surfing, Winston

Churchill, chimpanzees, and the philosophy of John Wooden—but I wasn't prepared to encounter a scholar of the American West. We talked about Comanches, about whom he knew a great deal, and we talked about his own childhood in Cody, Wyoming, and his lifelong interest in Native Americans. Then we got around to Apaches, who turned out to be his true love. I knew a little bit about them. Mike knew a lot about them, especially their war leader Geronimo. I listened, enraptured, much longer than I should have. I was there as a reporter and was supposed to be interviewing him about *football*, not talking about General Nelson Miles and Geronimo's renegade Chiricahuas. I had wasted valuable time. But it was fun just listening to him. I found out later that he used some of his Apache material in his talks with his players. Indians were an interest of mine. For Mike, they were a coaching tool.

It didn't occur to me at the time why Mike would be so interested in the character of Geronimo. But when he told me a couple of years later that he was working on a book about the Apache leader, it suddenly made perfect sense. Mike is not just a football coach. He is a *renegade* football coach, a man who has always done things differently, always operated on the margins of what the football world considered acceptable. That began with his decision, after having graduated in the top third of his law class at Pepperdine University, to attend a sports academy and then take a $3,000-a-year job coaching football at Cal State, San Luis Obispo. It continued in the form of his football teams, which did things that no one else did. I can remember moving to Austin and watching Mike's teams at Tech do things that seemed—back then—to stop just short of lunacy. He would spread his linemen out, four feet apart, leaving apparently giant gaps that just beckoned to defenders. He would empty out the backfield and cover the field with receivers. He threw almost every down. He never huddled. He rarely even punted, preferring to go for it—the ultimate football madness—on fourth down deep in his own territory. He didn't much like to kick field goals, either. Much of this is common in college and pro football today. Almost none of it was when Mike started out.

This sort of radically original behavior is what *Geronimo: Leadership*

Strategies of an American Warrior is all about. Geronimo's brilliance was both his eclecticism—he was a war leader, shaman, translator, negotiator, healer, and mentor, among other callings—and his defiance of conventional wisdom. With the entire post–Civil War world stacked against them, Indians were not *supposed to* be able to continue fighting past the mid-1870s. There was no way to win. Even the über-warriors of the Comanches, Cheyennes, and Sioux had surrendered. That did not deter Geronimo, who fought longer than anyone, finally tying up fully one-quarter of the active American army just to hunt down him and his band of Apaches. By the 1880s, write Leach and Levy, "only Geronimo and the Chiricahua were still free and fighting."

Thus Geronimo, the great—if brutal—war leader, becomes a classic paradigm of leadership. The book rightly focuses on how he was able to do what he did, on the parts of his character that led him to achieve greatness. Mike is ably helped in this endeavor by Buddy Levy, a historian who has written two excellent books about the Americas and who is steeped in the histories of Native Americans in the nineteenth century. Together they have written an enthralling little history that I found very hard to put down.

S. C. Gwynne

Gwynne is the author of *Empire of the Summer Moon,* a finalist for the Pulitzer Prize. His book *Rebel Yell: The Violence, Passion, and Redemption of Stonewall Jackson* will be published by Scribner in 2014.

CAST OF CHARACTERS

Key Apache Warriors

Cochise—one of the great Chiricahua (Chokonen) chiefs. Born c. 1805. No known pictures exist but he was said to be very tall and imposing, over six feet and very muscular. Son-in-law to Mangas Coloradas. Died in 1874, probably from stomach cancer.

Chihuahua—chief of the Warm Springs band (Red Paint people) of the Chiricahua. Fought alongside Geronimo in the resistance. Died in 1901.

Fun—probably a cousin to Geronimo and among his best, most trusted warriors. Fun committed suicide in captivity in 1892, after becoming jealous over his young wife, whom he also shot. Only slightly wounded, she recovered.

Juh—pronounced "Whoa," "Ho," or sometimes "Who." Chief of the Nedhni band of the Apache, he married Ishton, Geronimo's "favorite" sister. Juh and Geronimo were lifelong friends and battle brothers. Juh died in 1883.

Loco—chief of the Warm Springs band. Born in 1823, the same year as Geronimo. Once was mauled by a bear and killed it single-handedly with a knife, but his face was clawed and his left eye was blinded and disfigured. Known as the "Apache Peacemaker," he preferred peace to war and tried to live under reservation rules. Died as a prisoner of war from "causes unknown" in 1905, at age eighty-two.

Lozen—warrior woman and Chief Victorio's sister. She was a medicine woman and frequent messenger for Geronimo. She fought alongside Geronimo in his long resistance.

Mangas Coloradas—Born in 1790, he was the most noted chief of the Bedonkohe Apache. A massive man for his era, at 6'6" and 250 pounds, he was Geronimo's central mentor and influence. He was betrayed and murdered by the U.S. military in 1863. Geronimo called his murder "the greatest wrong ever done to the Indians."

Mangas—son of the great chief Mangas Coloradas, but did not succeed his father as chief because of his youth and lack of leadership. Died as a prisoner of war in 1901.

Naiche—Cochise's youngest son. Succeeded older brother Taza after he died, becoming the last chief of the free Chiricahua Apache.

Nana—brother-in-law to Geronimo and chief of the Warm Springs band. Sometimes referred to as "Old Nana." Died as a prisoner of war in 1896.

Victorio—chief of the Warm Springs band. Noted and courageous leader and a brilliant military strategist. Brother and mentor to warrior woman Lozen. Slain by Mexicans in the massacre of Tres Castillos in 1880.

Key Apache Adversaries—U.S. Military Figures and Civilian Apache Agents

Clum, John P.—born 1851. Civilian Apache agent at the San Carlos and Fort Apache reservations. Nicknamed "Turkey Gobbler" by the Apache for his strutting nature. Later became mayor of Tombstone, Arizona. His claim to fame was being the only person to successfully "capture" Geronimo. Died in 1932.

Crook, General George—born 1828. Called America's "greatest Indian fighter." He was the first to use Indian scouts and was crucial in ending the Apache Wars. Called Nantan Lupan ("the Tan Wolf") by the Apache, he advocated for Apache rights while at the same time becoming one of Geronimo's greatest adversaries. Crook negotiated Geronimo's "surrender" at the Cañon de los Embudos. He died in 1890.

Gatewood, Lieutenant Charles B.—born 1853. A latecomer to the Apache Wars, Gatewood used scouts but failed to bring in Victorio. However, Gatewood would ultimately negotiate the terms of Geronimo's final surrender to General Nelson A. Miles in 1886. He died in 1896.

Miles, General Nelson A.—born in 1839. Civil War veteran best known for accepting Geronimo's final surrender. Fought Sioux and Cheyenne Indians after the Battle of Little Big Horn. He died at the age of eighty-five in 1925 and was buried with full honors at Arlington National Cemetery.

Sieber, Al—born 1843. A German-American, he served as the army's chief of scouts during the Apache Wars. Died in 1907.

GERONIMO

Warrior, shaman, negotiator, and war leader Geronimo
riding a warhorse in Apache country.

Geronimo and the American Spirit

WHEN I WAS A KID growing up in Wyoming, there were cowboys and Indians, and I always wanted to be an Indian. We played to see which tribe was the toughest, which lasted the longest, which put up the most resistance. And because historically the last to surrender were the Apache, I viewed them as having the highest level of achievement. The Apache offered steady resistance and held out the longest. That started my interest. Geronimo was the best of them—he possessed a kind of greatness. Greatness is well respected by everyone in all cultures; people just want to be able to see it and feel it and be in the presence of it, even if just for a short time. Geronimo personified a life-way of excellence, and others around him rallied behind that excellence and followed him. It's compelling. In his life he was a living example of greatness, and people—even his adversaries—could feel it.

I admire his commitment to being the best. He possessed great integrity and commitment because of his pride in being an Apache. He was committed to his religion. He had for a long time an extremely high level of success—and, whether rational or irrational, he felt this was his destiny. Like he was a man of destiny. He believed it was what he was put on earth to do, and he pursued his convictions vigorously. He personified independence and assertive action. Geronimo and the Apache epitomize the American Spirit. There is much for us to learn from the man and his people—and insights to take away from his remarkable times.

The Geronimo story taken as a whole is a tragedy. It's tragic that the Apache were not allowed to continue to live as they had for centuries, but things change. Times change. In the end, the way the United States handled the Indians was not done in a fair and proper fashion, and the episode remains very much a black eye on this country. We weren't fair and true and right in the way we handled a proud people. It's tough to yank a people out of their time and setting. We took traditional no-madic hunter-gatherers and tried to turn them into sedentary farm-ers—how in the hell did we think that was going to turn out?

The triumph in this story, however, is in the process rather than the final destination, in the incredible feats that Geronimo and his people accomplished and how they pulled them off. I want to consider Geroni-mo's story and ask: What is greatness and how do we attain it? I hope you enjoy the story, the commentary, and the lessons.

Origins of the Apache: Who Were "The People"?

ONE THING THAT fascinates me about history is how hard it is to pin down. Example: The name *Apache* itself is unclear. It might be a Spanish pronunciation of the Zuni word *apachu*, which means "enemy." I like that explanation because I like the idea of enemies, and the Apache had their share. It's a fact that the Apache traded with the Zuni, the pueblo dwellers of northern New Mexico, and raided them whenever they could. Now, let's get something straight right out of the gate. The Apache were raiders. "Raiding" means stealing. Pillaging. Taking from others what you want or need. The

LESSON: *Be curious about everything. Read everything you can find about your obsessions.*

Greeks did it. The Vikings did it. The Huns did it. Pirates did it. Let's face it: The American pioneers and settlers did it. They stole the Indians' land. I'm not saying raiding is right, but it's a historical tradition, and some people were expert raiders. The Apache were expert raiders. In Apache, the word *raiding* meant literally "to search out enemy property."[1]

There's another theory that the term *Apache* comes from the Ute name for the tribe, *Awa'tehe,* which means "people of the mountains."[2] My favorite explanation is that the word *Apache* comes from the Spanish verb *apachurrar,* "to crush," referring to the Apache tendency to turn enemy captives over to the women and children of the tribe, who then pounded them to death with stones. It was best NOT to get captured by Apaches.

What we do know is that the Apache called themselves *N'de,* meaning "The People" (also spelled *Tinneh, Dine,* or *Tinde*).

Conventional wisdom (plus linguistic and DNA evidence) suggests that they arrived via Canada and Alaska as early as the thirteenth century.[3] The thing is, I'm not that conventional. There are other theories. I've never liked the theory that the Indians came over the Bering Strait land bridge. I have thought that theory absurd since I was a child. If that was such a good idea, why didn't the Europeans do it that way? Also, where are all the skeletons and artifacts that verify such a notion? In 1947 Norwegian researcher/explorer Thor Heyerdahl sailed his handmade balsa-wood raft *Kon-Tiki* 5,000 miles over 101 days from South America to Polynesia. His journey showed that ancient South American mariners had the capability of sailing great distances— which questioned accepted theories about the peopling of the Americas. Maybe the earliest Americans came from Asia by boat and landed in North America. Heyerdahl showed that the continent's inhabitants didn't necessarily come to North America via the Bering Strait land bridge and may have come from a variety of directions.[4]

Anyway, before contact with the Spaniards and their discovery of the horse (the Spaniards brought the horse back to North America after it had become extinct here—but that's another story), the Apache roamed on foot, following buffalo herds, using domesticated dogs to carry their belongings with packs, or towing travois (tepee poles wrapped with hides to make a kind of trailer). The Spanish conquistador Coronado came to North America in search of the Seven Cities of Gold and was probably the first Anglo to see "The People" (Geronimo's ancestors) wandering New Mexico in 1541. He called them "Querechos," a name he learned from the pueblo dwellers of Tiguex (originally twelve pueblos on the eastern Rio Grande of central New Mexico, which are now the Sandia Pueblo).

Coronado said that the Querechos had the most impressive physiques he had seen in the New World. They lived at that time off of the buffalo, making their tepees with their hides, wearing their skins, sewing with thread from their sinew, making awls and knives from their bones. They even made drinking jugs from the animal's bladders or intestines,

MONGOL WARLORDS AND STEAK TARTARE: A DIGRESSION

I once heard that thirteenth-century Mongol warlords like Genghis Khan rode around with meat under their saddles to tenderize it before they ate it—and I wondered if that was true. I also wondered if the Apache did it too. Turns out that while the Mongols (and Tartars) actually DID in fact put strips of raw meat beneath their saddles, the reason was to protect their horses' skin and also heal their saddle sores. According to *The Cambridge Medieval History*, 1924, after a day of riding with the meat under the saddle, the meat would have been downright inedible—rank and soaked with horsehair and horse sweat.

Despite the historical truth, the lore continues that "steak tartare" got its name from the Tartar peoples of central Asia—when in fact the dish originated in France in the twentieth century, named not for the Tartars who ate raw meat but for the sauce (tartar) served with it.

And no, there's no evidence that Geronimo and his Apaches rode around with strips of meat under their saddles (or under their butts when they were riding bareback). But they did carry their dried pemmican with them as they rode.

Source: Craig S. Smith, "The Raw Truth: Don't Blame the Mongols (or Their Horses)," *New York Times*, April 6, 2005.

and relied on its blood as a sustaining beverage. Coronado was fascinated by their technique. He said, "They clean a large intestine, fill it with blood, and hang it around their necks, to drink when they are thirsty. Cutting open the belly of an animal, they squeeze out the chewed grass and drink the juice."[5] I like that kind of ingenuity and resourcefulness.

They survived on buffalo meat, eating it slightly roasted or raw, depending on the situation. They dried the meat in the sun to make pemmican, or jerky, which made it highly portable. They were proud, fiercely independent, and dangerous. You did not want to fight them. But Coronado also said if you left them alone they were a "gentle people."[6] As we'll see, with the arrival of the white man, "The People," the Apache, would become less gentle.

CHAPTER ONE

The Making of a Warrior (Discipline)

They Called Him Geronimo: What's in a Name?

GERONIMO WAS BORN in 1823 at the headwaters of the Gila River east of the border of present-day Arizona and New Mexico.* His Bedonkohe (pronounced Bed-on-koh-hey) Apache name was Goyahkla, meaning "One Who Yawns." But he wasn't bored or boring. He was defiant, independent, and exceptional. The story of how he got his later name is a good one. In a revenge attack against the Mexicans, the young warrior Goyahkla fought like a fiend, rushing in repeatedly from cover, killing an enemy with every charge, and stealing the dead man's rifle. Each time he came at them, the Mexicans cried out in terror, "Look out, Geronimo!"—mispronouncing his given name or calling out for the help of Saint Jerome (which translates in Spanish to "Geronimo"). His Apache people took up the battle cry, and "Goyahkla" became "Geronimo."[1]

---

* The exact place of Geronimo's birth is unknown and contested. See the map at the front of the book. Historians are split—some say Arizona, some say New Mexico. Geronimo himself said Arizona, but back then it was neither Arizona nor Mexico—it was Apache country. See S. M. Barrett, *His Own Story*, 3–4; Debo, *Geronimo*, 7–8. His birth date is often cited as 1829, but it was more likely 1823.

During his raids and escapes across the American Southwest, the mention of his name had the power to enrage the highest brass of the U.S. military—including presidents—and to terrify white settlers who bolted their doors and windows and scribbled frantic letters to the White House begging for protection. Over time, Geronimo's name has come to symbolize courage, daring, wild abandon, and leadership. Revering his courage, World War II paratroopers shouted "GERONIMO!" as they leaped from airplanes into battle.

The first time I ever heard the name "Geronimo" was as a small child watching Bugs Bunny. I think it involved Yosemite Sam yelling "GERONIMO!" as he was preparing to pull one of his courageous and daring stunts. The last significant time I heard the name Geronimo was when U.S. Navy SEALs moved in to kill Osama bin Laden. The mission was code-named "Geronimo," which caused considerable controversy. I can't think of another historical figure whose name has withstood the test of time and been used in as many contexts as Geron-

THE CHIRICAHUA APACHE BANDS AND THEIR RANGE

Geronimo was a member of the Bedonkohe band of the Chiricahua Apache. The Chiricahua—the most warlike of all the Apache tribes—were split up into local bands, each band following one or more chiefs. Before the whites came, the Chiricahua range included what is today called southeastern Arizona, southwestern New Mexico, and the northern parts of the Mexican states of Sonora and Chihuahua.

Geronimo's Bedonkohe band was flanked by three other Chiricahua bands. Farthest south, below the border that in 1848 would divide the United States and Mexico, dwelled the Nednhi (Ned-nee) band. They inhabited the harsh, rugged terrain of the Sierra Madre in northern Sonora—a place Geronimo would come to deeply love and where he would spend much time. Southwest of the Bedonkohe—comprising the Dragoon and Chiricahua mountains and valleys in southeastern Arizona—lived the Chokonen (Cochise's band—he would become their greatest chieftain). The Chihenne (Chee-hen-ee) band lived to the east, between the Mimbres River and the Rio Grande. They were called the "Red Paint People."

The main bands were allies, and if necessary, they banded together in wartime when large numbers of warriors were needed. There were also subgroups within these main groups, with the Warm Springs band the most prominent of many Chihenne subgroups. All of the bands had similar life-ways, cultural practices, and language.

Not all the Apache tribes were friendly, however. The White Mountain Apache to the west—the largest division of the Western Apache—sometimes scrapped with the Chiricahua Apache; they raided each other's lands and even stole each other's women.

But throughout most of Geronimo's life, these groups all got along peacefully. During Geronimo's lifetime, the entire Chiricahua tribe at its height—including all bands—numbered just three thousand people. (There were probably never more than ten to twelve thousand Apache living at any one time in their entire history.) The population in Geronimo's day became severely depleted due to warfare, and later, as they succumbed to incarceration and disease.

Sources: Mails, *The People Called Apache*, 11–17, 207–210. Opler, *An Apache Life-Way*, 1–4. Sweeney, *Cochise*, 4–6. Utley, *Geronimo*, 7. There's also a great summary from remaining Fort Sill Apache members on their tribal history: http://www.fortsillapache-nsn.gov/index.php?option=com_content&view=article&id=5&Itemid=6.

imo's. His name is consistently associated with courage, ingenuity, and resourcefulness.

WARRIOR TRAINING—ONLY THE STRONG SURVIVE

>>Pre–Warrior Training and Apprenticeship

GERONIMO GREW UP on the middle fork of the Gila River, near the famous Gila cliff dwellings in southwestern New Mexico. Geronimo and his people camped there, protected by towering canyon walls. By now the buffalo were all but gone, and the Apache had become mountain people, tough and adaptable, able to thrive in mountains other humans found unlivable. In winter they'd move to the lower valleys to hunt. Though nomadic, the Apache did tend small tracts of beans, corn, melons, and pumpkins, stashing their harvest in secret caves for the lean, harsh winters. Geronimo's family lived in clusters of dome-shaped brush houses called *wickiups,* roofed with yucca-leaf strands. They also sometimes slept in taller, peak-shaped tepees like those used by Plains Indians.

Geronimo recalled his childhood fondly: "As a babe I rolled on the dirt floor of my father's tepee, hung in my *tsoch* [Apache name for cradleboard] at my mother's back, or suspended from the bough of a tree. I was warmed by the sun, rocked by the winds, and sheltered by the trees as other Indian babes."[2] His mother taught him the legends of his people, stories about the sky and stars; his father told him of the brave deeds of their warriors, about hunting, and about the "glories of the warpath."[3]

From Geronimo's earliest memories he was a warrior. He and the other boys played hide-and-seek among the rocks and cottonwoods along the river, pretending to be warriors. They practiced sneaking up on made-up enemies—rocks or trees—and hid for many hours, utterly silent, practicing the stealth and patience they would need when they became warriors. This early practice would pay dividends later.

Geronimo's entire boyhood was a long and rigorous apprenticeship in hunting, gathering, physical fitness, mental toughness, horsemanship, and warfare. To develop their deadly accuracy, the boys cut willow branches, then rolled little mud pellets in their hands and stuck them on the ends for spear points; these were whipped at birds on branches and rodents on the ground. They made slingshots from animal hide and sinew, and they shot bows and arrows from an early age, practicing hours on end for distance and accuracy. They were so into shooting their arrows that they sometimes stayed out all day, never stopping, not even to eat.[4]

LESSON: *Serve an apprenticeship to develop excellence and a useful set of skills.*

Geronimo could shoot a bow and arrow with skill by age five. He learned to hunt from his father and elder warriors, who taught him to crawl silently along the ground, snatching prey with his hands. To cele-brate his first kill, he ate the animal's raw heart, showing it respect and gaining his adversary's strength. To stalk larger game like deer and ante-lope, he learned how to crawl along the ground for hours wearing the hide, head, and antlers of a deer or antelope as a disguise. He studied his prey's habits, knew what they ate and where they grazed, knew their different tracks. He hunted rabbits, squirrels, turkeys, and grouse too. Geronimo learned to build small fires at night to lure bats, then heave his moccasins at the creatures in flight with enough accuracy to knock them to the ground—he'd then pounce on them and kill them with his bare hands.[5]

I really like the Apache technique for hunting ducks—it's innova-tive. In early winter, when ducks tend to flock in huge numbers on lakes, the Apache would take hundreds of gourds—dried and hollowed-out pumpkins and big squash—and set them afloat on the lakes. The gourds would blow across the lake and the Apache would go over and retrieve them, then repeat the process. At first the gourds would startle the ducks and they'd fly off. But over time the ducks would get used to the gourds bobbing along the water and floating past. Once the ducks had learned not to fear the gourds, the Apache would take gourds and cut holes for the eyes, nose, and mouth. Then they'd wade neck deep into the water, with only their gourd-head poking out above the surface. They'd sneak up on the ducks while imitating the bobbing gourd motion with their heads; when close enough, they'd drag the ducks under water by their feet and stuff them in a bag. It was ingenious and highly effective.[6]

>>Warrior Training

WARRIOR TRAINING WAS brutal. Geronimo had to wake up well be-fore dawn and run up to the top of a mountain and back before sunrise. The goals were discipline, a strong mind, and legs and lungs so devel-oped that no enemy could outrun

⮞⮞⮞⮜⮘⮞⮞⮜⮜⮜
LESSON: *Be physically better than others and take pride in your physical and mental well-being.*
⮞⮞⮞⮜⮘⮞⮞⮜⮜⮜

the Apache warrior. These goals were realized. One elder put it this way to his young son: "Your mind will be developed. . . . Getting up early in the morning, running to the top of that hill and back will give you a strong mind, a strong heart, and a strong body."[7]

Running was essential for the Apache way of life, and they worked at it endlessly. They were on foot more than on horseback because there were rarely enough horses to go around, and because they could sneak up on enemies better on foot. As they trained, the runs got longer and more difficult. Sometimes they had to carry heavy packs on their backs and, to prove their endurance and mental tenacity, remain awake continuously for a day and a night or even longer, without food. Part of this training included running many miles before daylight, then an icy morning plunge in a frozen stream in only their breechcloths, all before they were allowed to build a fire.

One of the training tactics I found most interesting was this: Young boys had to run more than ten miles, up and down mountains, carrying water or rocks in their mouths the entire time; they could spit out the rocks or water only at the end of the run. This proved their endurance and toughness. The exercise also taught them to breathe through their noses.[8] If they failed, they had to do it again—and again,

LESSON: *The best are those who know they are tougher than their competition.*

and again—until they got it right. Geronimo did not fail. Later, as a trainer, he would teach this skill to others.

The Apache were tougher—*much* tougher—than we are today. Apache warrior training was often a matter of life or death, and only the strongest survived. Besides running for miles and miles in the heat and cold with a mouthful of water or rocks, apprentice warriors were encouraged to fight until they bled. Teams of four stood across from each other in rock-slinging competitions. It was like playing dodgeball with stones. The object was to teach quickness and evasiveness—boys had to duck and dodge to keep from being hit. There were casualties. If a rock hit you in the head, you were often severely injured or died. If one hit you in the arm, the bone often broke. Such training developed nimble, evasive warriors.[9]

Rock slinging progressed to arrow shooting in the training regimen. The trainer placed teams of boys about fifty feet apart. On the trainer's command, they started shooting. The arrows were too small and light to be fatal, but sometimes they'd become embedded in their bodies. I like this quote from anthropologist Morris Opler, who lived among the Apache and studied their way of life and training: "I tell you they have fun too! They hardly ever hit each other. But I remember one boy who had been shot in the eye, and it put his eye out."[10] You just have to admire and revere such training, commitment, and dedication—especially at such a young age. Even this early, training was life or death.

Apache Weapons

BEFORE THEY GOT modern firearms, warriors used traditional weapons. They made five-foot-long bows from flexible wood like mulberry. The strings were stretched and dried deer sinew. They made arrows from three-foot cane shafts and fletched them with eagle or hawk feathers. The tips were sharpened and fire-hardened, then armed with obsidian or flint arrowheads. The Apache sometimes used poisoned arrowheads. There were a few ways of doing this. One was by cutting the heads off of rattlesnakes and squeezing venom from the fangs. Or they'd get poison juice from insects.

LESSON: *Always have the right tools for the job and know how to use all of them precisely.*

My favorite is this one: They'd take a deer's stomach, fill it with a mixture of animal blood and poison plants, and then bury it long enough for the contents to ferment and become toxic.[11] The Apache were so well trained that warriors could fire up to seven arrows at an enemy before the first hit its target—at a range of more than 150 yards.[12] You did not want to

THE NOVICE COMPLEX

Before an Apache could become a full-fledged warrior, he had to participate in four raids under the strict guidance of elders. It was a vital initiation period. There were very particular rules about the novice's conduct and treatment. He had to learn specific warpath language that only warriors knew, and on his novice raids he was not allowed to do any of the stealing of horses or cattle, or any of the fighting if it broke out. He had to remain away from the enemy camp, usually up on a hill or bluff where he could watch what went on and learn how things were done. An elder—a guide or trainer—stayed with him to explain the raid's tactics and strategies. During the raid, the novice was supposed to speak only when spoken to, and just listen. He could eat only cold food, and he had to stay awake until given permission to lie down and sleep. The novice did all the camp chores on a raid: fetched water, collected and cut wood, took care of the horses, and cooked all the food. The novice helped guard the camps too. The warriors watched the novice carefully—as did the elder in charge of his instruction. The novice wore a special cap or headdress with the feathers of four birds in it: quail, eagle, oriole, and hummingbird. The hummingbird feathers were to make him run fast and be hard to see as he moved, like a hummingbird. After returning from his fourth raid as a novice, if there was no objection from the warriors and if the novice performed all his duties with excellence, then he became a man and a warrior. On his fifth raid, he was sent to the front and allowed to participate fully. He could also now take a wife.

Sources: Opler, *An Apache Life-Way,* 137–139; Goodwin, *Western Apache Raiding,* 288–98; Mails, *The People Called Apache,* 260–262.

be hit with one of these. An informant noted, "A man hit with an arrow dipped in poison turns black."[13] He also died a horrible death.* The poisoned arrows were so toxic that the Apache had to be very, very careful

---

* I wondered about this turning-black condition and read about poisoned arrows used by tribes along the Amazon. A conquistador on Francisco Orellana's Amazon expedition in 1541 got hit in the foot with an arrow treated with the toxins of poison tree frogs, and witnesses reported that "the wound turned very black and the poison gradually made its way up the leg, like a living thing." When the poison reached his heart, he died (Levy, *River of Darkness,* 177).

handling them, making sure not to stick themselves while riding or running into battle. They usually waited until they were stationary and settled before busting out the poison and applying it.

The lance (or spear) was made from a fifteen-foot-long agave stalk, sometimes wrapped with skin from deer legs, then sharpened to a fine point or tipped with knives or bayonets taken from enemies. Warriors also armed themselves with war clubs and stone knives for hand-to-hand combat.[14]

Every aspect of Apache learning and apprenticeship systematically trained men for warfare: shooting; dodging and hiding; tracking; learning to map their surrounding terrain mentally; and remembering geographic features, landmasses, and rivers in order to find their way back to camp. Apprenticeship hardened the young warriors and prepared them for raiding and war—which was a life-or-death proposition every time out.

Geronimo Becomes a Warrior

BY AGE SEVENTEEN Geronimo was so skilled he could shoot poisoned arrows with deadly aim while dangling from a pony's neck. By then he had also completed four raiding expeditions, and because of his skill and bravery in attacking Mexicans and stealing their horses, he earned full warrior status. Geronimo had developed into an impressive young man—some described him as handsome, while others called his face mean-looking and scowling.

Warriors could take wives, so he courted Alope, a girl of the Nednhi Apache whom he'd been eyeing for a long time. Geronimo described her as "slender and delicate," adding that "as soon as the tribal council granted me the privileges of a warrior, I went to see her father concerning our marriage. He asked many ponies for her. I made no reply, but in a few days appeared before his lodge with the herd of ponies and took with me Alope. This was all the marriage ceremony necessary in our tribe."[15] Geronimo didn't say so, but he had most likely stolen the ponies from Mexico, his favorite raiding area.

Geronimo brought Alope back to his tepee. The Apache women built and maintained the tepees and wickiups, kept the camp organized, and did much more: They gathered food like piñon nuts, acorns, juniper berries, and mesquite beans; they collected and carried firewood, sometimes for many miles; they wove baskets and bowls from grasses and reeds (the Apache, being nomads, made very little pottery); they sewed saddlebags; and they made tiswin, their important corn liquor

SEXUAL PRACTICES AND RELATIONS BETWEEN THE SEXES

The sex lives of the Chiricahua, like all aspects of their existence, were dictated by long-standing customs and traditions. The Chiricahua were modest and undemonstrative when it came to sex, though obviously you have to account for individual differences. Sex two to three times a week was thought "normal" for married people—less when the men were hunting or raiding or warring. Adultery was a serious offense, though more so for the women than men—and there were repercussions on both sides. Relations between the sexes on this matter got very combative and violent, even fatal. If a woman cheated, the husband sometimes resorted to violence, even beating her or, in extreme cases, snipping the end of her nose off to mark her as an adulteress (the idea was to make her undesirable to other men). Wives who caught their husbands usually just scolded them, though some punished their husbands by stabbing them while they slept. It's said that Cochise's youngest wife, jealous of his first wife, bit him on both hands and left big teeth-mark scars. If they couldn't work it out, the couple would divorce. The Apache word for *divorce* meant "they walk away from each other." If the woman wanted the divorce she just put her husband's things outside the wickiup. He'd grab his belongings and start looking for another wife. If the husband wanted out, he told his wife he was going hunting and never came back to her. Neither had to have a very good reason for divorce, though some causes were sterility or frigidity. If the woman was frigid or sterile, the husband would leave. If the man couldn't get an erection, it was thought caused by witchcraft. If he couldn't be "cured," the woman would divorce him.

Sources: Opler, *An Apache Life-Way*, 401–426; Stockel, *Chiricahua Women and Children*, 9–15; Sweeney, *Cochise*, 377.

that they drank at major celebrations. The women were also skilled in medical treatments, from using chewed mescal to stop bleeding to making bone-fracture splints with slats cut from sotol cactus; these they wrapped around the break with buckskin strips.[16]

Family and community were deeply important in Apache culture, and Geronimo's tepee was right near his mother's, whom he had cared for and supported since his father's death. "Inside my tepee were many bear robes," Geronimo said, "mountain lion hides, and other trophies of the chase, as well as my spears, bows, and arrows."[17] Alope decorated buckskin with beads traded for or stolen from the Mexicans, and she drew pictures on the inside walls of their home.

Soon they had three children and were living well in the Apache way, just as their ancestors had always done. They traded peacefully with some of the Mexicans as well as raided them when they needed food or horses. But the American Southwest was a contested area. Geronimo's Apache territory bordered northern Mexico and the states of Chihuahua and Sonora to the south, and for centuries the Apache had raided the Mexicans when they needed food or horses.

Raiding versus War

RAIDING HAD BEEN the Apache way of life since the days before the Spanish conquistadors came. The Apache prided themselves on the stealth and speed of their raids, swooping silently through the darkness taking only enough food, provisions, and horses for their people to survive, then vanishing like wolves into the night. To the Apache, there was a huge difference between raiding and war. I like these distinctions and the different tactical approaches to each. *Raiding* meant "to search out enemy property," and *war* meant "death to the enemy."[18] Raids were used to steal what was needed, usually livestock, but also guns and ammunition. War was waged to avenge the death of kin who'd died at the

LESSON: *Have a purpose in everything you do.*

Geronimo and some of his warriors ready for war or raid. From right to left: Geronimo, Fun, Chappo (Geronimo's son), and Yahnoza.

hand of an enemy. Before a raid, the men who were going would meet in a sweat lodge to discuss their plans. Raiding parties were small and efficient—usually just five to fifteen warriors. Using smaller parties was really smart. It allowed the Apache to avoid being seen or heard, either coming or leaving. Stealth and silence were crucial. The raiders crept slowly and quietly until they reached enemy territory. Then they ducked behind trees, rocks, or cactus—anything they could hide under or behind.

Once in striking distance of their target, they stayed silent and motionless until just before dawn. Two or three warriors then crept up to the enemy's horses or cattle, picked out the animals they wanted, and, whistling quietly and using switches and rope and their outstretched hands, herded them to the other warriors at a chosen spot. There,

LESSON: *Be smart and disciplined, and develop the ability to communicate.*

mounted or on foot, they all drove the stolen animals toward home at breakneck speed, rarely stopping. To get away safely, they sometimes had to run and ride for days without stopping. If the Apache could conduct a raid without bloodshed, they would. Their strategy was to get in, then get out. They were tremendously efficient and successful at these raids.

War was different. War parties were larger—up to a few hundred men if required and available. Sometimes different bands teamed up. The object of war was to kill for revenge. War parties brought along a shaman or medicine man to advise the war leaders and sometimes even convince them to retreat if victory wasn't likely. Warriors were too valuable a resource to squander. The shaman also treated the wounded.

Warriors typically attacked a town or village where they were sure a kinsman had been killed. The war strategy was simple and efficient: scouts located the target and reported back to the leaders. Quietly, during the night, the entire force surrounded the target—and at first light the warriors launched an all-out attack, shooting arrows as they rode in hard, throwing spears, bashing with war clubs, and fighting hand to hand to the death. The object was to kill as many of the enemy as possible as quickly as possible, take any spoils, and then get out of there. Fast.[19]

Victorious war parties returned to celebrate and dance with their bands, breaking out the tiswin* and partying for four straight days.

Massacre at Janos

IN 1846, WAR erupted between Mexico and the United States. The U.S. victory resulted in the 1848 Treaty of Guadalupe Hidalgo and gave much of the Spanish Southwest—including California, New Mexico, and Texas—to the United States. The problem was, the Apache already lived there.

Geronimo's tribal homelands (called *Apacheria*) fell within the

---

* Fermented corn liquor. (See tiswin sidebar on pg. 66, Chapter Four.)

new boundaries. The treaty between the United States and Mexico stipulated that the U.S. authorities would restrain the Indians in the newly acquired lands from raiding Mexico. That turned out to be easier to agree to than accomplish. Without any say in the matter, Geronimo and his Apache had had their land taken from them. The Apache hadn't signed any treaty, and the new boundaries were arbitrary to them. The Apache felt no allegiance to the U.S. and Mexican governments who'd made the deal. But these boundaries would end up lassoing and eventually tying a noose around their lifestyle, as they'd soon find out.

While the Americans and the Mexicans made deals and drew borders, the Apache continued to roam and raid and trade. The Mexicans also tried to make deals with Geronimo's Chiricahua Apache to stop their incessant raiding. The Mexicans offered free food at "feeding stations" in northern Chihuahua—encouraging the Apache to use these rather than raiding.

But the state of Sonora refused to set up feeding stations, so many Chiricahua raids were focused there. Often these raids went uncontested, but sometimes the Sonorans resisted and fought back. Then there was fighting and bloodshed, and death on both sides. It created a raid-revenge cycle that went on for decades, broken only by brief periods of peaceful trading.

In 1851,[20] when Geronimo was twenty-eight years old, his band went south into Mexico on a peaceful trading mission. On such missions the Apache sent messengers ahead to a town, explaining that they came in peace and only wanted to trade. If the town's officials agreed, then the Apache would come in and trade. It was a handshake agreement for a peaceful exchange.

The Apache camped outside a village called Janos; the men went into town to trade, leaving their horses, weapons, and the women and children under a small guard. When they returned to the camp after trading, Geronimo and the other men were met by wailing women and children. They cried that Mexican troops from some other town had killed the guard, captured their horses and supplies, and massacred many of their people. Stunned, Geronimo found that his aged mother; his young wife, Alope, and his three small children had been brutally slain.

Though Geronimo wanted to perform a proper burial ceremony, there wasn't time—the attacking Mexicans were still nearby, and the Apache were greatly outnumbered. The great chief Mangas Coloradas ordered a retreat to the north, to their homes in Arizona. They needed to leave the dead where they lay. Geronimo hurriedly cut his long hair and spread the strands by his family as a sign of his mourning, then turned away. As the warriors and survivors retreated, Geronimo stood and stared, as if dead himself. "I stood until all had passed," he remembered. "I did not pray, nor did I resolve to do anything in particular, for I had no purpose left. I finally followed the tribe silently, keeping just within hearing distance of the soft noise of the feet of the retreating Apaches."[21]

The massacre of his family was one of the defining moments of his life. During the first march and while they camped that night, Geronimo spoke to no one, and no one spoke to him, for, as he put it, "There was nothing to say."[22] The Chiricahua considered showing one's emotions to be a sign of weakness, and they believed that deeply felt feelings, if shown, might later result in hasty actions.

After three days of walking, they arrived back at their settlement. Geronimo entered his tepee. "There were the decorations that Alope made—and there were the playthings of the little ones. I burned them all, even our tepee. I also burned my mother's tepee and destroyed all her property."[23] The Apache did not keep any of the property of a deceased relative. Their unwritten tribal customs forbade it, because they believed that otherwise the children or other relatives of one who had much property might be glad when their father or relatives died. The practice also avoided ugly family feuds over spoils.

Geronimo's heart ached. He traveled alone deep into Chiricahua country and prayed. After a long time he heard a voice calling his name, "Goyahkla!" Four times it called to him. Then it spoke: "No gun can ever kill you. I will take the bullets from the guns of the Mexicans, so they will have nothing but powder. And I will guide your arrows." Geronimo knew that he had been given a form of *Power*, something the Apache believed in deeply and accepted without question. Power was bestowed on certain people as special gifts—some got the gift of healing, some could predict weather, some understood animals, and some could foretell when enemies were coming before they arrived.[24] Geronimo had the Power to foretell events and even to know details of specific events that were happening great distances away. He also had

APACHE POWER

Much of Apache religious life centered around the all-powerful Ussen, the Life Giver, the supreme maker of the world, creator of their Apache lands and source of all supernatural power. Within that supernatural power, the Apache had access to particular kinds of individual abilities, which often came to them through four-day fasts that induced hallucinations and dreams that bestowed Power. Those who gained their Power in this way—through visitation via fasting, prayer, an important event (like the massacre of Geronimo's family)—became highly revered and respected by their peers. Power was meant for doing good: to heal the sick, to "see" enemies approaching, to "know" when it was time to leave. Power was beneficial—to heal, warn, or guard. There were other types too. The warrior Juh had the Power to handle and organize his men—he had leadership Power. Chief Chihuahua had Power over horses: He was said to be able to calm and ride the wildest of all horses easily, and he could heal wounded ones—he once cured a horse dying from a rattlesnake bite. Geronimo had multiple aspects of Power, and these helped him become the great leader he was.

But Power was complicated, even to those wielding it. Said Juh's son, Daklugie, "Power is a mysterious, intangible attribute difficult to explain, even by those possessing it. It was, even above his courage, the most valuable attribute of a chief."

Of Geronimo, Daklugie went on to say, "I don't know if Geronimo ever told his warriors that he had supernatural protection, but they were with him in many dangerous times and saw his miraculous escapes, his cures for wounds, and the results of his medicine."

Sources: Ball, *Indeh*, 61; Mails, *The People Called Apache*, 122–123. Opler, *An Apache Life-Way*, 204–205.

the Power of healing and, of course, the useful Power that no bullet could kill him.

It was another defining moment for Geronimo, and he knew what he had to do. He vowed that day to take revenge on the Mexicans—and this vengeance would fuel him for the rest of his life.

Commentary

Remember That Everyone Is a Product of His or Her Environment. *Geronimo was shaped by his landscape, his people's history and traditions, his religion, and his core beliefs. It's hard—if not impossible—to rip people from their environment and expect things to go smoothly. The U.S. military tried to yank Geronimo and his people from their environment, and that didn't go very well, as we'll see.*

Embrace Discipline, Practice, Daily Routine. *We can learn a lot by observing the Chiricahua discipline, practice, and daily routines—which were all a part of their daily lives and all related and interconnected. Even back then, the Apache culture already had training methods that are still in modern times proven to be effective. Anything that they wanted to be good at, they practiced and trained for with as much precision as possible. Especially impressive is how they competed at everything. Also, they were tougher than other people because they practiced it. To be tough you have to do tough things. Then they went beyond that and practiced preparation for emergency situations like hunger, sleep deprivation, and finding alternative food sources.*

At a young age they began learning and developing as many of these skills as possible, and they incorporated all these skills into their daily routine.

Respect Family. *The family was the very core of Apache society. The Apache people were deeply devoted to family, and most of Geronimo's decisions were driven by his core commitment to his family. Geronimo's father, Taklishim ("The Gray One") was the son of a great chief named Mahco, a man of tremendous size, strength, and wisdom, and Geronimo heard many stories of his* *grandfather's exploits in battle. After Mahco died, for reasons that are not clear, a Bedonkohe named Teboka, and not Taklishim, became chief. This explains why Geronimo did not become a chief, since chiefdom usually passed from father to son. Still, Geronimo's father was well respected and revered, and when Taklishim died after a long illness, Geronimo, the family relatives, and friends dressed him in his best clothes, painted his face for the afterworld, wrapped him in a special blanket, loaded him on his favorite horse, and, carrying all of his belongings, took him to a cave deep in the mountains. They placed his body on the ground among his possessions, then sealed the entrance with stones to keep it undisturbed and hidden.*[25]

When his father died, Geronimo took over the care of his mother, Juana, supporting her and the rest of his family from the time he was about twenty years old. Care of one's parents was an expected duty; if an Apache neglected

APACHE WORLDVIEW AND CORE BELIEFS

For the Chiricahua Apache, Ussen created supernatural powers and provided certain people access to these powers. Shamans and other individuals connected to the supernatural (as Geronimo was) conducted various ceremonies for improving luck in battle, healing, confusing or defeating enemies, and many others. The most important of all Chiricahua Apache ceremonies was the girl's Womanhood Ceremony. The Chiricahua had numerous creation myths to explain the origins of their world. The two central figures in these myths were White Painted Woman and her son Child-of-the-Water. Some of these myths involve great floods. Geronimo recalled one creation story in which there was a battle between the birds and the beasts over light and darkness. The birds desired light, the beasts darkness. The birds won. White Painted Woman was one of the last people alive after the battle, and she gave birth to a son. She hid him in a cave to protect him from the last living beast, a dragon. The boy left the cave to face the dragon, slaying the beast with his bow and arrow. The boy was then named Apache. Lore tells that all Chiricahua descend from this boy warrior.

Sources: Stockel, *Chiricahua Women and Children*, 3–5; Stout, *Geronimo*, 5–6; Opler, *An Apache Life-Way*, 196–197; Barrett, *Geronimo, His Own Story*, 49–53.

his parents in any way, if he denied them food or shelter at any time, he was banished from the tribe. Banishment was the worst form of punishment because most members of a band were immediate family members, and banishment meant being forever disassociated from your family. Banishment prohibited the joining of any other Apache band as well—so it was a great dishonor. They were on their own. We should all learn from that kind of dedication to family. It was an inherent code of honor and expectation to take care of one's family.

The Apache were polygamous, with prominent leaders like Geronimo able to take multiple wives. Throughout his life Geronimo was married to nine women and had numerous children. He supported and loved them all, as well as their many children and grandchildren.

Understand Faith and Power. *After his family was slain, Geronimo heard the voice of his god Ussen, and he listened. The spiritual experience gave him direction and made him fearless in the field—and why wouldn't it? His faith, his spiritual core, allowed him to handle a difficult situation and go on, making some sense out of the hardship. He did not act rashly, or on the spur of the moment. He planned and pursued his goals and objectives for decades, guided always by his inner faith. Power was bestowed upon special people, sometimes obtained or received through long fasting and meditation. It might take the form of an animal, a tree, a plant, or a mountain—and this Power, this medicine, served as a guide or consultant for the rest of his life. Geronimo knew this: However you acquire Power, guard it with your life and wield it wisely. You don't know whether you'll ever get more, and it could also be taken away. Power can be called a lot of different things: intuition, déjà vu, sense of destiny, spiritual experience, or faith. All are hard to articulate but clearly very real to a lot of people. The Apache took such things very seriously.*

Leave an Impression. *Geronimo always left an impression. When he flew about the battlefield in a killing frenzy, he left Mexicans chanting his name in awe. Geronimo chose an extreme way to go about making an impression, but folks definitely remembered him. Mentors Cochise and Mangas Coloradas, who were impressed by his leadership skills, noticed him too. Getting noticed* like this allowed Geronimo's fast ascent among his peers, granting him more status as a shaman, guide, mentor, battle leader, negotiator, and translator. He earned these positions based on merit and performance, for an Apache tribe was an authentic meritocracy. His first impression had made him unforgettable.

CHAPTER TWO

Geronimo's Warpath Begins (Fortitude)

IMMEDIATELY AFTER THE MASSACRE AT JANOS IN 1851, Geronimo wanted to try out his Power and avenge the deaths of his wife, mother, and children. But the Apache were not impulsive, and they calculated warfare carefully, with detailed planning and patience. So it was almost a year before Geronimo finally met with Mangas Coloradas and the war council and asked if they could take the warpath against the Mexicans. At war councils, the chiefs and leading warriors met, sometimes around a fire, sometimes on a hill or area away from the camp. They sat in a circle and spoke one at a time, making their case. A leader's speaking skills gained him status and also maintained it—if he kept failing to get results from his speeches, he wouldn't be a leader for very long.[1]

LESSON: *Leaders plan, down to the smallest possible details.*

Geronimo felt they now had enough weapons, ammunition, and supplies to go on the attack. Mangas Coloradas was receptive, but he

MENTORS MANGAS COLORADAS AND COCHISE

Geronimo's most influential mentor was, without a doubt, Mangas Coloradas—a fellow Bedonkohe and the band's most noted chief. Born about 1790 (died 1863), he was a massive man—considered a giant by Apache standards—towering nearly 6'6" and said to weigh 250 pounds. With bulging muscles, a barrel chest, broad shoulders, and burly legs, his posture was "straight as a reed from which his arrows were made." Severe, intense black eyes and a wide, high forehead were punctuated by prominent cheekbones and a jutting jaw. Known for his assertive leadership and the political skill of uniting tribes and bands to follow his lead, he was unrivaled in hand-to-hand combat and he personally coached Geronimo in fighting technique. Geronimo developed a very tight kinship with Mangas Coloradas, learning the Apache trait of courage as well as his dislike for the Sonoran Mexicans. Also, because Mangas Coloradas ultimately took on the leadership role left by Chief Mahco, Geronimo's grandfather, and because his own father died when he was relatively young, Geronimo developed a deep affinity and connection to his central mentor and became his protégé.

Cochise, a Chokonen Apache chief, was thirteen years older than Geronimo and a major mentor. He was also Mangas Coloradas's son-in-law. Like Mangas Coloradas, Cochise became a superior leader and devastating fighter, and he was also quite tall for an Apache, standing at just over six feet. Powerfully built and thickly muscled, with long black hair to his shoulders, a sharply bridged Roman nose, high cheekbones, and high forehead, he struck fear and awe even among his own people. He was not as politically savvy as Mangas Coloradas, but he was a powerful, charismatic leader whom Geronimo observed carefully, learning all he could by example.

Sources: Quote is from Sweeney, *Mangas Coloradas*, xxi. On Mangas Coloradas: Utley, *Geronimo*, 9–10; Sweeney, *Mangas Coloradas*, xix–xxi. The incredibly detailed physical description of Mangas Coloradas is from the army surgeon who examined his corpse just after death. See Sweeney, *Mangas Coloradas*, xxi. There's a great description of Mangas Coloradas in Sweeney, *Mangas Coloradas*, 450. Also see Sweeney, *Cochise*, xxi–xxiii; Utley, *Geronimo*, 19; Roberts, *Once They Moved*, 21–22.

asked Geronimo to go as an emissary seeking support from the great Cochise of the Chiricahua. Cochise called for a council at dawn and listened to Geronimo's story. Geronimo stood before Cochise and his warriors and asked them all to join him: "I will fight in the front of the battle—I only ask that you follow me to avenge this wrong done by these Mexicans. . . . If I am killed no one need mourn for me. My people have all been killed in that country and I, too, will die if need be."[2]

Geronimo's speech was convincing, and Cochise agreed, but he still had to ask for his warriors' allegiance too. I find it fascinating that he "asked" them and did not "command" them. The Apache operated with a much different kind of leadership system than ours. They believed in both individual and tribal

LESSON: *Listen to the desires of your people.*

independence and self-governance. Even a chief as powerful as Cochise couldn't order his warriors into battle. Each man made his personal choice about every battle or raid, made of his own free will.[3] In this case, Cochise and his warriors accepted.

Next Geronimo visited Juh (pronounced *Whoa* in Apache, or sometimes like an explosive "Who"[4]) to recruit the Nednhi, and he got the same result. Juh and Geronimo were boyhood friends and remained close their entire lives. Juh also married Geronimo's sister Ishton, so Juh was his brother-in-law. Geronimo's leadership and persuasive oration rallied a three-pronged army under Cochise, Mangas Coloradas, and Juh. With two hundred warriors, it was one of the

LESSON:

Great performances are usually not the result of inspirational speeches—they are the result of great preparation. But it doesn't hurt to be a powerful and impassioned orator who can work people into a frenzy.

most intimidating Chiricahua forces ever assembled.[5]

They met at the Mexican border and prepared for war, decorating their faces with ocher and chalk warpaint and strapping buckskin warbands over their foreheads. They donned earrings* made of mouse skins, turquoise, feathers, even seashells. Geronimo, directed by his Power as a shaman, decorated members of his own group with white paint, marking their foreheads, the sides of their faces, and with a band across the nose.[6] Some of the markings distinguished their own warriors so that they would not accidentally be killed in battle. Before engagement Geronimo, as leader, inspired his men with words of encouragement, and he also led at the front of his warriors both on the attack and in retreat. As battle leader he was responsible for leading them to safety and making sure they had sufficient food and water.

Each warrior was self-contained and self-sufficient, carrying his war club, stone knife, bow and arrows, and a bag of pollen and herbs in case of sickness. The pollen was crucial, as it symbolized life and renewal; they traditionally used tulle pollen, but also oak, sunflower, piñon, or corn.[7] They brought three days' rations of mescal (the widely used agave plant, which was plentiful and versatile; they could roast it or bake it, or dry it to preserve for raids)

LESSON: *As a leader, make sure your people know their jobs and do their jobs. Self-sufficiency is key.*

and dried meat in a buckskin or hide bag slung on their shoulder strap (a precursor to the modern bandolier, or bullet sling). Each warrior slung from his neck a water bladder sort of like a bota bag—a kind of canteen—made from animal intestines. The container was tied shut at the top so as not to leak. Some of these were really ingenious—precursors to modern-day hydration systems. They were made out of horse intestines and formed into flexible tubes up to thirty feet long that could hold a lot of water. The men wore only their loincloth and moccasins,

---

* All Chiricahua children had their ears pierced with a bone or sharp thorn by the time they were about two months old. They believed that the child learned "to hear things sooner" and obeyed better with their ears pierced. They were also thought to grow faster (Mails, *The People Called Apache*, 60; Opler; *An Apache Life-Way,* 13).

and the material they would unwrap to use as a bedroll for sleeping.[8] Speed and mobility were keys to Apache attack and retreat. They knew it was important to execute plans as fast and efficiently as possible.

All warriors carried bone awls, sinew for thread, and animal hide to make moccasins wherever they were. The terrain was so rough, and it was so hot, that they often wore their moccasins out and had to be prepared to sew new ones fast. They made them with extra leather layers and upturned fronts to protect them from bashing their toes as they ran over rocks. They made them thigh-high and then turned a flap down over the knee. Moccasins were an essential piece of equipment— and good moccasins sometimes saved their lives, allowing them to move fast over sharp rocks and prickly cacti.

⤜⤜⤜⤜⤜⤜⤜

LESSON: *Teams and individuals excel best at what they do most often, rather than constantly changing what they do.*

⤜⤜⤜⤜⤜⤜⤜

The Revenge Battle for the Massacre at Janos

GERONIMO WAS THE guide for this battle, since he knew where the Mexicans who had massacred his people at Janos lived. They went south on foot, leaving their horses and families behind to ensure surprise. With scouts running up ahead and returning to report, and scouts on their sides and at the rear, Geronimo's group moved in clusters two abreast, stealing through Sonora's riverways and mountain trails. They jogged about forty to forty-five miles a day until they neared Arispe. There they camped. Soon eight Mexican soldiers rode out from the nearby town to parley with the Apaches, but Geronimo wasn't in a talking mood. "These we killed," he recalled, "to draw the troops from the city."[9] The technique worked, for the next day some more Mexicans came, and after a full day's battle, the Apache captured the enemy supply train, so now they had plenty of guns and ammunition.

The next morning, the rest of the Mexican force showed up—two companies of cavalry and two on foot—about one hundred soldiers total. The battle to follow was rare for two reasons. First, it was among the few times that the Apache were not outnumbered. And second, it was also unusual for the Apache to engage in a pitched battle, as they almost always used the surprise attack: ambush followed by sudden flight. Swoop in, attack, and then scatter was the Apache style. But with their strong numbers and newly acquired guns and ammo, they felt confident. Plus they were fueled by Geronimo's passion for vengeance.

Even though Geronimo was not a chief, he was given the honor of leading the battle because he had lost his entire family to these Mexicans. Concealed in timber near the river, he arranged his warriors in a crescent and waited. When the Mexican infantry came within about four hundred yards, Geronimo led an all-out charge, the Apache firing guns and zinging arrows as they sprinted into battle. They fought viciously with spears and war clubs. Throughout the fight, Geronimo remembered his family: "I thought of my murdered mother, wife, and babies—of my father's grave and my vow of vengeance, and I fought with fury."[10] Geronimo raged across the plain, dodging and running with bullets landing all around him. He killed every enemy he encountered. The battle lasted two hours.

At last Geronimo stood in a dusty clearing with three other warriors, a distance from their compatriots. They were out of arrows and their spears were broken off in the bodies of the dead and dying enemies. They were down to their knives and war clubs. Then two armed Mexicans arrived from another part of the battlefield, firing their guns as they came. Two of Geronimo's warriors were hit and they slumped to the ground, dead.

Geronimo and his companion fled to their own ranks for more weapons, and as they ran, his comrade was struck down. Geronimo reached his other warriors, seized a spear, and spun around. The two oncoming Mexicans fired again but missed, so Geronimo charged, killing the first one with his spear. He quickly grabbed the dead soldier's sword and engaged the last one hand to hand with sword and knife. They grappled to the ground. Geronimo killed him with his knife and stood over him, holding his weapons high, daring anyone else to fight him. None were left. Geronimo relished the victory, remembering: "Over the bloody field, covered with the bodies of Mexicans, rang the fierce Apache war-whoop."[11] It was on this day, legend holds, that Geronimo got his name.[12]

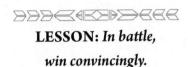

LESSON: *In battle,*
win convincingly.

Apache warriors surrounded Geronimo and cheered him. Both Cochise and Mangas Coloradas witnessed his fury and his courage, and the massacre at Janos had been avenged. To reward his exploits and

APACHE POLYGAMY

Polygamy made sense for the nomadic Apache for a number of reasons. First of all, one of the main points of marriage was to produce children, so the more wives one had, the more children he could produce. Also, in Apache culture, when a woman gave birth she refrained from sex until the child was weaned—at about four years old. Extra wives gave men an outlet for this inconvenience. Great warriors were the most powerful, had the most influence and economic power, and thus were given the right to take many wives—it was a badge of honor. Leadership and wealth gave a warrior the privilege to take multiple wives, but since leadership and status took many years and great trials to attain, only about 10 to 20 percent of the Chiricahua men were wealthy or powerful enough to earn the privilege. There was a definite pecking order among the wives, with the first wife having control of the whole household. Things went smoothly if the other wives respected her position of authority. They usually all ate together, and sometimes they all slept in the same dwelling, although sometimes a wife or two would have a separate dwelling. For purposes of sex and procreation, the man could divide his time between the women as he chose. Often the first wife had been married to her husband for many years and she would suggest his taking a second wife to help with household duties and even to provide sex for the husband if she was no longer interested or was unable to bear children.

Sources: Stockel, *Chiricahua Women and Children*, 14; Opler, *An Apache Life-Way*, 419–20; Mails, *The People Called Apache*, 312–13.

leadership, the two chiefs allowed him to take many wives, including She-gha, a relative of Cochise himself.[13]

Memorable Battles, Near Death Experiences, Failures and Successes

AMONG HIS PEOPLE, Geronimo had gained much respect. He had not earned the stature of Cochise or Mangas Coloradas, but his individual heroism in avenging the Janos massacre elevated his leadership and

THE APACHES AND HORSES

The Apaches got their first horses from the invading Spaniards in the sixteenth century, and by 1660 they could properly be called "Horse Indians." They were the first Plains tribe to have the horse, and they quickly became masterful on horseback. Initially they hunted buffalo (until there were none left), and the Apaches got so good on horses that they could ride down rabbits at a full gallop, swing down while holding on, and bash the rabbit with a club. Mounted, the Apache rider could also herd turkeys, flush them into the air, and knock them from flight with a stick. Starting at a very young age, the Apaches were such skilled horsemen that they could break a new horse in less than an hour, and they were expert at riding bareback as well as saddled. They often rode bareback because saddles were scarce and time consuming. The horse was the perfect raiding tool, allowing the Apaches to swoop in fast and escape quickly. They viewed horses as tools and also as food. Because they were always moving, always raiding and running and warring, there wasn't really time to develop deep emotional connections with their horses. When a horse wore out, they'd shoot it and eat it right there on the spot. If a horse got shot from under a warrior, he'd quickly dive behind it and use it as cover in a firefight, shooting over its still-warm flanks. They'd ride them until they died, then replenish supplies by stealing more. But because they were important tools, the Apaches learned to make cowhide "horse moccasins" to protect the hooves of their animals in raid or war.

Sources: Mails, *The People Called Apache*, 281–82; Opler, *An Apache Life-Way*, 396; S. C. Gwynne, e-mail to Buddy Levy 7/18/13; Robinson, *Apache Voices*, 170.

also fired him up for more raiding. For the next decade he led numerous raids and war parties into Mexico; some raids had war parties of up to twenty-five or thirty warriors, while other riskier attacks included just him and two other men. The first of these was probably foolhardy, and it nearly ended Geronimo's legend before it began.

Geronimo persuaded two warriors to accompany him to northern Sonora. On foot, with the usual three days' rations, they followed the Sierra de Antunez to their southern end, deciding to attack a small village there. At first light they crept from the mountains into the outskirts of the village. The plan was to steal five horses hitched outside some buildings. But just as they reached the horses, the Mexican villagers opened fire, killing Geronimo's two companions on the spot. Instantly, armed men on horseback and on foot arrived from all sides, but Geronimo darted for cover, firing arrows as he ran. "Three times that day I was surrounded," he said, "but I kept fighting, dodging, and hiding."[14] Throughout that day he hid and shot sniper-style, picking off Mexicans with arrows as they aimed their rifles at him. He did not miss a single time, his silent arrows impaling his pursuers before they could pull the trigger.

Geronimo ran all night, but the Mexicans tracked him on horseback for two full days, firing bullets at him whenever they had a fleeting shot. When he ran out of arrows, Geronimo called upon his years of warrior training: "I depended on running and hiding, although I was very tired. I had not eaten since the chase began, nor had I dared to stop for rest. The second night I got clear of my pursuers, but I never slackened my pace until I reached our home in Arizona."[15]

It was a miraculous getaway, but he returned home with no spoils and, worse, no companions. He reported the deaths of his comrades to the people, and the wives and children of the slain were consoled by the rest of the group. Some of the Bedonkohe Apache held Geronimo personally responsible for the two men's deaths, although they had gone along of their own will. Geronimo made no excuses. "I said nothing," he recalled. "Having failed, it was only proper that I should remain silent."[16]

Once during this time Geronimo led twenty-five warriors into the Sierra de Sahuaripa, hoping to surprise and defeat a larger, mounted, and better-armed troop of Mexicans. The Apaches ambushed them in a narrow canyon, Geronimo leading the charge and launching into hand-to-hand fighting. He came upon a Mexican whose gun was leveled at him, but before the man could fire his rifle, Geronimo slipped on slick, bloody ground and crashed at the Mexican's feet. The soldier slammed the butt of his rifle into the side of Geronimo's head, knocking him unconscious.

When Geronimo awoke he learned that just as the soldier was about to kill him, an Apache warrior impaled the enemy with a spear. It turns out that, inspired by Geronimo's charge, the Apaches had routed the rest of their enemies and stolen many of their horses. They'd dragged Geronimo off to a stream. He had lost much blood and looked to be dying. They'd doused him in the stream and bandaged the deep gash in his head. Slowly he revived, and by the next morning he was able to walk on his own again, making the mountainous trek back north to Arizona. He had a severe concussion and skull fracture that took many months to heal, and he would wear the scar from the rifle butt to the end of his days.[17]

Another time, in 1861 during a raid on a Mexican mule train in the Sierra de Sahuaripa, Geronimo took a gunshot to the face. The bullet glanced off him at the outer corner of his left eye and knocked him unconscious. The attacking Mexicans left him for dead and chased the other warriors fleeing for cover in the trees. Geronimo came to and sprinted for the woods with bullets landing all around him. His left eye was swollen completely shut, yet he remained calm, recalling that "bullets whistled in every direction and at close range to me. One inflicted a slight flesh wound in my side, but I kept running, dodging, and fighting until I got clear of my pursuers. I climbed a steep canyon, where the cavalry could not follow. The troopers saw me, but did not dismount and

LESSON: *Stay calm under pressure at all times, and those around you will be calm too.*

try to follow. I think they were wise not to come on."[18] I imagine a wry smile on his face when he says this, remembering what a dangerous man he was in his prime. His tone borders on cocky, but it isn't bragging if it's a fact, I guess. Sounds like they *were* wise not to follow him up the canyon.

More than a decade of constant raiding honed Geronimo into a masterful tactician of guerrilla warfare and a fearless, revered leader of warriors. He learned from his failures, and successful raids followed. He was now paired with Mangas Coloradas on some raids, Mangas Coloradas commanding one division, Geronimo the other. And he served as a liaison between Mangas Coloradas and Cochise. The honor was great, as were the spoils. Once Geronimo returned from Mexico laden with plunder and leading a herd of "all the horses, mules, and cattle we wanted." The people praised him, for in one raid he'd brought in enough supplies, weapons, and ammunition to last his entire tribe for more than a year.

Though he did not know it at the time, as the decade-plus of raiding drew to a close, Geronimo's world was about to change forever—for the white men were coming. The warrior-shaman that the interlopers would encounter was by now a sculpted fighting machine—about 5'8" tall, about 165 to 170 pounds of muscle and sinew who could run for days on end and kill you with his bare hands, even though the third finger on his right hand was bent backward from a bullet wound. The whites who first saw Geronimo described him as "proportioned like [a] deer . . . [a] perfect specimen of the racing type of athlete," adding that his legs were "sinewed as though with steel cords."[19] He was somewhat bigger than the average Apache warrior, who were between 5 feet 6 and 5 feet 7 and around 135 to 145 pounds.[20] One military officer, in describing Geronimo and his warriors, said, "In muscular development, in lung and heart power,

LESSON: *It's important to be more concerned with your character than your reputation.*

they were, without exception, the finest body of human beings I had ever looked upon."[21]

At the same time, his complex character was being molded. Already he was defiant and determined and crafty. Highly intelligent, he was a shrewd manipulator and a fearsome force on a battlefield. He was also a devoted family man. His lifelong vendetta against the Mexicans burned deep within him. His eyes were clear and sharp. His face, creased by bullet wounds across his forehead, eye, and cheek, instilled fear and awe in his enemies. His face was called "a vicious one made more repulsive by the scars upon it."[22] The face, and the man, were poised to become notorious, then legendary.

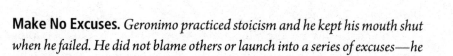

Commentary

Make No Excuses. *Geronimo practiced stoicism and he kept his mouth shut when he failed. He did not blame others or launch into a series of excuses—he simply bore the responsibility for his actions on his own shoulders, learned from his mistakes, and moved on. Stay stoic and don't make excuses. Excuses don't get you anywhere and only make you look bad and make matters worse.*

Foster Mentorship. *We have to revere our mentors—and Geronimo had some impressive mentors in Mangas Coloradas and Cochise. Geronimo was his own man, but he had the wisdom to learn from his mentors and take those teachings and adhere to them in every aspect of his life.*

Nearly every successful person has drawn from the wisdom of mentors. The object is not to reinvent the wheel but, rather, to push the wheel forward. Mentors are not just valuable to teach you how to do things and do them right, but they also provide examples of mistakes to avoid. It is important to have a base philosophy so that you have direction and keep your thinking from getting scattered. From there you want to learn as much as you can from as many sources as possible. In order to draw from the past and the experience of others, you need a humble appreciation and an open mind. Geronimo never stopped learning.

Focus on Yourself and Your Abilities when Battling an Adversary.
Revenge in the Apache culture was sacred, a social duty that bound war-
rior brothers. Geronimo's revenge was not necessarily a case of blind emotion.
Sure, vengeance drove Geronimo and revenge kept him committed. He re-
acted intensely to the injustices perpetrated on his people and he was aggres-
sive in his reactions to those injustices. But I've always felt that revenge can
have an unfocusing effect in that the effort becomes frantic; your execution
goes downhill because you are focusing on the opponent and not yourself. As
Geronimo and the Apache pursued their enemies, they focused on their exe-
cution and their own tactics that they had developed and enhanced since they
were children. Geronimo focused his revenge FOR his people.

Geronimo's vengeance dictated many of his actions, and revenge festered
in him to the end of his days. At the end of his life, Geronimo mused on his
revenge against the Mexicans, and his position had never wavered in more
than sixty years: "I am old now and shall never go on the warpath again,
but if I were young and followed a warpath, it would lead into Old Mexico."

Take Calculated Risks. *Some of Geronimo's earliest raids were very risky;*
they nearly cost him his life and definitely cost the lives of some of his fellow
warriors. But taking calculated risks is crucial if you want to succeed. Geron-
imo understood this, and he kept taking calculated risks throughout his life.
People who don't take risks are often those who are afraid to fail. This can
prevent success as well.

Learn from Loss or Failure—Don't Be Discouraged. *Geronimo's early*
failures were followed by great successes. He never became discouraged, even
when he had to report grim news to his people. Sometimes you learn more
from failure than you do from success. For one, you learn that you don't want
that empty feeling failure brings, and you learn not to make the same mis-
takes again.

Diversify Your Skills—Make Yourself Needed. *Geronimo was not nec-*
essarily born a leader; he became one through deeds and actions and by earn-
ing the respect of his mentors and his colleagues. He worked hard to become
a great warrior, but he also paid attention and learned the practice of medi-

cine/shamanism too, which doubled his usefulness to his tribe. He surfaced as a confidant to Mangas Coloradas and Cochise, offering them tactical battle advice and opinions, and serving as a translator, negotiator, and mentor to younger apprentice warriors. Eventually, because he was multifaceted, the people sought his advice in war campaigns, strategy, and tactics, and they knew he could be counted on to cure or treat wounded warriors.

CHAPTER THREE

The Coming of the White Men (Lore)

THE FIRST WHITE MEN Geronimo saw were surveyors during the summer of 1851. They were mapping out the new territory acquired in the U.S.-Mexican treaty of 1848. The Apache traded with them through hand gestures, and the white men seemed peaceable—they all even shook hands. Geronimo was fascinated by their cash currency—which he later learned was very valuable—and by their surveying instruments: "Every day they measured land with curious instruments and put down marks which we could not understand. They were good men, and we were sorry when they had gone on into the west. They were not soldiers. These were the first white men I ever saw."[1] Pretty soon he'd be sorry he ever saw them in the first place. They'd hardly be the last.

The great California gold discovery of 1848 had brought flocks of Americans across the southern route to California. The Overland Trail (also known as the Butterfield Stage Route) bisected Arizona and New Mexico, going from Tucson all the way to El Paso, Texas. U.S. mail traveling from St. Louis to San Francisco went this way. The stagecoaches labored through the high and difficult Apache Pass, which skirted the southern edge of the Apache ranges. The Apache had controlled this pass for as long as they could remember.

At first this traffic didn't seriously encroach on their tribal homelands. The Apache kept their distance, watching the arriving whites from the high, forested ravines and peaks of the Pinos Altos and Mongollon mountains rising over eight thousand feet above the valley floors. For a while, Geronimo, Cochise, and Mangas Coloradas avoided contact with them. Cochise hoped that the Americans were merely an inconvenience and would eventually go away. But of course they did not.

LESSON: *Understanding each other is important to any mutually beneficial relationship.*

Miners struck a rich gold vein in the mountains northwest of Santa Rita in 1859. They found copper too. Soon the town of Pinos Altos was booming. Like most frontier boomtowns, the place was pretty much lawless. Many of the miners were rough and violent, hoping to strike it rich. They didn't care that the Apache had been there first, and for several hundred years. Many of the miners hated and feared any Indians they saw, and they shot at them as they would coyotes or wolves. Uneasy relations loomed between the settlers and the Apache.

During this time Cochise and Mangas Coloradas each tried to maintain peaceful relations with the ever-growing white population, even agreeing to certain deals. Cochise pledged not to attack white travelers on the Overland Trail, and even to supply the Butterfield Station at Apache Pass with firewood. For its part, the U.S. government provided provisions, including food and blankets, to the Apache. What the Apache didn't know was that at the same time, the U.S. government was making plans to round all of them up and put them on reservations. This they'd find out soon enough. In the meantime, the Apache continued to raid Mexico.[2]

LESSON: *Good leaders must sometimes be peacemakers.*

Cut the Tent (The Bascom Affair)

WHITE DECEIT WOULD soon fracture the peace. It wasn't just one thing but a series of events that led to decades of war. Actually, the Apache Wars, as they're called, raged on and off from 1849 until 1886. Two famous stories in Apache lore say a lot about Cochise and Mangas Coloradas, and I'll retell them here—because they bear retelling and because these were Geronimo's main mentors. The episodes also say a lot about the background of white-Apache relations during Geronimo's lifetime.

The first, which the Apaches called "Cut the Tent," goes like this: On February 3, 1861, just after Cochise had returned from a raid to Sonora and while Mangas Coloradas and Geronimo were away on another, Cochise received a message that soldiers were camped near Butterfield Station at Apache Pass and that their officer wanted to speak with him. The next day Cochise went to see what the officer wanted, and, sensing no danger, he brought a few of his family with him—his brother Coyuntura, two nephews, a wife, and two of his children.[3]

The army men—headed by a second lieutenant named George Bascom and his interpreter—greeted Cochise, invited him and his brother into a tent, and then immediately began accusing Cochise of having led a raid that resulted in the kidnapping of the stepson of the interpreter, a boy named Felix Ward, and some of his oxen. The soldiers wanted them back. Cochise denied the charge and claimed, truthfully, that he did not have the child. Cochise knew about the raid, but it had been done by other Apache. He did not have the child, but he told Bascom that, given a week, he could find him and bring him back.

LESSON:

Try cooperating first.

Bascom had the audacity to threaten Cochise, among the greatest Apache warriors of all time. Through his interpreter he told Cochise that he would hold him and his family hostage until the boy was returned. Cochise acted instinctively. In a flash he drew his war knife, slashed a hole in the wall of the canvas tent, and bounded like a deer up the steep slope behind the soldiers' encampment. The interpreter fired his pistol, but Cochise had already disappeared over the hill. Some reports say that he flew so fast up the hill that at the top he was still holding his coffee cup. But his relatives had been rounded up and captured.

LESSON: *Great leaders do not hesitate when it's time to act.*

Cochise returned an hour later and yelled from the top of the ridgeline, asking for his family. Bascom's response was a blast of gunfire from his soldiers. Cochise then raised his hand, swore revenge, and yelled out, "Indian blood is as good as a white man's blood."[4]

The next morning Cochise returned with a lot of warriors. From the hills above the station they held up a white flag of truce. Cochise just wanted to talk; he still hoped to work something out. Stating again that he did not have the missing boy, Felix Ward, he demanded that Bascom return his family, to which Bascom replied that he would not until the boy was returned. Seeing this stalemate from near the station, an older, experienced stagecoach driver named James Wallace, who spoke some Apache, came out to try to assist and set things right. Bad idea. Some of Cochise's men on the hillside swooped in, kidnapped Wallace, and fled as Bascom's men fired on them. Cochise and his warriors sprinted for cover. But now Cochise had a bargaining chip.

The next day, Cochise paraded Wallace along the hilltop, his hands tied behind his back and a noose around his neck. Cochise's demand was simple: Wallace's life—and sixteen mules—in exchange for his family. Nope. Bascom was too stubborn. Cochise turned away in disdain and hatred, for he would do anything to get his family back. It was time to plot revenge and action.

By now, Mangas Coloradas and Geronimo had returned from a recent raid in Mexico, and they joined Cochise.[5] Cochise's scouts had spotted a freight train of five wagons headed toward Apache Pass. He sent Geronimo and Mangas Coloradas to spring a trap, in order to get more hostages for bargaining. Geronimo and Mangas Coloradas hid near the summit, then ambushed the wagon train, surprising the nine men—three Americans and six Mexicans. They seized the mules, took three Americans prisoner, then bound the Mexicans to the wheels and set the wagons on fire.

Now Cochise had four hostages. He tried one last time, writing a note to Bascom that said, in English, "Treat my people well, and I will do the same by yours." Cochise would trade his four Americans for his family. But Bascom still did nothing. He still believed, wrongly, that Cochise had this kid named Felix Ward. Bascom claimed he saw the note but remained unwilling to make a deal.

>>>≼≼≽>≼≼≼

LESSON: *Be wary of "shape-shifters," people who have divided allegiances.*

>>>≼≼≽>≼≼≼

MICKEY FREE

Mickey Free deserves a digression. His abduction prompted the "Cut the Tent" episode, in which Cochise was falsely accused of harboring him. The real story is that this Mickey Free was an illegitimate full-blooded Mexican, born Felix Telles, in 1847 just north of the Sonora, Mexico, border and west of Tombstone, Arizona. His mother took up with an Irish immigrant farmer-rancher named John Ward, who raised the young boy as his own and renamed him Felix Ward. In 1861 an Apache raiding party attacked the Ward ranch. John Ward was away and nine Apache warriors swept in, stole livestock, and abducted young Felix. He lived with them for the next ten years, raised as a White Mountain Apache, learning their language and their customs. He became a warrior and he even went on Apache raids.

By 1872, Felix's White Mountain band had been rounded up and placed on reservations by none other than George Crook. Felix Telles, aka Felix Ward, ended up at Fort Apache, and there, because he could speak fluent English, Spanish, and Apache, he was enlisted

The controversial Mickey Free
(born Felix Telles, aka Felix Ward).

as one of Crook's scouts and given the name Mickey Free. Geronimo encountered him numerous times and had to live near him. But he never trusted him. Perhaps this was because—though everyone thought he was half-Irish and half-Mexican—he was in fact a full-blooded Mexican, and Geronimo knew it. By the time he became a scout, he was a slight, shifty, 5'5" 135-pound twenty-four-year old whom Al Sieber described as "half Mexican, half Irish, and whole son of a bitch." Geronimo hated him because he served as one of the San Carlos Indian police and was always against the renegade Apache. He was a turncoat's turncoat. He sold prohibited liquor to the other scouts for a profit, and he constantly provided (sometimes false) information on Geronimo's activities to try to get him in trouble. At the end of the Apache Wars, Mickey Free was temporarily sent with the other Apache to prison in Florida, but he was then discharged as an army officer and returned to Arizona, where he farmed twenty acres until he died in 1910.

Sources: Thrapp, *Al Sieber, Chief of Scouts,* 262; Radbourne, *Mickey Free.*

Cochise was enraged but he was out of diplomatic options. This hardheaded Bascom would not reason or make sensible deals. Cochise considered an all-out attack, but there were too many soldiers. The military camp they had set up at Butterfield Station was too heavily fortified with stone walls. With the help of Geronimo and Mangas Coloradas, Cochise could probably have won a battle, but the cost to his warriors would be too high. The Apache always calculated carefully. Warriors were a highly valuable resource that were needed for raiding—they could not be wasted. Instead, Cochise left on a raid to Sonora. He would try to retrieve his family at another time, when surprise and stealth were on his side.

Geronimo and Mangas Coloradas struck for their homes on the

Son of Cochise, Naiche fought with Geronimo
and was the last chief of the free Chiricahua.

upper Gila River. Before departing, though, they carried out Cochise's wishes: They tortured and killed the American prisoners, leaving their mutilated bodies near the summit of Apache Pass for the vultures and coyotes to find.

Find them they did. A few days later reinforcements arrived for Bascom. They discovered the slain and mutilated corpses of the Americans. In retaliation, Bascom took Coyuntara, Cochise's brother and valuable warrior, and Cochise's two nephews to a stand of oak trees and hanged them by their necks until dead, while Cochise's wife and two children watched. They were mercifully released. One of the children was Cochise's son Naiche, who would grow up to team up with Geronimo in the Apaches' long freedom fight against the whites. Naiche would become the last chief of the free Chiricahua.

The catastrophe of the Bascom Affair became lore among the Apache, a story elders would tell to their children called "Cut the Tent" or "Cut through the Tent." Geronimo mentioned it in his memoir, proud to be retelling the story. But at the time for Geronimo, "Cut the Tent" cemented his distrust of the invading Americans, a people who would kidnap your family for no good reason and hold them hostage. "After this trouble," Geronimo recalled, "all the Indians agreed not to be friendly with the white men any more."[6]

The Betrayal of Mangas Coloradas: "The Greatest Wrong Ever Done to the Indians"

GERONIMO COULD SEE what was happening in his country, to his people. Even to Mangas Coloradas. Mangas Coloradas is the subject of the second anecdote, which I'll retell here. The need for gold was making the white prospectors crazy. It made no sense to the Apache, who had a completely different relationship with gold. First off, gold was a symbol of the sun, sacred to their god Ussen. Mining for it was taboo—for it was believed to cause earthquakes orchestrated by the wrath of Ussen.[7] The Apache found gold of little use, as it is too soft for making either arrowheads or spear points.

exterminate the Apache. The Confederate governor of the new territory called the Apache "cursed pests" and issued the following order:

> You will . . . use all means to persuade the Apaches or any tribe to come in for the purpose of making peace, and when you get them together kill all the grown Indians and take the children prisoners and sell them to defray the expense of killing the Indians. . . . Leave nothing undone to insure success, and have sufficient number of men around to allow no Indian to escape.[8]

Union troops stationed in Mescalero, in Apache country, had similar orders: "All Indian men of that tribe are to be killed whenever or wherever you can find them. The women and children will not be harmed, but you will take them prisoners."[9]

LESSON: *Avoid dealing with people who have proven to be treacherous and dishonest.*

The Apache leaders learned of these directives, and they moved nervously through their own country. It's amazing that all this was going on right in the middle of the Civil War. In fact, with so many soldiers leaving and going back east to fight in the Civil War, the Apache had the false sense that they might actually be winning—and driving the White Eyes (as the Apache called the whites) away. Of course, they would return.

In January of 1863, Mangas Coloradas was seventy-three. He was old and tired and frustrated by the pressure his people were under. He returned to Pinos Altos when a large party of gold seekers began to move into the area. He met with the prospectors, ex-soldiers who offered the Apache blankets, flour, and beef if the Indians came in peace. Mangas Coloradas thought it seemed like a good idea and agreed to return in two weeks with an answer. Geronimo and other leaders counseled Mangas Coloradas against making any deals with the whites, who

But the gold at Pinos Altos brought in enough prospect
Mangas Coloradas nervous about their growing numbers, a
he tried to do something about it. He knew that there was g
south, in Mexico, and he decided to visit the mining camps,
to them that there were vast deposits in old Mexico—he said
personally guide them there. The prospectors, drunk and su
believed it was a trick—that Mangas Coloradas had come to c
from their camps and kill them. So they seized the giant chie
him to a tree, and whipped him brutally, then let him go. It wa
rage that Mangas Coloradas would never forget but would ra
about. But all the Apache knew
about it. Certainly, Geronimo, as
the chief's prime protégé, would
have known the story and filed it
away to draw on for revenge. And
after the "Cut the Tent" treachery, it
was time for revenge.

LESSON: *Study the*
your opponents think
the way they act. They
betray themselves.

By 1862 Geronimo was thirty-
nine. He'd lost two wives, four chil-
dren, and his mother to Mexican troops. The whites kept encroach
Mangas Coloradas and Geronimo met with Cochise in a war cou
Now the region was being overrun, not only by miners, but also by
diers from Civil War regiments charged with taking the New Mexico
gion for the Confederacy. There were also Union troops in the area,
the Apache found themselves literally in the crossfire. They would m
war on the intruders.

In a two-day battle at Apache Pass, the Apache had their first e
counter with the guns called howitzers, large cannon that proved to
much for them. Mangas Coloradas took a carbine ball to the chest (
was later removed, and he survived), and the combined force of Apache
relinquished the spring at Apache Pass, an important water source
Worse, within just three months of this encounter (the first true battle
between the resident Apache and the encroaching American soldiers),
both the Confederacy and the Union had developed official policies to

had proven before that they could not be trusted. But for whatever reason—pride, arrogance, overconfidence, or even the realization that there were just too many whites to keep fighting—Mangas Coloradas trusted the Americans and returned with only some bodyguards to try to strike a deal.

Mangas Coloradas should have listened to Geronimo and Cochise. When he got within 150 yards of Pinos Altos, armed men arrived and told him that his bodyguards could go—he would no longer need them. Mangas Coloradas dismissed them, by now realizing that he had been tricked. Soldiers led him to a crude adobe building and forced him to the dirt floor, tossing him a single blanket. They built a fire for themselves, away from him. At around midnight four new soldiers arrived, replacing the others. Two served as outside sentries, while two stayed inside with Mangas Coloradas. They heated their bayonets in the fire and seared the great chief's bare legs, laughing at him and taunting him. As Mangas Coloradas rose to fight back, the soldiers fired musketballs into his chest at point-blank range. He slumped to the ground. Another soldier put a bullet into the warrior's head.

The next morning a soldier used the cook's butcher knife to scalp Mangas Coloradas, pocketing the trophy. Around midday they tossed the body into a ravine, covering it with rocks and sticks. A few days later, some soldiers uncovered the body, cut off its head, and boiled it in a black pot. Later, the skull was shipped to an East Coast phrenologist, who weighed and measured it and reported it to be larger than Daniel Webster's (a leading American statesman and senator from Massachusetts who died in 1852). The skull was said to have been put on display at the Smithsonian, though the institution denied ever having it.[10]

Geronimo called the betrayal and murder of his mentor "the greatest wrong ever done to the Indians."[11]

A FEW WORDS ON SCALPING

The Apache rarely scalped. Almost never, in fact. If they did, it was always in direct retaliation. I love this explanation from *An Apache Life-Way*: "The Mexicans used to take scalps. They started it first—before the Chiricahua. They used to take scalps, including the ears, and sometimes they took the whole head. The Chiricahua would make peace with the Mexicans. Then the Mexicans would give them liquor, get them drunk, take them in their houses, and cut their heads off. Then the war would start again." It was a vicious cycle. In fact, evidence suggests that the Apache began scalping in retaliation, only in response to a bounty system offered by the Mexican state of Sonora, which required vigilantes to produce the scalp as proof they had killed an Apache. The prices were twenty-five dollars for a child, fifty for a woman, and a hundred for an Apache warrior's scalp. Faced with this system, the Apache sometimes scalped back. Cormac McCarthy based his masterpiece *Blood Meridian* on this very sequence of events, by the way. It's a great book, though too violent to have a movie made out of it yet.

Sources: Opler, *An Apache Life-Way,* 349–50; Clum, *Apache Agent,* 194.

 **Commentary**

Embrace Lore. *Remember your people through their stories ("Cut the Tent" became Apache lore). Families and firms have their own sets of stories that recall their history and define them through recollections of great deeds, amazing feats, et cetera.*

Guard Against Betrayal. *What the whites did to Mangas Coloradas, even in the context of war, was unthinkable. The behavior broke Apache codes of honor and decorum, and it created tense relations and mistrust that would last until the very end of the Apache Wars. Acts of betrayal have severe consequences that can last lifetimes, creating blood grudges held for centuries afterward.*

Weigh Grudges. *Geronimo held grudges. If the wrong done to him was great enough—as with the slaughter of his family—he held them for life. No question that the dirty dealings with Cochise in the Bascom Affair, and later the torturing and then brutal killing of Mangas Coloradas, cemented grudges against the whites that he'd never manage to shake. Where there is no trust, there can never be any real relationship. Try to make the grudge the burden of the other party by not being consumed with it. However, in many instances, getting even is vital in order to protect your interests (and your people) from future damage.*

Try to Avoid Dealing with Irrational People. *If you encounter them, try to eliminate them from your life. Nothing good or logical comes out of them. Maintain your credibility in your own dealings.*

CHAPTER FOUR

The Tan Wolf and the Turkey Gobbler
(Independence)

T HE DEATH OF MANGAS COLORADAS in 1863 weighed heavily on Geronimo, Cochise, and the rest of the Apache. It wasn't just the trickery and the murder—it was the mutilation of his body that shocked and enraged the Apache. According to Juh's son Daklugie, "To an Apache the mutilation of the body is much worse than death, because the body must go through eternity in the mutilated condition. Little did the White Eyes know what they were starting when they mutilated Mangas Coloradas. Where there was little mutilation previously [Apaches mutilating whites], it was nothing compared to what was to follow."[1] A member of Chief Victorio's Chihenne band added, "The killing of an unarmed man who has gone to an enemy under truce was an incomprehensible act, but infinitely worse was the mutilation of his body."[2]

The Apache believed that the dead went on to another life just as they were on earth at the moment of their death, transferred to the afterworld in that state. Geronimo spoke of the afterlife near the end of his own life, saying:

As to the future state, the teachings of our tribe were not specific, that is, we had no definite idea of our relations and surroundings in after life. We believed that there is a life after this one, but no one ever told me as to what part of man lived after death. . . . Perhaps it is as well that we are not certain.[3]

THE AFTERLIFE

The Apache believed in an afterlife, an "underworld." That's why they buried a dead warrior with his favorite horse, favorite dog, best weapons, and burned everything else. He'd need his best warrior items in the underworld. An Apache must not arrive in the underworld without the things he needed. As with all peoples, the details of the underworld or afterlife were matters of speculation. Some Apache claimed to have seen the underworld during near-death visions. The general belief was that it was a place beneath the ground, and that the whole body, as it was on earth, went below to the other world.

This meant that you arrived there literally as you left the earth, which might mean in a mutilated state (like Mangas Coloradas). If you got hanged, you arrived in the afterlife with a stretched and broken neck. You carried your battle wounds and scars with you—and you remain the same age, just as you were when you died. This belief shaped the way the Apache thought and behaved, forming notions about their role on earth while here.

Sources: Mails, *The People Called Apache,* 179–82; Opler, *An Apache Life-Way,* 472–78.

Geronimo and Cochise headed to the mountains near Apache Pass and plotted revenge. Within two months, they had attacked a new military outpost in the Pinos Mountains, stealing more than sixty horses.[4] Raiding and scattering, Geronimo and Cochise took revenge continuously for the next two years, mostly stealing military stock and killing soldiers. During this time, Geronimo joined forces with Juh, their blood-bond deepening with every year on the warpath.

The Apache tried to live as they always had, frequently roaming south to Mexico to raid. But the whites kept coming in increasing numbers. Then the U.S. government made plans to officially administer the Apache homelands—splitting the western half of New Mexico to form the Territory of Arizona and establishing the boundaries of the states we know today. Between 1869 and 1872, the government determined to round up all the Apache of Arizona and New Mexico and place them on reservations. They'd give them some subsistence: food, blankets, and seeds; it was hoped that this would keep them from raiding Mexico, to keep them from going rogue. That was the theory, anyway.

But many of the area's white settlers resisted the reservation system from the beginning. They even sometimes took matters into their own hands. In April 1871, a group of Tucson vigilantes secretly bonded together angry Mexicans and Papago Indians—traditional enemies of the Apache. A mob of 146 crept up on a group of peaceful Apaches camped near Fort Grant, just north of Tucson. Most of the Apache band's warriors were away hunting. The Tucson mob caught the rest still sleeping in their wickiups. They shot, cut, and clubbed all the women and most of the children to death, killing between 125 and 144 Apaches, only two of them grown men. The military didn't bother to count the mutilated bodies when they came in to quickly bury them. Thirty infants were sold into slavery in Sonora, Mexico.[5]

President Ulysses S. Grant, who was humane and thought that prior Indian removal policies of extermination were wrong, was furious and called for immediate action. He threatened to place all of Arizona under martial law unless the governor brought the murderers to justice by proper trial. In due time a hundred of the vigilantes were indicted and tried, but the trial was a sham. A Tucson jury of the conspirators' peers deliberated for nineteen minutes before declaring every single one of the vigilantes "not guilty."[6]

President Grant, largely as a result of this massacre and the growing tensions in the region, instituted a formal Peace Policy in Arizona. The "Apache Problem" now had national attention, and it required presidential action. The Peace Policy was directed by the federal government and overseen by the Bureau of Indian Affairs in Washington, as well as the War Department. The plan was to round up and settle all Apache and place them on reservations near military forts, where they'd be protected from angry white citizens. It wasn't a great deal for the Indians, as the reservations would be located in places that the whites didn't want—usually pretty undesirable spots. It was a thickly layered bureaucracy with a lot of slow-moving parts. And as we'll see, not all the Apache bought into being herded up to become farmers and ranchers.[7] Geronimo never did.

The reservation plan turned out to be much harder in practice than on paper. Many of the Apache—especially Geronimo—had no intention of being rounded up and fenced in. Instead, they scattered and resisted.

The Arrival of the "Tan Wolf," a Worthy Adversary

IN THE SUMMER of 1871, President Grant sent Brigadier General George Crook, a Civil War vet and the greatest Indian fighter ever produced by the U.S. army, to deal with the Apache Problem.[8] Crook had years of experience fighting the Indians of the Pacific Northwest—but he had yet to encounter the likes of the Apache. Crook was courageous, determined, and curious. He learned Indian languages and life-ways, trying to comprehend every aspect of their culture. He sought to understand the "secrets of the inner Indian,"[9] and he admired their cunning and industriousness. He was impressed by how they'd carved a life out of that harsh landscape. Because of his own guile, cunning, and dogged persistence (and for the color of khaki he wore), the Apache called him Nantan Lupan, the "Tan Wolf."[10]

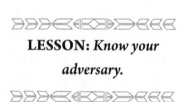

LESSON: *Know your adversary.*

Crook was quirky too. He rode a pack mule (which he named, ironically, Apache), rather than a horse. He liked a mule's surefootedness in the broken terrain. Crook dressed in the tan canvas garb of his hired mule packers rather than in military uniform. He always had a shotgun

GERONIMO'S ADVERSARIES: GEORGE CROOK, ARMY OFFICER (SEPTEMBER 23, 1829–MARCH 21, 1890)

Brigadier General George Crook "The Tan Wolf," dressed in his tan packer's garb and riding his favorite mule, Apache. He always rode with his double-barrel shotgun at the ready.

Born near Taylorville, Ohio, he went to West Point and would serve a distinguished career over nearly forty years, becoming the most successful and experienced Indian fighter ever produced by the U.S. military. Crook served in California during the 1850s and alternately in California-Oregon country, skirmishing with the Klamath Indians and then the Yakima Indians in Washington state up to the Civil War. His Civil War record was exceptional. In 1866 he commanded the district of Boise, Idaho, fighting against hostile Snake River Indians. By the time he was assigned to the Department of Arizona in 1871, his reputation as fair-minded, intelligent, and hardworking preceded him. Crook understood the temperament and worldview of the Indians as well as—or probably better than—any officer ever to fight them. Passionate about hunting and fishing, Crook preferred the wilderness to civilized life. His expeditions after Geronimo in the Sierra Madre are considered some of the most remarkable in the history of the Indian Wars. After he was relieved of his duties in Arizona Territory (following Geronimo's last escape), Crook commanded the Division of the Missouri from 1888 until his death from a heart attack in 1890.

Sources: Thrapp, *Encyclopedia of Frontier Biography;* Lamar, *The New Encyclopedia of the American West;* PBS—*The West.*

slung across his saddle, and his passion for hunting bordered on addiction. He sported huge, bushy sideburns—like a full beard coming off either side of his face—and had steely blue eyes. He loved to hunt so much that he sometimes took time to go after turkeys or deer, even while chasing Indians around the country. Here's a little-known fact: He once arrested Calamity Jane for posing as a man to get a job as a packer on a mule train. (She was exposed for her lack of swearing, which is ironic since she was known for swearing!) But that's another story.

Crook's job was to smooth out Indian-settler relations and implement the reservation system. Crook did things his own way. The minute he arrived in Arizona, he made his intentions clear: If the Apaches would stay in the designated reservation areas, he'd help them and provide sustenance for them. He'd even provide education, since he believed they could be assimilated into white culture. But if they left the reservation and kept raiding, he'd hunt them to the ends of the earth and kill them all if he must.

Crook's innovation was his understanding that it would take an Apache to catch an Apache who didn't want to be caught. So he bribed them, giving monetary and tangible incentives to so-called scouts who agreed to help hunt down any rogue Indians. Scouts got to keep their horses and their weapons, and they were paid handsomely for their jobs: Late in the campaign, Crook offered hundred-dollar cash bounties for the head of each hostile Apache brought in.[11]

Crook traveled as far as Utah to recruit Paiute scouts, but he tried to use as many Apaches, and Chiricahua Apaches in particular, as he could. They were tougher, they knew the terrain, and they were the best trackers and fighters. To maintain discipline and keep scouts from going rogue again or mutinying, Crook hired on the incredibly able Al Sieber as chief of scouts. Sieber kept the scouts in line with an unwavering and brutal policy: They either did what he said or he'd kill them. "I do not deceive them but always tell them the truth," he said. "When I tell them I am going to kill them, I do it, and when I tell them I am their friend, they know it."[12]

Scouts (and other Apaches who stayed on the reservation) came to be called "good Indians" by the U.S. authorities. "Good Indians" did what they were told. Geronimo, of course, was called a "bad Indian." He would eventually be called "the worst Indian that ever lived." Crook's other clever tactic was the use of pack mules, which were hardier, required less water, could carry more weight than horses, and did better in the spooky-steep mountains of the Apache hideouts. Horses were

AL SIEBER, CHIEF OF SCOUTS

General Crook's credo that "only an Apache can catch an Apache" required white scouts to control and command the recruited Indian scouts, and the best of the best was Al Sieber, chief of scouts.

German-born (February 29, 1844) Al Sieber was engaged in more Indian fights than Daniel Boone, Kit Carson, and Jim Bridger COMBINED—and he killed more Indians than all of them put together as well. Sieber fought in the Civil War—he was severely wounded in the Battle of Gettysburg but survived and moved out west to California. He drove horse herds to the Arizona Territory, managed a ranch near Prescott for a couple of years, and in 1872 was signed on as a scout by Crook during the first years of his initial campaign rounding up Apache. Sieber would gain Crook's trust, become chief of scouts, and fight Apache for the next two decades. He was a mentor to the notable scout Tom Horn, and Sieber earned the reputation as the finest tracker in the territory.

In 1907, at the age of sixty-three, Sieber was managing San Carlos Indian work crews constructing the Roosevelt Dam (then called the Tonto Dam) when he was crushed by a boulder on a job site. Though ruled an accident, there's at least one account that says the Apache pushed the giant rock onto him intentionally, as payback.

Incidentally, Robert Duvall played the role of Al Sieber in the movie *Geronimo: An American Legend*. Pretty impressive cast. Gene Hackman played Crook, Matt Damon played Britton Davis, Jason Patric played Charles Gatewood, and Wes Studi played Geronimo.

Sources: Thrapp, *Al Sieber, Chief of Scouts;* Thrapp, *Encyclopedia of Frontier Biography.*

faster, though, and since the Apache were such experts on them, they preferred horses.

Geronimo considered Apache who became scouts turncoats—their willingness to help the White Eyes hunt down their own Apache brothers made him bitter. He would kill them like U.S. soldiers if he had to, in order to remain free.

Geronimo, Cochise, and the Chiricahua held out and fought while other Apache bands weakened and gave up. But even Cochise could see that his Chiricahua were greatly outnumbered. For a couple of years, as his health declined from what was likely stomach or colon cancer, Cochise started to make peace overtures with the American government. He even reluctantly agreed to cease raiding parties into Mexico and remain on the Chiricahua reservation within the boundaries of his tribal homeland. The reservation encompassed a good chunk of Chiricahua land from the Mexican border, extending west of the Arizona–New Mexico line about sixty miles and including the Dragoon and Chiricahua Mountains to the north.[13] The place he agreed to had streams, canyons, and foothills that at least his people could hunt. But they were not allowed to leave the reservation area. Geronimo, by the way, was never thrilled with this deal Cochise made.

Death of a Mentor

IN EARLY SUMMER 1874, while the United States was rounding up Apache and putting compliant ones on the reservations, Cochise became gravely ill. He slipped in and out of comas. He called his son Taza to his side and asked him to lead his people after he died. The men of the tribe consented, vowing to follow Taza. The great Chiricahua chief Cochise died early on the morning of June 8 in his stronghold. He had predicted the time of his death to within the hour. News of his death, and deep sorrow, spread quickly across Apache country.

Custom called for a close relative (probably his wife or his sister) to bathe his body, comb his long hair, and dress Cochise in his finest clothes to prepare him for the afterlife. They decorated him with warpaint and head feathers, wrapped him in a heavy red woolen blanket, and placed him on his favorite horse for his journey. His burial was attended by his sons, his three wives, a shaman, and select members of his extended family. A warrior guided him on horseback through tumbled rocks and chasms to a deep crevice amid granite spires. There, his relatives took Cochise from the horse. As was Apache custom, they shot his horse as well as his favorite dog. His best gun—a shotgun-rifle combo inlaid with silver and gold—was hurled into the gorge. Then, using lariats, first the horse, then the dog, and finally Cochise were lowered down into the abyss.[14]

Mourning lasted four full days. This lengthy period was reserved for only the greatest shamans and leaders. Nearby Chiricahua—probably Geronimo among them—howled and wailed in lament.

LESSON: *Honor and pay homage to the great leaders who have come before. Know their stories and what made them great.*

They say that for a few days warriors traversed their horses all around the burial site to obscure any trail leading to it. Because Cochise was so important, the entire Chokonen band stripped and burned their clothes to honor him. They believed that burning the clothes of the dead, as well as their own, would keep the ghost of the dead person from returning to haunt them.[15] Such reverence, such honor, is impressive. None of his people ever revealed the location of his grave. It remained a secret they would take to their own.[16]

Taza, son of Cochise, was now chief, but Geronimo knew what his mentor's passing meant to the people. It was now up to Geronimo to lead the Chiricahua resistance.

The Tan Wolf Leaves

AFTER COCHISE DIED, Taza kept a promise he'd made to his father to live in peace on the Chiricahua lands. But with Cochise gone, the U.S. authorities reneged, breaking their end of the bargain. The area where

Cochise had agreed to go was prime land for mining and ranching, and the government wanted it. After Cochise died, Washington quickly made a couple of moves that would have immediate consequences for Geronimo and his people. First they'd transfer Crook, who was sympathetic to the Chiricahua having their own reservation. Then they'd move the Chiricahua to a hellhole called San Carlos.

Because Indian-settler relations were relatively calm now, President Grant transferred Crook to the Platte in the Dakotas. Grant needed America's most accomplished Indian fighter to deal with a volatile situation in the Black Hills. Gold had been discovered on Sioux lands, and miners had illegally invaded the Sioux reservation area, scattering Sioux and Cheyenne. Leaders Crazy Horse and Sitting Bull refused to come in for talks (like Geronimo, they were "bad Indians"), so Crook left Arizona to go there and assist General George Armstrong Custer in getting these Indians back on the reservation. Before he left, Crook issued stern protests against forcing the Chiricahua away from their tribal homelands, but the Interior and War Departments ignored him.

Turkey Gobbler

WITH CROOK LEAVING to go fight the Sioux, a new man was needed to run things. In August of 1874 a brash young twenty-two-year-old upstart named John Clum arrived, a man noteworthy for his religious devotion. In fact, as part of President Grant's Peace Policy, the Dutch Reformed Church got to nominate the person to fill the San Carlos vacancy, and they chose Clum, who hired on as a civilian contractor to be the Apache agent. There's a great little-known anecdote about Clum: As a student at Rutgers, he was on the team that played against Princeton in the first college football game ever contested in America. Back then (the game was in November 1869) teams were twenty-five to a side; the sport resembled rugby, and there was no passing. Rutgers won the game 6–4.*

---

* Although Clum was a team member of the Rutgers squad, he didn't suit up until the second college football game ever played between rivals Rutgers and Princeton.

GERONIMO'S ADVERSARIES: JOHN P. CLUM, FRONTIERSMAN, INDIAN AGENT, EDITOR (SEPTEMBER 1, 1851–MAY 2, 1932)

John Clum, nicknamed "Turkey Gobbler" by the Chiricahua, posing with white gloves and his hat cocked sideways.

Born on a farm near Claverack, New York, Clum spent one year at Rutgers before taking a position as a weather observer with the U.S. Signal Corps in Santa Fe, New Mexico. At age twenty-two, in 1874, Clum became agent of the San Carlos Apache Reservation. He was no military man and found the army authorities extremely difficult to work with. After only three years, he quit his post as Apache agent at San Carlos and bought the *Arizona Citizen* newspaper. He sold the paper in 1880 and moved to Tombstone, where he founded the *Epitaph* and then became mayor and postmaster. Clum left Tombstone in 1882, moved east to Washington, D.C., for some years, then returned to Tombstone in 1885. Clum was a postal inspector in Alaska during the 1898 gold rush (he's a member of the Alaska Mining Hall of Fame), where he reconnected with Wyatt Earp, whom he'd met back in Tombstone. Clum (and Wyatt Earp, incidentally) settled down in Los Angeles after the Alaska gold rush. Clum wrote articles about his frontier life until he died of a heart attack in 1932, at the age of eighty-one.

Source: Thrapp, *Encyclopedia of Frontier Biography,* 287.

Clum was cocky, headstrong, and pompous. When he arrived in Arizona in 1874, he strutted about so much that the Chiricahua immediately gave him the nickname "Turkey Gobbler." I laugh when I imagine the Apache imitating his gobble and strut. Within a year Clum was charged with removing all the Chiricahua from their livable reservation

TISWIN

The Apache made their own alcoholic drink from fermented corn. The women prepared the beverage, and the kids helped in the process. It is uncertain whether they learned it from Spanish-speaking Mexicans or from Indians of Old Mexico. They first soaked corn in water overnight. Then they dug a long trench in the ground and lined it with grass, placing the soaked corn along the length of the trench and covering the soaked corn with more grass. They carefully sprinkled the corn twice a day with water—morning and evening—for ten days, until it sprouted. Then they removed the sprouted corn, ground it, and boiled it for up to five hours. Last, they strained off the liquid and let it bubble and ferment for a day or so—until it stopped bubbling. Then it was ready to drink. They say the taste is salty, and although the alcohol content is relatively low, it gets the job done. I love this quote about tiswin's kick: "One drink of tiswin . . . would make a jack-rabbit slap a wild cat in the face." The Apache especially liked to drink tiswin after returning from raids or wars, but they were careful with it because it was addictive and riled the men to disorderliness and fighting. The U.S. military's banning of tiswin would have serious consequences in the events of Geronimo's life, as we will see.

Sources: Barnes, *Apaches and Longhorns,* 51. On the making of tiswin, see Opler, *An Apache Life-Way,* 369–370; Debo, *Geronimo,* 22; Mails, *The People Called Apache,* 330–31.

(against Crook's parting advice). They'd be transferred to a sweltering place a hundred and fifty miles north called San Carlos. San Carlos was a division of the White Mountain Reservation, east of present-day Phoenix. There Clum would strictly forbid the making or drinking of tiswin, personally leading midnight raids on tiswin stills along stream banks, disposing of found containers and jailing for two weeks any Apache caught making it.[17]

Clum rode out from San Carlos with a strong bodyguard of nearly sixty Apache scouts and met first with Taza to inform him of the move. Still mourning the loss of his father, Taza reluctantly agreed to relinquish the Chiricahua reservation and lead his people north to San Carlos. Clum rounded up others in the area, and within just days he was riding at the head of a column of Indians that included some 325 Nednhi, Bedonkohe, and Chokonen bands of Chiricahua Apache.[18]

But Geronimo and Juh had other ideas. They agreed to meet with Clum near Apache Pass to talk. Geronimo did the talking for Juh, who had a severe stutter. During what Clum later called "a big smoke and big talk,"[19] Geronimo begrudgingly agreed that his Bedonkohe and Juh's Nednhi would consider going to San Carlos. Geronimo, always a shrewd negotiator, said he would need some time—twenty days at least—to think about it. He had to ride out and round up his people, some of whom, he said, were a few miles south of the Mexican border. Clum, strutting as usual, said he'd give Geronimo four days to comply and come in. Clum was suspicious about Geronimo's intentions, saying, "The general demeanor of this renegade did not inspire confidence."[20] He even ordered some of his spies to shadow Geronimo's movements and report back.

Threatened, Geronimo acted quickly. He conferred with Juh and the others, who all wondered, "What right had this arrogant young man to tell [us] what to do?"[21] Geronimo agreed that Clum had no right. No one did.

That night Geronimo and Juh slunk about the camp, extinguishing fires. They silently killed any feeble or disabled horses that might slow them up, then strangled all the dogs to keep their barking from giving them away. Right under the noses of Clum's army and scouts, Geronimo and Juh rallied seven hundred of their followers and snuck into the desert night, undetected. By the time the sun rose the next day and Clum had figured out he'd been tricked, Geronimo, Juh, and their bands were already safe in the canyons of the Sierra Madre, still free. They would continue raiding to live, avoiding being penned up and confined and told where they could and could not go.

CHIRICAHUA APACHE DOGS

The Apache had dogs before they had horses, and they used them much the same way, as tools. Originally dogs pulled travois or were loaded with packs to carry goods. Then after the Apache got horses, dogs were used to hunt small game and birds—squirrels, rabbits, turkey, and quail. The dogs also guarded camps and warned the people of approaching intruders. The dogs the Apache had in Geronimo's time were a mixture of the wolf-coyote descendants native to North America, combined with dogs that the Spanish and other Europeans brought over later.

The Chiricahua seemed to have more dogs after the advent of the reservation system: When they were moving a lot, or on the run, it wasn't practical to have dogs along with them. Mixed in sizes and colors, the typical Apache dog had a curved tail, white paws, and yellow patches over each eye.

The Apache did not eat dogs—that was considered taboo.

Sources: Schwartz, *A History of Dogs in the Early Americas,* 52, 84, 190n; Opler, *An Apache Life-Way,* 226–27; Bolton, *Coronado,* 247.

Clum fumed at their getaway, and he grew obsessed with catching Geronimo. First, he escorted the Apache who'd agreed to go to San Carlos. The much more desirable Chiricahua reservation was now officially shut down by President Grant. At San Carlos, Clum bided his time and plotted some way to ensnare the shifty renegade Geronimo.

Geronimo knew there was nothing for him or his people at San Carlos. The place was so dry that it was devoid of grass. Juh's son Daklugie called it "the worst place in all the great territory stolen from the Apache."[22] He described it like this: "If anybody had ever lived there permanently, no Apache knew of it. Where there is no grass there is no game. Nearly all the vegetation is cacti. . . . The heat was terrible. The insects were terrible. The water was terrible."[23] The parched ground teemed with scorpions and tarantulas.

Apache Thespians

GERONIMO HAD ALSO heard about Clum's plans for some of those Indians who had turned themselves in, like Taza. Agent Clum had a fiancée back in Ohio whom he wished to visit (and he probably wanted to get out of San Carlos for a bit), so he devised a scheme to pay for his trip. Clum's brainstorm was a touring company of Apache thespians, including Cochise's son Chief Taza, who would attend the Centennial Exposition in Philadelphia, visit "The Great Father" in Washington, and perform along the way in Clum's "Wild Apache Show."[24] It was a precursor to the later, more famous, and much more successful Buffalo Bill's "Wild West Show."

The whole idea was a distasteful scam, a way for Clum to use the Apache for his own benefit, even though he said (and perhaps believed) that it was for their benefit. "I wanted my Indians [yes, he said "*my Indians*"] to see the greatness of our United States and become impressed by the progress of their white brothers."[25] But really, Clum wanted to use the Apache to pay for his trip back east to marry his fiancée. He uprooted twenty prominent Apaches, including Taza and a number of chiefs and their wives, and put them on a train bound for a world unknown to them. Many Apache onlookers wailed in fear, certain that they would never return. "When their people saw their young chief [Taza] and his men depart, they mourned for them as dead, for their experiences had caused them to feel that they were being taken away to be executed."[26]

Clum thought it was a stroke of brilliance, claiming, "The idea went over big with the Indians."[27] Not exactly. The shows were pathetic and sad. Clum took proud, recently free-roaming American Indians, forced them onstage, and had them act out scalp dances, despite his knowledge that Apache very rarely scalped. Clum even admitted his blunder, saying, "The scalping acts should not have been included in our program. . . . While scalping an enemy was common practice among Plains Indians, as well as some of the eastern tribes, the Apache did not scalp their victims."[28] Yet that did not stop Clum from perpetrating a lie. The performance would end with the Apache attacked and defeated by white men. Clum's show flopped financially. It's a wonder the Apache didn't break their tradition and actually scalp the white "thespians" on the stage, or scalp Clum while they had the chance. After just a few performances, Clum ran low on funds and had to quit show business.

But the worst was yet to come. Clum took the Apache to Washington, where they met President Grant—but while there, Taza came down with pneumonia and promptly died. Instead of transporting the chief of the Chiricahua back to his tribal lands for proper burial, Chief Taza, son of Cochise, was buried in the congressional cemetery. Clum sent the rest of the Apache back to the San Carlos reservation by train, while he went off to Ohio to get married, then to San Francisco and San Diego for his honeymoon. When the Apache returned without Taza, many at San Carlos believed their chief had been poisoned. The Chiricahua elected Naiche chief after Taza's death.

By the time Clum returned from his honeymoon on New Year's Day, 1877, most of the Apache—and definitely Geronimo and Juh— were deeply suspicious of the Turkey Gobbler. They were certain that he had intentionally taken Taza east with the plan to kill him.

Tricked at Ojo Caliente

THERE WERE THEN some forty-five hundred Indians being kept on the San Carlos reservation, including members of all the Apache tribes—but not Geronimo. He remained riding free, refusing to come in, still out roaming and raiding. Recent Apache raids—possibly led by Geronimo—resulted in the deaths of nine ranchers and the theft of more than a hundred head of stock. Clum sent troops of cavalry to catch the culprits, but they found none. Clum's obsession over Geronimo grew, and he blamed him for the recent attacks and raids, though he had no proof. But he did have a good lead: He learned that Geronimo had been recognized at Ojo Caliente (Warm Springs) Reservation Agency in New Mexico, some four hundred miles to the east (about halfway between Las Cruces and Albuquerque). And the kicker: He was riding at the head of one hundred horses.

Clum hurriedly organized one hundred Apache scouts and prepared to chase after Geronimo. Cocky as always, he and some of the scouts placed bets on when and where they would find Geronimo, and on whether they would be able to capture him or have to kill him. Clum and his scouts rode and walked twenty-five miles a day (the Apache wanted to make forty, but apparently Clum could not keep up that pace), and they arrived on the outskirts of Ojo Caliente on April 20, 1877.

Ojo Caliente was a sacred spring known to the Apache for its curative properties. The Warm Springs Apache, or "Red Paint People," got the red warpaint to cover their faces from its clay-rich waters. The healing pool* was shrouded by alders on a small tributary of the Rio Grande and was a vital watering hole for antelope and deer. Nearby the U.S. government had built an agency of adobe structures from which they administered the reservation, including handing out rations to compliant Apache. Geronimo was hardly compliant, but he was in the neighborhood, and he sometimes pilfered rations for his people if he could get away with it.

When Clum arrived, he confirmed that Geronimo and one hundred of his followers were camped just three miles away.[29] That evening, Clum and twenty of his most trusted Apache scouts went ahead and encamped at the agency in full sight, so that if Geronimo's spies were

---

* Ojo Caliente is today a swanky new-age mineral pool resort and spa.

watching, they would see only a small force. The other eighty of Clum's scouts snuck in after sundown and hid in the commissary building to await their signal.

At sunrise the next morning, Clum sent an Apache messenger to Geronimo, asking if he would come to the agency to talk. Since it was ration day anyway, which was always peaceful, Geronimo figured it was safe. He rode toward the agency with a small retinue of armed followers. Said Geronimo, "The messengers did not say what they wanted with us, but as they seemed friendly we thought they wanted a council, and rode in to meet the officers."[30] It was a mistake, one of the few such tactical blunders Geronimo ever made. To my mind, Geronimo must certainly have believed in his heart that he was headed for a friendly talk. If he had suspected any kind of trap he would never have come in—especially given the foul play and dirty dealings that befell Mangas Coloradas and Cochise.

LESSON:

Never become complacent.

Clum would later exaggerate that Geronimo came with "some 250–400 well armed, desperate Indians . . . rude and ruthless redskins."[31] Thinking he was here only to talk and maybe leave with some rations, Geronimo rode right up, flanked by five or six of his most trusted warriors. Geronimo dismounted, rifle in hand, and walked up to within ten feet of John Clum. Clum stood before the main building's front porch, guarded on either side by a line of Apache scouts, each holding a rifle at the ready.

Clum greeted Geronimo by berating him for killing ranchers, stealing cattle, and for refusing to come in with the other Apache to San Carlos. He barked that Geronimo would have to come now.

According to Clum, Geronimo responded like this: "You talk very brave, but we do not like that kind of talk. We are not going to San Carlos with you, and unless you are very careful, you and your Apache police will not go back to San Carlos, either. Your bodies will stay here at Ojo Caliente to make food for the coyotes."[32]

At that moment Clum gave his signal. The commissary doors flung open, and out jumped the other scouts, surrounding Geronimo and his warriors. They leveled their rifles at Geronimo's head. Geronimo was outnumbered and he knew he had been tricked. The hot air grew tense, with all eyes on Geronimo. He started to cock his rifle with his thumb, then thought better of it. While his Power told him that he himself would not die by bullets, he wasn't willing to risk the lives of his finest leaders. The odds were against them. Duped and now held at gunpoint, Geronimo had no choice: He'd have to fight another day. This Turkey Gobbler wasn't worth it.

Clum ordered Geronimo and his entourage to the blacksmith shop at gunpoint and shackled them in leg irons. Tricked by Clum and by his own people—the turncoat scouts under Clum's orders—Geronimo was hauled away in chains and loaded onto a wagon bound for San Carlos. He was disgusted—both at the scouts and at himself for falling for the trap. As the wagon creaked

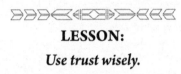

LESSON:

Use trust wisely.

and bumped along the rutted tracks, perhaps for the first time in his life Geronimo had reason to doubt his Power—for although his Power told him he would never die by bullets—it said nothing of the gallows.[33]

 | **Commentary** | ◁─────

Organize and Plan. *Sneaking undetected into the night with seven hundred family and friends, while surrounded by armed troops, requires a fail-proof game plan. The Chiricahua prided themselves on stealth—and for hundreds of people to silently slink into the hillsides or deserts undetected required planning, discipline, and execution of the highest order. There could be no missed assignments. Everyone had to know their role, do their job, and move in unison. The Apache stronghold proved that having a plan and a backup*

plan mattered. The Apache knew where to seek refuge, and they'd planned their escape routes long in advance. They left nothing to chance and had orchestrated a protected, defensible hideout.

Live to Fight Another Day. *Once he'd been tricked at Ojo Caliente, Geronimo had sense enough not to do something rash and get all of his best warriors killed. Geronimo said once, "It is senseless to fight when you cannot hope to win."[34] Sometimes you have to save your best warriors (and yourself) for another day if annihilation is certain. Making tactical judgments and understanding the big picture are keys to long-term success.*

Respect Everyone but Fear No One. *John Wooden said, "Respect everyone but fear no one." Both Geronimo and Crook seemed to live by this credo. Geronimo's biggest tactical failure, when he went to meet Clum at Ojo Caliente, illustrates this point. He probably didn't have enough respect for Clum's force and treachery.*

Understand Rivalries. *What made Geronimo and Crook great rivals is that they both had a lot of respect for the other's abilities. They also both studied and worked hard to understand each other. What makes great rivals is when you are fully invested in defeating the other, and this includes a healthy dose of familiarity and respect.*

CHAPTER FIVE

Women Warriors and Dreamers (Isolation)

AT SAN CARLOS ON MAY 20, 1877, the Turkey Gobbler John Clum threw Geronimo, now fifty-four, into the guardhouse. Geronimo, still in chains, stared out of barred windows with just a tiny view of the sky. The trip from Ojo Caliente had taken nearly a month, with Clum leading a long train of Indians that included more than a hundred from Geronimo's band. During the trip, some had contracted smallpox, the dreaded "spotted sickness" brought by the whites. Between the disease, and rumors that he was to be hanged, Geronimo wondered whether his days were seriously numbered. Geronimo later said that this moment "might easily have been death to me."[1] He was shackled and imprisoned, able to see only a sliver of the sky. He spent all his time chained up indoors, a brutal form of punishment that solidified his distrust for the U.S government and its authority.

With Geronimo locked up, Clum told the rest of the Indian band they could camp where they wanted to, as long as it was on the reservation and as long as they came in once a week to be counted and to receive their rations of food and clothing. The Chiricahua were made to wear ID tags and had to get permission to leave the immediate area around San Carlos and go to other parts of the reservation. Geronimo's followers built their wickiups on the cracked, arid flats while he languished for months in the guardhouse. Clum made plans to execute Geronimo.

Miraculously, Geronimo's life was spared because of Clum's greed and Washington's bureaucratic confusion. Arrogant and even bossy, Clum requested a raise and more Indian police to oversee San Carlos. He was flatly denied, prompting him to resign in anger—citing insufficient pay and an unworkable bureaucracy. He moved to nearby Tombstone and became mayor, leaving Geronimo to rot. There would be no hanging.

LESSON: *Outlast your competition. Stay prepared and focused.*

Geronimo's case got lost in the shuffle. Geronimo later remembered that the authorities held a trial or two without their prisoner present. Sometime later Indian inspector William Vandever, on someone's orders, removed his ankle chains and released him. Vandever thought that Geronimo was "thoroughly subdued."[2] It turns out he was wrong. As for Clum, he stayed obsessed with Geronimo for the rest of his life and later fumed at his release: "Upon whose orders this murderer of at least a hundred men . . . was turned loose, has been a mystery."[3]

With Clum gone, Geronimo decided to camp on the reservation with the Chihenne Apache for a time while he plotted his next move. The hunting proved horrible, and the tepid, standing waters along the Gila bred malaria. Geronimo was forced to wear an identification tag and seek permission to go anywhere. He had to agree to plant crops and dig irrigation ditches in scorched ground where nothing grew. "Not even the dogs liked it there,"[4] he muttered. The place was so hot and horrible that the U.S. military who ran it nicknamed it "Hell's Forty Acres."[5] Geronimo wasn't allowed to carry a weapon of any kind. For the next seven months he bided his time miserably, watching the white man's "spotted sickness" continue to kill his people. He secretly organized small groups of his warriors to steal weapons and ammunition, stashing these near his camp for the right time.

Then a tragic incident involving a family member told Geronimo it was time to bolt. Though tiswin was still outlawed, with Clum gone, production on the creekside stills had ramped up again, and during a huge tiswin party one night Geronimo drank too much and got into a loud, nearly violent argument with his nephew. The young man took his berating so hard that he committed suicide. It broke Geronimo's heart. On April 4, 1878—after near execution, four months of incarceration, and confinement at San Carlos—Geronimo knew he'd had enough. On top of everything else, Geronimo now felt responsible for his own nephew's death.

He gathered his immediate family, including two of his wives and their children, grabbed the stashed weapons, and fled south for Mexico. Along the way he joined up with Juh, who was still on the loose. During their flight, they attacked a wagon train, killed the drivers, and stole more ammunition and guns. A small group of soldiers pursued them, but Geronimo and Juh escaped by traveling light and fast. They made for Juh's stronghold in the Sierra Madre.

Geronimo returned to the life he was born for—living free in the Sierra Madre, raiding with his best friend, Juh, pillaging Mexican villages. They swept in and stole horses and cattle, selling the stock for more guns, ammo, and whiskey. Their raids struck like lightning and the Mexicans never seemed prepared. Geronimo and Juh would at-

LESSON: *Be consumed and passionate about what you are doing with your life.*
Think about it every day.
Live it. It is fulfilling to be consumed with what you are doing. If you aren't consumed by what you are doing, do something else.

tack, vanish, and attack again the next day, forty miles away. They lived like this, in the old way, for about eighteen months.

Woman Warriors: Lozen

BECAUSE THEY NEEDED all of their scarce resources, the Apache trained and fought with a few highly skilled women warriors. One of the most celebrated was a woman named Lozen, sister to the great Chihenne chieftain Victorio. She's got a fantastic story. Geronimo called her simply "Woman Warrior." As a young girl she could outrun any of the men, and she was courted by numerous men for her beauty and fine features. After her womanhood ceremony, many men courted her but she refused to marry, preferring the path of the warrior woman. She rode alongside the men, shot her bow and rifle with deadly accuracy, and was fierce wielding her war club or spear. In war or raid, Lozen rode right beside her famous brother, Chief Victorio. "Lozen is my right hand," Victorio said of her, "strong as a man, braver than most, and cunning in strategy. Lozen is a shield to her people."[6] She was a superb horse rider and excelled in roping, so she led many horse-stealing raids, shooting her rifle at pursuers with deadly accuracy. They said she was tough as rawhide and could kill you with her bare hands, yet those hands could be gentle too, for as a medicine woman she was skilled in midwifery and healing.

Like Geronimo, Lozen possessed Power. Her Power was the unique ability to locate the enemy. She would stand with her arms outstretched and turn in a slow circle, singing a prayer to Ussen until her palms tingled—then she knew the direction of the enemy and sometimes even their exact location.[7] There is a great image of her that comes from a firsthand account while she was on the warpath with Victorio. Once during a retreat they came upon a raging river. All halted, refusing to enter the roiling water. The current looked too dangerous. No one was brave enough to go first. Then there was a commotion and the line of warriors parted to let a lone rider through. According to Kaywaykla, whose mother was also a woman warrior, "I saw a magnificent woman on a beautiful black horse . . . Lozen, the woman warrior! High above her head she held her rifle. There was a glitter as her right foot lifted and struck the shoulder of her horse. He reared, then plunged into the torrent. She turned his head upstream and he began swimming."[8] Inspired by her courage, the rest followed her lead and they escaped.

Lozen was good enough to eventually ride with Geronimo's band. My favorite story of her is one of sheer courage, ingenuity, and toughness. Once, after a raid, Victorio's band was being closely pursued by the U.S. cavalry near the Rio Grande in Texas. Lozen was riding alongside a young, pregnant Mescalero Apache when the girl went into labor. Lozen quickly dismounted, grabbed the girl from her horse, gave their horses to her fleeing companions, and went off into thick brush to hide from the cavalry and act as midwife. With soldiers riding just nearby, Lozen managed to deliver

LESSON: *Treat all people with dignity. You never know what skills or talents will emerge in someone. Lozen was a woman who turned into one of the great Apache warriors.*

the baby and keep the Mescalero girl healthy, all without being heard. But now they were all alone and on foot.

Lozen still had her rifle, bandolier, and knife, and she guided the woman and her baby through the barren wilderness. Lozen had enough food with her for only three days. The first night they camped quietly along the river. She feared the enemies in the vicinity (both the cavalry and the Mexicans just across the Rio Grande) and knew she could not fire her rifle or they'd be detected. She crept into a herd of cattle, killed a longhorn steer with her bone knife, then cut and cured strips of meat for their journey. She swam across the river, stole a horse, and returned to build a crude cradle out of willows for the woman to carry her infant on her back. Lozen sliced lengths of hide from the steer to fashion a bridle, and the next morning before sunrise they set off through the mesquite scrub, with Lozen on foot leading the young girl and her infant on horseback.

Lozen knew where the girl lived, and she traveled southwest mile after mile, day after day. When they ran out of water, she found a herd of Mexican cattle, killed a calf, cured more meat, and made a canteen from the animal's stomach. She filled it with river water and they kept going.

Along the way she stole another horse from Mexicans, but these men detected her and she barely escaped as bullets whirred past her head and ricocheted off rocks at her feet. After many weeks of survival and countless miles, Lozen guided the woman back to her Mescalero reservation, delivering her. Then she set off alone to reunite with her own people. When she finally found them, she learned that during her absence, her brother Victorio had been slain by the Mexicans in a massacre at Tres Castillos. She rejoined the surviving members of her band and vowed revenge, soon joining up to ride beside Geronimo to the

THE AMAZON WARRIOR WOMEN

Legends of the Amazon women are fascinating, and the Spanish conquistadors had a number of encounters with women warriors. Columbus, in 1493, made reference to an island peopled only by women. These women periodically took men from nearby islands for procreation and kept only female offspring. Hernan Cortes in 1524 wrote about a place in the province of Ciguatan, south of Panama, "an island inhabited only by women, without a single man . . . and many of the chiefs had been there and seen it."

On the first European descent of the Amazon River in 1541–1542, Conquistador Francisco Orellana battled with women warriors. "They were very robust," reported Orellana's priest, "and go about naked, but with their privy parts covered, with their bows and arrows in their hands, doing as much fighting as ten Indian men, and indeed there was one who shot an arrow a span deep into one of the brigantines [boats], and others less deep, so that our brigantines looked like porcupines." According to the priest, the conquistadors battled hand to hand against the Amazon women warriors, finally killing seven or eight of them. "These we actually saw," said the priest. They lay there right in front of them, slain on the blood-soaked beach.

Source: Levy, *River of Darkness*, 72–73, 161.

very end.[9] Her remarkable exploits remind me of those of the Amazon women warriors reported by the Spanish conquistadors.

Near the beginning of the year 1880, after a year and a half of living free, Geronimo did something strange and unlike him. Geronimo and Juh suddenly arrived, voluntarily, back at San Carlos. The reasons for this aren't entirely clear, but I have a few hunches. Let's face it: To voluntarily go back to the worst place he'd ever lived, he had to have good reasons. It may have been that increased Mexican troops around the Sierra Madre, coupled with all the U.S. troops chasing Victorio's remaining band

LESSON:

Disguise your intentions.

around, made further raiding for Geronimo too difficult. Geronimo had left San Carlos with only a few family members, and Juh's numbers were not large—so Geronimo may also have wanted to return to recruit more of his own followers in the resistance, including the rest of his family, whom he missed. This seems most likely given what would happen next. At any rate, Geronimo's return was in no way an official surrender. He simply chose, until it suited him otherwise, to stop raiding and live on the reservation with his family. He was fifty-seven years old.

The Dreamer

AROUND THE SAME time, early 1880, Geronimo and Juh also heard rumors of a powerful medicine man, a prophet and seer named Nock-ay-det-klinne (pronounced *Noch-ay-det-kle-nay*), nicknamed "The Dreamer." Geronimo knew well who he was, though it's unclear whether he knew him personally.

The Dreamer was small in stature, just 5'6" and 125 pounds, but his presence was large. A chief of the Cibecue Apache band, he is said to have attended a school run by white missionaries and to have served as one of Crook's first scouts. Seeking a vision from Ussen, he ascended a mountain, fasted and prayed for many days, and descended as a self-proclaimed healer and mystic with a message for the People. He said that Ussen had sent the white settlers to Apache lands as a test, to ensure that the People believed in him fully. But the most compelling aspect of his vision—and the one that intrigued Geronimo the most— was this: The whites would one day soon vanish from Apache land, and all the great dead chiefs would be resurrected.[10] Nock-ay-det-klinne claimed to communicate directly with his supernatural Power.

Shortly after Geronimo's return to San Carlos, he learned that Nock-ay-det-klinne had earned a large following. Members of the Tonto, White Mountain, Mimbreno, and even some Chiricahua Apache began to flock to see this Dreamer who preached a message of peace, but one that promised the extinguishing of the White Eyes at the hands of Ussen and the return of their fallen chiefs. At first, Geronimo was in- trigued. He wondered about this man and what his vision might mean for his people.

After a time Nock-ay-det-klinne began to hold elaborate ghost dances on Cibecue Creek, about fifty miles north of the San Carlos agency. The ghost dances were spiritual celebrations honoring tradi- tional life-ways and dead ancestors. The ghost dance was started by a northern Paiute leader and medicine man named Wowoka. His vision foretold the resurrection of the Paiute dead and the removal of the white invaders from North America. Now, that was something worth dancing for! The dances evoked and conjured times past when there were no white people. The ghost dance would later spread to the Lakota Sioux and in 1890 result in the Wounded Knee Massacre and the death of Sitting Bull, as the U.S. military interpreted the dance as an Indian uprising.[11] The military authorities at San Carlos had similar concerns about the Dreamer causing rebellion.

Geronimo and Juh decided to attend a few dances on Cibecue Creek. They watched but did not participate in the dance. Indians came from far and wide to line up like spokes on a wheel and dance for days on end, moving around in a slow circle, their chants rising to ecstatic frenzy as they conjured the spirits of the dead while Nock-ay-det-klinne

sprinkled them with sacred cattail pollen. Pollen symbolized life and renewal, and they used various types in ceremonies. Cattail pollen was
used most often, but they also used pollen from piñon or other pine
trees or sunflowers.

Large numbers of San Carlos Apache began requesting passes to attend the ghost dances, and some would be gone for weeks at a time. The
Dreamer's following grew so large that it eventually did alarm the white
authorities, who began to fear that the dances would result in widespread uprisings. The reservation authorities had learned what the
dances meant, that they called for white removal. The authorities at San
Carlos sent a request to higher military persons to either kill or capture
Nock-ay-det-klinne to quell the frenzy around him. The military dispatched a Colonel Carr, who marched toward Cibecue Creek with one
hundred men, including twenty-three Apache scouts. They arrived at
the Dreamer's camp on August 30, 1881.

Colonel Carr found the rail-thin prophet standing before his wickiup surrounded by a throng of warriors, and he promptly arrested Nock-
ay-det-klinne, who did not resist. Carr began a forced march back
toward Fort Apache, which Carr administered. Geronimo, Juh, Lozen,
and a large group of Apaches trailed along very close, not trusting the
U.S. military. They worried for the prophet's life. Late that afternoon,
Carr called for a halt to set up camp, and he sent word that the Apache
riding and walking alongside were too close—that they needed to back
off or go away. But the Apache pressed in still closer. Tensions rose, then
shots rang out across the plain.

No one knows who fired first, but soon all were at arms. As the
Apaches attacked, Carr called out, "Kill the medicine man!" Nock-ay-
det-klinne took a bullet through his thighs; he fell to the ground and
crawled away until another soldier caught him, stuck a pistol in his
mouth, and fired. Nock-ay-det-klinne kept crawling, now trying to
reach his wife. Before he got there, a white civilian guide got to him and
split his head with an ax.[12]

The fighting went on until darkness fell. Amid rifle and pistol fire,
Lozen charged her horse through deep brush into the enemy's camp

and rode off with fifty-five army horses and mules. Remarkably, the Dreamer's influence was so great that for the first and only time in the Apache campaigns, all but one of the Apache scouts serving for the military mutinied. Angered by the death of the Dreamer (who had earned prophet status) and inspired by Geronimo's courage, they deserted their posts and fought side by side with Geronimo, Juh, and Lozen. Some of them were killed in the battle; the rest would be hunted down, captured, and court-martialed. Two of these were sent to Alcatraz, and three were hanged. As the sun set, the gunsmoke cleared and the war whoops died down. Six American soldiers and one officer lay lifeless. Eighteen Apaches, including six scouts, had died in the fight. And Nock-ay-det-klinne, the Dreamer, had been made a martyr.

LESSON: *Live, and fight for, your principles. People admire it and you'll inspire them.*

For Geronimo, he now saw only one course of action: He would strike for the stronghold once more and fight—to his death, if need be—for his freedom.

Commentary

Be Careful Who You Follow. *Be clear-minded and don't get caught up in the hype.*

>>>>◄◄◄►►►◄◄◄

CHAPTER SIX

The Great Escape (Audacity)

T HE U.S. MILITARY KILLED THE DREAMER, the prophet Nock-ay-det-klinne, at the Battle of Cibecue Creek on August 30, 1881. Geronimo was now more distrustful of white authority than ever. He had seen firsthand that the whites would kill Indians simply for dancing, for expressing their beliefs in ceremony and ritual. So Geronimo and Juh immediately held secret war councils with other Chiricahua leaders to discuss what to do.

The military moved seven hundred new troops around the perimeter of the San Carlos agency, confirming Geronimo's suspicions that something bad—like what had happened to the Dreamer—was about to happen to him. "A rumor was current that the officers were again planning to imprison our leaders," Geronimo said, adding that "this rumor served to revive the memory of all our past wrongs—the massacre in the tent at Apache Pass, the fate of Mangas Coloradas, and my own unjust imprisonment"[1] There were also rumors, which came on good authority, that the government planned to hang any and all Apache who had participated in the battle at Cibecue Creek, and this included both Geronimo and Juh.[2]

The Chiricahua chief Chatto could see that the increased military presence made Geronimo anxious. "Geronimo was just like a wild animal," he said, "troops made him nervous."[3] Geronimo felt that treachery was imminent, so in councils he rallied warriors for departure, and some agreed. "We thought it more manly to die on the warpath than be killed in prison,"[4] Geronimo reasoned. Geronimo used his verbal powers of persuasion to rouse as many warriors as possible to go along with his plan.

LESSON:

Communicate as quickly and efficiently as possible during a crisis or a challenge.

The Getaway

AT TEN THIRTY on the night of September 30, 1881, just a month after the vicious slaying of the Dreamer, Geronimo and Juh led the second major breakout from San Carlos. Naiche, son of Cochise, as well as the chiefs Chatto and Chihuahua, agreed to come along. They rounded up guns and ammunition, their finest stock, packed only the most necessary food and belongings, and planned the route and tactics for their flight south. Then, with remarkable silence and stealth, into the light of the half moon crept some 375 Chiricahua—including just seventy-four full-fledged warriors and twenty-two older boys who could fight; the rest were women and children.[5] Everyone knew exactly what to do and what was expected of them.

LESSON: *Have everyone know their roles and rely on them to perform these roles— this gives them the best chance for success.*

Now fifty-eight, Geronimo called on all of his guile and experience to lead his people to the safety of the Sierra Madre. He figured on being pursued by the soldiers and took premeditated countermeasures. Instead of taking their usual route toward Mexico, they chose a different, more direct but less mountainous route. This way they avoided the hundreds of U.S. troops they knew were stationed along their normal route.

Geronimo led the advance, while Juh took charge of the main body and rear. The women carried the children on their backs and rode horses, the warriors ran. Sometimes they switched mounts to rest the

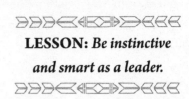

LESSON: *Be instinctive and smart as a leader.*

runners. They moved through the night, paralleling the Gila River for about twelve miles.

Then they cleverly divided into four groups to throw off and slow down the troops tracking them. Smaller bands left fainter tracks, and they could move faster. They split and then rendezvoused at a predetermined place called Black Rock—a jutting rock mass rising nearly a thousand feet above the desert floor. On his way there, Geronimo took a small band and raided a ranch and two freighters (tall, mule-drawn covered wagons—also called freight trains or freight wagons), stealing fifty horses and mules.[6] From the rendezvous point at Black Rock they hurried on, traveling another ten miles to the southeast, where they set up camp at the lower elevations of the Santa Teresa Mountains. It was late afternoon, and they'd been running and riding (and Geronimo had been raiding) for more than fifteen straight hours, but they would have little time for rest.[7]

By one o'clock on the morning of October 1 the authorities at San Carlos had learned from an Apache scout of the daring escape. A sub-agent dispatched the controversial Felix Ward, the child whose disappearance had been blamed on Cochise and who was now grown up and employed as a scout and interpreter, to alert the area officials of the breakout.

The U.S. authorities sent two troops (usually about a hundred men per troop) of cavalry and ten Apache scouts to follow the Chiricahua trail and to cut them off if they could. By the time the troops reached Black Rock, the Chiricahua were already gone, racing their way south. Juh and Naiche commanded the main body of warriors, while Geronimo led his band. Said Jason Betzinez,* who joined the renegades, "Geronimo was pretty much the main leader. . . . He seemed to be the most intelligent and resourceful as well as the most vigorous and farsighted. In times of danger he was the man to be relied on."[8]

LESSON: *Have a clearly defined, simple plan that you can lead and others can execute—but make sure to have a few variations to offset the opposition.*

Geronimo determined to travel about twelve hours each day, from midnight to noon, when the temperatures were cooler and they would need less water—then rest for a few hours each day in the hottest part of the afternoon and into the evening. Using this strategy, they could make up to forty or forty-five miles in a day. Sometimes Geronimo sent small groups of women and children to travel just behind the warriors, wanting to ensure that they would make it safely to their sanctuary in Mexico. The warriors would defend them from the front and flanks.

Remarkably, even while outmaneuvering the U.S. cavalry, Geronimo and Juh conducted raids at the ranches they passed because they needed guns, ammo, and stock for their stand in the mountains. Geronimo was on the serious warpath now, fueled by the events at Cibecue Creek and the masses of troops surrounding them. During their flight, Geronimo and Juh would attack and kill anyone in their path. They wanted to leave no witnesses who could say which direction they had gone. They came upon a large mule train of twelve wagons and 108 mules transporting more than fourteen thousand pounds of cargo for

---

* I know, hold the presses: *Jason Betzinez* sounds like an outfielder and not an Apache. His childhood Apache name was *Nah-delthy*, which means "Going-to-Run," but on the reservation at San Carlos people started calling him *Batsinas*, after an old Apache. Later, when he got shipped to the Carlisle School in Pennsylvania, his first teacher, Miss Flora F. Low, gave all the Chiricahua children new names and taught them to write them on the blackboard. *Batsinas* (which he thought was Apache) became *Betzinez*, and she gave him a first name too: *Jason*. That's the story (Betzinez, *I Fought with Geronimo*, 149–159).

San Carlos. Without warning, the Apache attacked the wagons, killing six Mexican contractors and seizing revolvers, Winchester rifles, and hundreds of cartridges, and they rounded up 102 mules. They also took brown sugar, flour, and cookware. The ambush was over in less than half an hour; dust settled over the bodies of the dead men as Geronimo galloped off. All this happened with the pursuing American troops less than an hour away.[9]

Geronimo and Juh pressed south toward the Fort Grant area, moving through the large, flat valley between the Pinaleno and Galiuro mountains. They killed a lone traveler carrying supplies, taking four horses; then they ambushed and slew four Fort Grant soldiers who were repairing a telegraph line. In the upper Sulphur Spring Valley, Geronimo directed the women and children to stay close to the foothills and hide among rocks and trees if necessary as the renegade bands passed through rancher Henry Hooker's large Sierra Bonita Ranch. With news of their rampage now circulating through the area, they met no resistance from ranchers and stole 135 of Hooker's horses, killing another dozen for food.[10]

A few miles farther south they attacked another ranch owned by a man named A. J. Hudson and stole every one of his stock animals (thirty-three horses and colts) within sight of his ranch house. As they bolted for their hideaways in the Dragoon Mountains, they harvested from herds of cattle they encountered, butchering as many as they could and packing the fresh meat on horses.[11]

By now news of Geronimo's escape and his attacks on ranchers and mule trains had spread through the area's newspapers. As he rode and raided, he earned the reputation among reporters as "the worst Indian who ever lived."[12] Geronimo's nemesis John Clum, now mayor of Tombstone, took the news hard and reacted fast. Clum organized a posse of thirty-five that included three of the five famous Earp brothers—Wyatt, Virgil, and Morgan—and other frontier notables like Curly Bill Brocius and Billy Breakenridge. Clum was still miffed that Geronimo had not been hanged, and he charged his posse to take no prisoners and offer them no quarter. "Remember, men," he called out as his followers reined in their horses, "I delivered Geronimo to the army once, in irons. They turned him loose. If we get him this time, we will send him back to the army, nailed up in a long, narrow box, with a paper lily on his chest."[13]

Wishful thinking and boastful words. Clum and his posse followed Geronimo and Juh through Antelope Pass to the western rim of the Sulphur Springs Valley, but heavy rains slowed him and his men and they grew wet, weary, and saddle sore after a couple of days. Though they pushed all the way to Mexico, Clum's posse never caught so much as a glimpse of Geronimo, and at the border they were forced to turn back because Mexico and the United States still had no legal agreement to pursue criminals or renegades across the other's boundaries. Said Clum, "We had no right to invade Mexico; we were not equipped for an indefinite campaign; were out of grub; so we headed our horses northward, toward the U.S.A."[14] (This is pretty amazing: Less than three weeks later, on October 26, 1881, Wyatt and Virgil Earp would battle Tom and Frank McLaury in the famous shootout at the O.K. Corral. Both McLaury brothers died in the gunfight, as did Billy Clanton. Interesting too that Tombstone photographer C. S. Fly was there. He seemed to be pretty adventurous, always in harm's way. His studio was right next to the site of the shootout. He also ended up taking some of the most famous photos of Geronimo ever.)

On October 7, 1881, after one week of running and raiding and terrorizing the American Southwest, Geronimo, Juh, and some 375 Apaches reached their stronghold in the Sierra Madre, a place they called home named the Devil's Backbone. Geronimo's escape was astonishing, supremely well orchestrated, and courageous. From the moment of their breakout, they moved fast and furious for more than twelve hours a day, in ninety-degree heat, across more than two hundred miles of rugged terrain. Raiding ranches as they went, they hugged the rolling foothills of southern Arizona's mountains, on their way to the border via the Dragoon Mountains. Geronimo supplied his people with stores of weapons and ammunition and enough horses and mules—between three hundred and fifty to five hundred—to mount every member of his and Juh's bands! He'd executed his guerrilla-style tactics remarkably well. The flight from San Carlos—called "the Great Escape"—consisted of masterfully conceived and conducted military maneuvers that garnered Geronimo much notoriety in the newspapers and began to form his legend. It also made him America's "Most Wanted Man."

The Chiricahua ascended to Juh's favorite retreat, "an immense, flat-topped mountain upon which there is a forest, streams, grass, and abundance of game."[15] Juh liked the natural fortress because of the steep, exposed switchback climb to get there. All along this trail were huge boulders they could roll down onto invaders. The Mexicans tried to get up there once, and young warriors rolled stones and logs down on them—leaving many dead and buried under the debris. The exact location of Juh's stronghold remains debatable. Juh's son Daklugie places it "just west of the Chihuahua-Sonora line in the Sierra Madre, about a three-day walk from Casas Grandes, Mexico."[16] This description is vague enough that no one would ever find it.

Once in the stronghold, Geronimo and Juh joined forces with a Chihenne chief named Nana to assemble almost 450 people, the most formidable Chiricahua fighting force since the celebrated days of Cochise.[17] With them was Lozen, the woman warrior. The Chiricahua were the only Indians in America still fighting for their freedom. The Comanche under the great war leader Quanah Parker, the Kiowa, the Cheyenne of the Great Plains—they'd all been forced onto reservations over the last two decades. The Lakota bands had finally fallen in the Great Sioux War of 1877; Chief Joseph had agreed to "fight no more forever," and his Pacific Northwest Nez Perce had given up. Only Geronimo and the Chiricahua were still free, still fighting.[18]

LESSON:

Everything is preparing you for something else.

 **| Commentary |**

Have Superior Skills. *Geronimo was a superior survivalist, a woodsman, and a tracker. He had exceptional vision and hearing, and he learned from every previous experience. He seemed to understand that everything was preparing him for something else. He was a cut above the other warriors around him, and he even dominated the Apache scouts sent to pursue him—able to remain ahead of them through his superior skill set. This he managed to do even with a team comprised mainly of women and children. All of the Apache, whether a warrior in his prime, a fifty-year-old woman, or a child, could blaze across the desert and over mountains. They knew where to hide and how to find food and water on the run. That says a lot about how tough the women and children were, true. But Geronimo was the best of everyone. It also says a lot about what a great leader he was, able to move his band to keep from getting captured.*

Know What You Want to Do. *Geronimo always knew what he wanted to do, and his opposition did not. He also spent more time planning than his opposition for what HE wanted to do. This is important. Every time he ran or raided, he had planned and practiced what he wanted to do, and his adversaries never had time to plan or develop a defensive strategy to combat his preparation.*

CHAPTER SEVEN

The Great "Rescue" (Passion)

IN THE LATE FALL OF 1881, Geronimo and Juh celebrated their arrival at the stronghold with a dance ceremony. To ensure that there were no enemies near, Lozen first used her Power. She lifted her palms skyward and spun in a slow circle, her face uplifted, singing:

> *Over all this world*
> *Ussen has Power*
> *Sometimes He shares it*
> *With those of this earth.*
> *This Power He has given me*
> *For the benefit of my people.*
> *This Power is good.*
> *It is good, as He is good.*
> *This Power I may use*
> *For the good of my people.[1]*

As she sang, no tingling came to her hands, and her palms did not turn red. "No enemy is near,"[2] she said. The singing and dancing could commence. Juh, whose stutter was so severe that Geronimo did most of his talking for him, could sing beautifully in a deep, soft voice, and he was "skillful in improvising rhythmic accounts of the exploits of his band."[3] He did not stutter when he sang. For days the bands feasted and sang and celebrated.

For several months the men raided and hunted; the women collected piñon nuts and baked mescal. They dried deer meat when the hunters returned, and made clothes from stolen Mexican cloth.[4] They prepared for future raids and warfare, since they knew that both U.S. and Mexican militaries would be searching for them. Geronimo personally directed the training for the young apprentice warriors in the stronghold. Juh's son Daklugie was one of his students, and he recalled the difficult training Geronimo put him and the other boys through:

LESSON:

To be a good leader you have to be a good teacher.

> He lined the boys up along the stream, after having them build a fire, and at his command had them jump into the cold water, even when it meant breaking the ice. When we climbed up the bank with our teeth chattering, he let us go to the fire for a short time, but then we had to jump in the water again. Of course, nobody wanted to obey, but one look at the stout switch in Geronimo's hand prevented any refusal. I never saw him strike anybody with it, but that club worked wonders.[5]

Geronimo toughened the young men for the rigors of war and raiding. He also taught them to study animals—horses and dogs—for their reactions to sounds and for their ability to alert one to the presence of the enemy. He taught the boys to watch rabbits, deer, and birds, and to read their reactions for

LESSON: *You should always be planning and strategizing, building and improving.*

warnings of danger, because animals have better hearing and smell and vision than people.

When not raiding or training, Geronimo and the other leaders talked about their future. They planned what steps they should take to remain free. Their numbers were considerable, and all but a few Chiricahua now resided in the Sierra Madre in Mexico. But there remained back at San Carlos a group of Warm Springs Chihenne under the leadership of Chief Loco, and Geronimo argued that Loco and his band should be with them in the stronghold. For one thing, Geronimo resented that Loco had grown so complacent and comfortable on the reservation. He'd gone soft. Geronimo would even have figured that Loco had been soft for a long time, because he was known to have opted for peace over war with the whites for the better part of his life. It was said that he got the Spanish name Loco because "he was crazy enough to trust the white men."[6] While he desired peace, Loco certainly did not lack courage. Once, while drinking at a watering hole, he was attacked

LESSON: *"Fortune favors the bold." Cortes said this. He was right.*

by a grizzly bear and fought the animal with only his hunting knife. He killed the bear single-handedly, but he was mauled in the process, his face clawed and disfigured and his left eye nearly blinded. After that, the lid sagged over it, and he had to hold the lid up to see out of the eye.[7]

Geronimo proposed a bold plan: to swoop back onto the San Carlos reservation and "rescue" Chief Loco and his band from the clutches of the White Eyes. The plan was controversial, and the leaders in the stronghold launched into heated debate. Chief Nana, who, after the death of Victorio, had been granted a co-chiefdom of the Chihenne along with Loco, argued that Loco had the right to choose peace and live on the reservation if that's what he wanted. Every Chiricahua warrior made his own choices. Several times since the great escape, Nana had sent messengers to Loco urging him to leave the reservation and join them in the mountains, but he hadn't responded. Geronimo argued that remaining at San Carlos meant certain death for Loco and his band, for they would die from hunger and malaria, suffering from the "bad water and the bites of the insects with the long beaks. They will die of that terrible sickness that causes people to shake like leaves in the wind, and to burn one minute and freeze the next."[8]

Geronimo, always persuasive and passionate, managed to convince the council that adding warriors (Loco had some thirty to fifty able fighting men and a few hundred women and children in his band) was worth the risk. If successful, then essentially ALL the Chiricahua left would be together, able to live in freedom. Nana agreed to stay in the stronghold with the women and children, and Geronimo, Juh, and Lozen would lead a group of warriors on the mission to San Carlos.[9]

LESSON: *As a leader, you must have patience and keep things stable.*

While the tribal councils and discussions had been going on, Geronimo and Juh had also sent a series of messengers to San Carlos to try to recruit Loco to Mexico. The messengers told Loco that Geronimo was coming. They just did not say exactly when. Geronimo was so bold that he warned everyone that he was coming. This put them all on edge. Loco replied that he'd rather stay on the reservation, riling Geronimo up even more. Loco reported the news of Geronimo's plan to the white authorities, who tightened security around the reservation, placing 2,630 well-trained troops in the vicinity of Loco's camp.

Everyone waited nervously for Geronimo to make his move. What Loco didn't realize was that even while he wished to live peacefully on the reservation, the U.S. government was making other plans. Since the battle at Cibecue Creek and Geronimo's escape to Mexico, settlers across the region were writing desperate pleas to Washington and their regional representatives to do something about the Apache Problem, to end the reign of terror. A grand jury in Gila County declared the policy of "taming, Christianizing, and civilizing the Apache"[10] an abject failure and called for all Apache to be removed immediately from the territory.

So, while Loco believed that his band would be taken care of, at that very moment the government was making a plan behind their backs to move them all far away from their tribal homelands, somewhere outside of New Mexico or Arizona. They'd be shipped off to some remote place that none of them had ever seen. Swampland in Florida seemed like as good a place as any to the government.

Rescue Family and Friends Who Need to Be Rescued

ON THE EARLY morning of April 12, 1882, around sixty Chiricahua Apache warriors slipped silently across the border and into the United States. Geronimo's war party crept stealthily along in two separate groups, twenty on foot and forty mounted. They followed the Peloncillo Mountains due north toward the San Simon Valley. The war parties regrouped at Doubtful Canyon, then continued on together toward the Gila River.[11] They headed for a ranch on Ash Flats owned by a man named George Stevens, who was away at the time but who had hired on a dozen Mexicans and a few White Mountain Apaches to run the place in his absence. Riding and trotting in silently, Geronimo and his warriors killed all the Mexicans except the foreman's nine-year-old son. The raiders moved fast, sneaking by the Camp Goodwin subagency (twenty miles west of San Carlos) at twilight the next evening and cleverly cutting the telegraph line there, severing communication and hampering the spread of news of their whereabouts and movements.[12]

At daybreak on April 19, 1882, a week after reentering the United States, Geronimo and his warriors arrived at Loco's village on the Gila, three miles away from the San Carlos agency. Jason Betzinez awoke to some noise and saw "a line of Apache warriors spread out along the west side of the camp and coming our way with guns in their hands. Others were swimming horses across the river or pushing floating logs ahead of themselves."[13] The Apache were good swimmers, since boys and girls learned to swim by the time they were around eight years old. Geronimo led the mission, calling out: "Take them all! No one is to be left in the camp. . . . Some of you men lead them out."[14] Jason Betzinez, who was among those rescued, recalled the suddenness of Geronimo's arrival: "Its surprise effect . . . threw us all into a tremendous flurry of excitement and fear. We did everything they told us to. We were given no time to look for our horses and round them up but we were driven from our village on foot. We weren't allowed to snatch up anything but a handful of clothing and other belongings."[15]

LESSON:

Use the element of surprise.

Get in, get out. That was Geronimo's style.

Loco attempted to negotiate, but Geronimo was in no mood to talk. He'd just ridden through a gauntlet of soldiers and was outnumbered forty to one. He knew he had to move fast. When Loco kept protesting, one of Geronimo's men, Chatto, pointed his rifle at Loco's chest and said he'd best come now. Loco wisely gave in. Geronimo led Loco's entire band of nearly three hundred, rescuing them. Others have called it kidnapping. But by whatever perspective, in all there were about four hundred Apache (including Geronimo's warriors) leaving the reservation. Some rode horses and others mules, with women and children driving stock. The group was strung out for about a mile and a half, with Geronimo's warriors protecting the flanks and rear and Geronimo riding out front, leading them east along the foothills north of the Gila.[16]

During the previous night, the telegraph line had been repaired and word of the "Loco breakout" traveled fast around the territory. Within a few hours Geronimo and the others were being pursued by a hodge-podge force that included "the San Carlos agency police force; cavalry units from Fort Thomas, Fort Apache, and Camp Grant; auxiliary scouts and trackers; and a few tag-along civilians."[17]

Geronimo moved the people through the rugged mountains where he knew of springs and watering holes. They kept to the ridges of the foothills so they could see any troops following below. The army carried weapons, ammunition, and water in wagons, and therefore the soldiers had to stay in the flatter valleys, giving Geronimo the advantage. They rested at a spring late in the day, and then Geronimo pushed them on a night march to gain some distance over their pursuers. Around midnight Geronimo halted at another spring he knew of, and here they rested and drank. Geronimo sent warriors to go find food at a sheepherder's camp down below in the valley. He would rendezvous with them the next morning at a predetermined spot on the Gila River. Geronimo had to urge Loco's band on, prodding them. He was right: They were soft. They had not been out raiding or on the warpath in more than thirteen years, and they were out of shape, slow, and tired.[18]

Loco's unfit Chihenne were glad when they arrived the next day at the rendezvous after nearly twenty-four hours of constant movement. They were even happier when they saw that the foragers had stolen and herded in some two hundred sheep. Despite being chased by nearly three thousand troops and several hundred Indian scouts, Geronimo chose to stop and slaughter sheep and feed his band. They'd need their strength for the final push into Mexico. They camped there for a day, gorging on good roast mutton and resting up for the next stage of the journey. An Apache kills a sheep by grabbing it by the legs, throwing it on its back, and cutting its throat. Then he tosses the carcass, skin and all, on a brush fire, barbecuing the meat while the hide protects it from the dirt.[19] Simple, fast, and effective.

While they refueled on roasted sheep, Geronimo and his leaders strategized. They admitted Loco to the council of elders and allowed him to help form strategy for moving a group so large across the border. To move fast and avoid capture, they would break into many smaller groups and scatter, all planning to rendezvous at a predetermined location which Geronimo knew of and described to the leaders. Some of the fastest warriors—those able to make between fifty and seventy-five miles a day on foot—were sent north on a horse-stealing raid to gain mounts for the women and children to ride so that they could all move faster and also raid as they went. They'd attack ranches in their path, kill ranchers, steal horses and mules, and ride off with any guns and ammo they could carry.

CHIRICAHUA HORSEMANSHIP

By the time they were just six or seven, Chiricahua kids could sling themselves onto the back of a horse and ride, using only a rope around the horse's nose as a bridle and reins. To practice their skills they would gallop down steep slopes, slinging down and holding on to the mane while scooping objects off the ground. They also were taught to ride at a full gallop toward a barrier and either come to a skidding halt just before it, or jump the horse over it. The Chiricahua developed tremendous thigh strength and, like all great horsemen, could influence a horse's movements through leg pressure alone if needed. Geronimo was so good with horses that he trained his to come from long distances at one shrill whistle—they'd gallop to him at full speed. At first he reinforced them with food, and later they'd just come. This allowed him to dismount, separate from his horse, then call it to him when he needed it. Geronimo and other warriors trained their horses to stop and stay put when they leaped off and dropped the reins. Shamans and others with Power like Geronimo also performed "horse ceremonies" to tame wild horses. They sang and prayed to them. They were the precursors to what we'd call today "horse whisperers."

Sources: Opler, *An Apache Life-Way*, 298; Ball, *Indeh*, 95, 95n; Barrett, *Geronimo, His Own Story*, 120; Mails, *The People Called Apache*, 281–82.

Soon the warriors returned with a small herd of horses, and they spent a day breaking horses for riding—either bareback or with crude saddles. They were expert at slipping a thong or rope noose over the horse's nose and making a bridle and bit, also with rope. They hobbled horses with woven yucca rope.[20] The Chiricahua fashioned makeshift saddles by wrapping either skins or woven cloth around bundles of tulles or reeds and lashing it over the animal's backs.[21] They were ingenious and functional on the run. It didn't take them long to jump on completely wild horses and break them enough to ride. Well fed and with freshly broken horses, Geronimo moved southward again.

Womanhood Ceremony

SHORTLY AFTERWARD, THE main body joined the advance guard and they moved as one. Before they had gone far, one of the young girls with them reached puberty. Immediately her parents stopped and arranged the traditional ceremony to honor her arrival at womanhood. The womanhood ceremony signifies the woman's readiness to marry and it is one of the most important events in a woman's life. The ceremony is never neglected, not even when the tribe is being chased by thousands of troops.

Normally the elaborate ritual takes four full days, with the girl bedecked in the finest buckskin dress embroidered with elaborate beadwork and tin bells. The ceremony is conducted by an experienced elder tribeswoman versed in the rituals, and there is sacred drumming, prayers to the four cardinal directions, chanting and singing, gift exchanges between the parents of the girl and the woman in charge, all culminating in a grand feast lasting four days and four nights. In this case, because they were on the run and in danger, the parents held a shortened ceremony and they all took off again that night.[22] Geronimo led them through the dark and moonless night, heading for a water hole he knew of near the foot of Steins Peak. He directed everyone to stay close together in a tight column. His best warriors flanked the main body to keep them all together. They bore south toward the Peloncillos into Mexico.

By now, Loco and his band had become resigned to being part of the renegades. They followed Geronimo's lead without question. The next day, at the rendezvous four miles north of Stein's Peak, the Apache made camp on the level canyon bottom, placing sentries on elevated canyon rim rocks. The

LESSON: *You must deal with the circumstances you have, those right in front of you. To do this well, you have to stay committed to technique.*

place was called Horseshoe Canyon. The sentries did not have to wait long before they saw a small group of horsemen winding up the canyon after them. It was the 4th Cavalry battalions commanded by Lieutenant Colonel George A. Forsyth. The sentries hurried to the leaders and Geronimo ordered the campfires doused and warriors into position on the canyon tops and craggy rim rocks. From there they could ambush their army pursuers.

When the cavalry came within a mile of their hiding places, the warriors stripped off their shirts and readied for battle. Geronimo ordered all able warriors to prepare for battle, and he sent some down the ravine. Shooting started immediately. Jason Betzinez, still a novice, watched from behind rocks high up on the mountainside: "The firing grew very heavy, almost continuous. The soldiers fired ferocious volleys. Those of us who were watching were shivering with excitement as our men slowly withdrew under this fire."[23] Around sunset, the shots died out and the entire band moved quietly southwest. One warrior had been killed and three or four wounded. Forsyth, unwilling to follow the renegade Apache at night farther into the mountains, turned back north toward San Carlos. He'd lost one man and five had been wounded. Apparently Forsyth did not like his chances in the narrow canyons ahead, saying he had never seen a more rugged place.[24]

Geronimo ordered everyone to move silently down the mountainside. They descended into the San Simon Valley to the west. They moved through sharp cactus and yucca thorns and knife-sharp rock as they walked and rode, stopping to rendezvous and rest at a spring in the Chiricahua Mountains on the morning of April 24. They watered the stock and themselves, filling their intestine-bladder canteens. They then proceeded to yet another spring farther south, near a mining town called Galeyville just north of the Mexican border.[25]

The bands rested and drank and ate what they had. That afternoon Geronimo's sentries saw a large cloud of dust not far off up the valley, and Geronimo sprang into action, renewing their flight. He orchestrated a long, difficult night march, cutting across the San Simon Valley in a southeasterly arc, then pushing all the next day across the rough

Peloncillos, rising to near seven thousand feet. After another night march they slipped down into Sonora on April 26, 1882, exactly one week since taking Loco and his band from San Carlos.[26] They had been running, walking, and riding now for thirty-six straight hours and had covered more than one hundred miles. This last marathon effort was a tremendous feat, and one of the band later claimed that Geronimo used his Power to sing so that the night would last two or three hours longer, allowing his people to safely reach the Chiricahua Mountains.[27] Maybe he did.

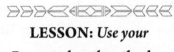

LESSON: *Use your Power to lengthen the day. Work harder, do more.*

For Geronimo, it had been a masterful week of leadership, cunning, and daring. He had swooped into San Carlos and, despite warning everyone that he was coming, had removed Loco and his entire band from the reservation. He'd avoided nearly three thousand U.S. troops, had successfully raided sheep and cattle ranches in his retreat, and during all this had managed to convert Loco into his renegade ranks. Finally, in a wide valley near the Enmedio Mountains—about twenty miles south of the border—Geronimo ordered the people to halt and to celebrate. They were safely in Mexico. They made camp west of a cool, clear spring near a rocky butte and prepared for two nights of feasting, merriment, and dancing.[28]

| Commentary |

Be Tactical and Strategize. *Geronimo's "rescue" of Loco's Apache confined to the reservation at San Carlos was an example of tactical genius and cunning. Geronimo showed an uncanny ability to improvise, to think creatively, to go on the offensive with the element of surprise. He confused the authorities with bravado by warning them that he was coming—and then he waited,*

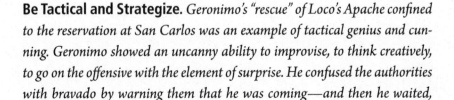

using patience, and came on his own terms, even though they were expecting him. When the moment was right for him, he charged forward. Having lived before on the reservation, he understood his opponent extraordinarily well, and this knowledge—gained through observation and study—allowed him to know where sentries would be posted at what times of night, and where all the escape routes were for his exit strategy. It was brilliant and bold.

Have Ambition. *Geronimo always had a high level of ambition. His was not solely for individual gain but for what he believed was the good of the tribe. He was taught ambition at a young age—not just to be a good warrior but to be the best warrior. Ambition was an integral part of who Geronimo was.*

Have a plan and a backup plan or exit strategy. *Geronimo planned his raids meticulously, and the "rescue" of Loco was no different. He knew exactly where the springs were (the pursuing soldiers did not) and had also planned their rendezvous points along the route well ahead of time. This way, when things did not go as expected (they rarely do) or the main group got split up (it often did), everyone in the tribe knew where to rendezvous along the route.*

Take Calculated Risks. *Geronimo understood the risks involved in infiltrating San Carlos. He knew there were thousands of soldiers around. But he calculated his arrival and departure moments, and he knew exactly where the soldiers were when he came. There was some risk of failure, but his calculations and planning lessened that risk.*

Do What You Have to Do. *Loco was a respected chief, but Geronimo viewed him as weak and compliant to the whites. Geronimo needed warriors if he wanted to save his people, so he overrode Loco's wishes and removed him from San Carlos at gunpoint. Everyone needs an external push now and then. Loco did. Geronimo provided that push.*

CHAPTER EIGHT

Tragedy in Sonora (Fallibility)

WHILE GERONIMO WAS CELEBRATING the successful rescue of Loco's band and their escape back to Mexico in the early spring of 1882, the Arizona and New Mexico newspapers were wild with stories of his mayhem. It's true that Geronimo and Juh had been violent in their weeklong flight from San Carlos. They had raided their way from the reservation to the border, leaving a trail of blood and death. The count: Forty-two settlers were dead and five wounded; seven soldiers and scouts were dead, and five wounded in combat. According to an army inquiry, Geronimo and his renegades had raided over $30,000 worth of civilian livestock and property.[1]

> **LESSON:** *Don't let what others think or say about you cloud your vision or your judgment. Leaders expose themselves to massive criticism, especially from the media. Remain true to your vision and judgment.*

These were hard numbers and facts. But the newspapers told sensational, exaggerated tales of Geronimo's trail of wrath. In one account Geronimo tortured a sheepherder until tiring of the game and splitting his head with an axe, then he took stones and beat to death the herder's wife and two sons. Another account from Tombstone claimed that Geronimo attacked a ranch, murdered three adults and took a teenage girl hostage, then grabbed a small child by the feet, swung the child, and battered its brains against the side of a house.[2] Yet another gruesome tale had Geronimo's men slaying two children, "one of whom they roasted alive and the other tossed screaming into a net of needle-crowned cactus."[3] The unreliable and fabricated accounts fed on and fueled a climate of fear.

So while Geronimo, Juh, and Loco were singing and celebrating, news of their "depredations" (as the whites called them) spread through the newspapers and telegraph wires north of the border. Geronimo's name was becoming a household word synonymous with terror and cold-blooded murder. He was Public Enemy Number 1.

As a result, a small contingent of army troops (about 110 men), including one of Crook's finest trackers—Chief of Scouts Al Sieber—stalked Geronimo all the way into Mexico. They broke the U.S.-Mexico border agreement and entered foreign soil without permission. On the second day of celebrations, as the campfires burned down just before dawn, three Apache women and a young man (a grandson of Mangas Coloradas, it turns out) went to attend a pit in which mescal was roasting. The agave plants, an Apache food staple they'd not had at San Carlos, were plentiful here, and the women had been roasting the fleshy stalks since they'd stopped to rest and celebrate.

LESSON: *Always be ready for your opponent to attack or strike with an offensive.*

About a dozen of the American army guides and scouts had found their way to the camp. In a rare letdown of his guard and lapse of defensive preparation, Geronimo had failed to post lookouts the night before. Now a sergeant leveled his rifle on the shadowy form of one of the girls turning the mescal in the pit. He fired, dropping the young woman dead. The others sprinted back to the camp as bullets ricocheted around them. Loco's son fell to his death during the attack.[4]

Some of the Chiricahua were still awake from the previous evening's dancing. Now all the others were shocked awake by the surprise attack, and they scrambled into action. Geronimo hollered directions, calling warriors to positions on the west side of the canyon. Armed with Sharps, Winchesters, and Springfields, the Chiricahua returned fire, reloading as fast as they could. The women and children took cover between rocks and in crevices on the butte. The firing went back and forth until nearly noon. The soldiers and scouts unloaded some five thousand rounds during the half-day battle.[5] But the army men and scouts couldn't get close enough to flush Geronimo and his warriors from their defensive positions in the rocks. By early afternoon the soldiers were low on ammunition and brutally thirsty and hungry. They'd gone nearly twenty-four hours without food or water. The Apache, on the other hand, knew where to find water and usually carried some with them. Plus they thrived on discomfort. They could stay there indefinitely. So the army withdrew.

Loco, who lost his son in the battle and was wounded in the leg, had no time to mourn. He led the main column from the rocky butte down to the foothills of the Enmedio Mountains. An advance guard had departed earlier while the firefight was still raging. The Apaches had lost the bulk of their horses to the Americans and left fourteen of their people dead in the mountains.[6]

The Chiricahua were now mostly on foot. A number of their women and children had been wounded in the onslaught of bullets ricocheting off the rim rocks. They made a reed stretcher for one woman who had been shot in the leg and dragged her for a while, then mounted her on one of their remaining horses, but she was unfit to ride and was bucked off. Not wanting to slow her family's progress and risk their capture, she asked them to leave her there and they eventually abandoned her on the side of the trail.[7]

Geronimo's people limped southward through the night, battle weary. They'd set as their final rendezvous point the crags of the Carcay Mountains and Juh's stronghold. Snaking in a long convoy, Geronimo remained a couple of miles behind with the best fighting men, protecting the rear; Loco led his people, mainly women and children; a small advance guard of fifteen warriors led the march toward their mountain sanctuary.[8]

Ambush at Alisos Creek

GERONIMO KNEW THEY must keep moving to distance themselves from the persistent American army. They moved across a sand-swept plain riddled with shallow ravines that slowed their progress, and at daybreak they arrived at the dry streambed of Alisos Creek. Beyond the creek they could see the foothills of the mountains where they were headed, just a mile farther ahead. Juh's stronghold lay some thirty or forty miles beyond that. The advance guard trotted through the ravine and headed for the foothills. They were in the home stretch.[9]

Then, just as Loco led his people into the creek bottom, gunfire rang out and bullets pounded them. It was an ambush by two hundred and fifty men led by a Colonel Lorenzo Garcia of the 6th Mexican Infantry.[10] Garcia, one of Mexico's finest Indian fighters, had learned that Geronimo and Juh were moving their people from the United States to Juh's stronghold. Garcia had let the small advance guard pass by first to allow an attack on the larger main body of Apache.

LESSON: *Be fearless and lead by example. There is a lot of risk in being a leader and directing others. Have faith in yourself and those battling with you.*

Jason Betzinez witnessed and recorded the ambush:

> Almost immediately Mexicans were right among us all, shooting down women and children right and left. . . . It was a dreadful, pitiful sight and one I will never forget. People were falling and bleeding, and dying on all sides of us. Whole fam-

ilies were slaughtered on the spot, wholly unable to defend themselves. . . . Those who could run the fastest and the farthest managed to escape.[11]

Geronimo acted fast, leading thirty-two of his finest warriors into the fighting. He called for warriors to protect the women and children even if it cost them their lives. Some of the women dug holes in the creek bank and hid children in them. Geronimo and his men hacked footholds in the bank and fired from these makeshift trenches as the women handed out ammunition and reloaded rifles. Accounts say Lozen, hidden behind a large cactus, fired constantly, dropping a Mexican with every shot.[12] Loco and his few men fired arrows at the Mexicans.

Geronimo and the Mexicans fought back and forth for hours. Around midmorning, the Mexicans decided to mount a full-on charge, pointing bayonets at the Apache as they ran and calling out: "Geronimo, this is your last day!"[13] Geronimo shouldered his rifle, aimed, and shot their commander dead with his first shot. This caused the rest of the Mexican soldiers to retreat, but the sporadic sniping kept on through the afternoon, with both sides now running low on ammunition. At one point an unarmed Chihenne woman sprang from the arroyo, sprinted to a downed Mexican horse, and used her knife to cut loose a large cartridge bag of five hundred rounds. She courageously dragged the ammo back to the safety of the ditch—all while Lozen covered her.[14]

As sunset fell on Alisos Creek, the firing died down. Geronimo whispered for small groups of his people to begin sneaking from the arroyo.[15] Throughout the night, the rest of the Apache snuck from the arroyo and fled to the mountain foothills, where they hunkered down and regrouped. "All during the night," remembered Jason Betzinez, "we could hear people mourning and wailing for their relatives who had been killed or captured. There was no help for the wounded, no food, no chance of getting reinforcements. . . . We lost nearly half our families in this tragedy."[16]

It was a devastating ambush. Seventy-eight Apaches died at Alisos

Creek, mostly unarmed women and children of Loco's Chihenne band. The Mexican military also captured Loco's beautiful sixteen-year-old daughter and another thirty-two women and children, taking them hostage.[17] Loco would never see his daughter again, and he was devastated by the loss. Juh's son Daklugie said, "Loco had been a brave and fearless warrior; perhaps his spirit was broken. When that happens, a man is finished."[18]

The costs were very high—Loco lost nearly 40 percent of his band—and Geronimo was criticized for taking Loco and his people from the comfort of San Carlos and leading them to slaughter. Always stoic in defeat, Geronimo said nothing about this. He'd done what he thought was right—that's what leaders must do. He led the survivors to reunite with Juh and Nana, who had gotten away and were camped in the lower Carcay Mountains.

They moved higher and higher into the massive, thousand-mile-long range, with snow-covered peaks rising to nearly eleven thousand feet. Upward they went, moving beneath great towering waterfalls and across plummeting, sheer-sided ravines called *barancas*. They followed game trails made by deer, bears, and wolves, going deep into the mountains, until Geronimo finally felt safe. Now he had what he wanted: Six hundred and fifty Chiricahua, nearly the entire living tribe, were all together in mountains where they had never been attacked.[19] Gathered here in this sanctuary, Geronimo believed, they could never be defeated.

Commentary

Don't Celebrate Too Soon, It Weakens You. *For all his tactical genius in the flight from San Carlos, the premature celebrations after crossing back into Sonora showed Geronimo to be fallible, vulnerable, even arrogant. Interestingly, James Kaywaykla, a Warm Springs Apache who knew Geronimo well, said he was arrogant, to which Kaywaykla's mother replied: "All Apaches are*

arrogant; they have a right to be."[20] *Also, the sheer magnitude and fatigue of their journey could have contributed to their letting their guard down. Whether it was arrogance or the belief that the Americans would honor the border agreement and not cross illegally into Mexico—whatever the reason—Geronimo had celebrated too soon. It cost him dearly. It's dangerous to celebrate your victories too soon or too enthusiastically, since there is likely another challenge just ahead.*

Be Calm under Fire or Pressure, and You Will Keep the Rest of Your Group, Team, or Unit Calm. *Although his followers suffered losses and were under extreme duress, Geronimo remained calm as a leader and he illustrated this calmness through his actions.*

Learn from Your Mistakes. *Rather than dwell on your mistakes, no matter how catastrophic, it is important to learn and move on. All you can control is the future. It is crucial to draw wisdom from your mistakes to constantly improve your skill and your resolve.*

arrogant; they have a right to be."[20] Also, the sheer magnitude and fatigue of their journey could have contributed to their letting their guard down. Whether it was arrogance or the belief that the Americans would honor the border agreement and not cross illegally into Mexico—whatever the reason—Geronimo had celebrated too soon. It cost him dearly. It's dangerous to celebrate your victories too soon or too enthusiastically, since there is likely another challenge just ahead.

Be Calm under Fire or Pressure, and You Will Keep the Rest of Your Group, Team, or Unit Calm. Although his followers suffered losses and were under extreme duress, Geronimo remained calm as a leader and he illustrated this calmness through his actions.

Learn from Your Mistakes. Rather than dwell on your mistakes, no matter how catastrophic, it is important to learn and move on. All you can control is the future. It is crucial to draw wisdom from your mistakes to constantly improve your skill and your resolve.

CHAPTER NINE

Raiding from the Stronghold
(Perseverance)

IT WAS MAY 1882 when Geronimo guided the survivors of the Alisos Creek massacre deep into the mountains to Juh's primary stronghold in the high Sierra Madre. The place was called Bugatseka, which means "On Top Rocks White."[1] It was a perfect spot on top of a level pine forest, flat and yet protected. Large pine trees lined a small stream. Although this was the main hideout, the Apache never stayed in one place for very long. They frequently moved from camp to camp for the next year within this immense maze of deep gorges and canyons—an area said to be several times larger than the Grand Canyon.

Now that they were back in Mexico, Geronimo and Juh wanted to resume their old ways of raiding and trading, but they saw an increased Mexican military presence in the lowlands. Sometimes the Apache made deals with certain towns, promising not to raid them if they'd reciprocate with peaceful trade. The Apache had traditionally raided ranches throughout Sonora and Chihuahua, then traded many of their goods in nearby Chihuahuan towns like Corralitos, Casas

Grandes, and Janos—always seeking guns and ammunition, as well as booze.

Many of the Apache, including Geronimo and Juh, liked the strong kick of whiskey and mescal, which were both more potent than tiswin. To make mescal, they baked the center or heart of the maguey (American aloe or agave) cactus and allowed its juice to ferment and distill. They then boiled the juice of the trunk marrow with water and spices. They knew how to add different roots and berries, as well as lime juice and chilchipin—the basis for tabasco sauce—to the mescal, which gave it even more kick.*[2] The Mexicans brewed their own concoctions of mescal and knew that Geronimo and Juh loved it; so they made it available whenever they could because they knew the Apache would then go on multiday drinking binges that made them vulnerable. Geronimo had an uneasy relationship at best with all Mexicans and bad memories of his family's slaughter at Janos, so he was generally suspicious of any deals struck.

Less than a month after their return to Bugatseka, Geronimo and Juh held a council with the other leaders and decided to seek peace with the Mexican authorities at Casas Grandes. Nearly a third of the whole band went along, some two hundred and fifty of their people, and they camped about four miles southwest of Casas Grandes. On May 18, 1882, Geronimo and Juh spoke with town officials: "We shook hands and promised to be brothers," Geronimo said of the meeting. The town's officials smiled and assured the Apache that all the troubles from the past were forgiven—it was a clean slate. They invited the Apache to enter the town and enjoy themselves. Geronimo remembered it well: "Then we began to trade, and the Mexicans gave us mescal. Soon nearly all the Indians were drunk."[3]

We're talking rip-roaring, spin-around, and fall-on-the-ground drunk. Jason Betzinez, now an apprentice warrior under Geronimo, recalled: "During the night I could hear the drunken Indians in their

---

* Columbus witnessed mescal being distilled and drunk by the native peoples in South America. The word *mescal* comes from the Aztec Nahuatl words meaning "oven-cooked agave."

camp, howling and dancing."[4] This went on for a few days. Then, on the third morning, as the Apache lay drunk and hungover at their camp, the Mexicans attacked with a force of 560 men.[5]

Gunshots ripped through their camp at dawn. Geronimo, Juh, and other leaders sober enough to function sprang up and quickly herded the women and children away from the camp. They left all their belongings and even their horses behind. Geronimo and Juh managed to get most of their people to safe positions under the cover of darkness. The Mexicans did not pursue them up into the mountains. The Apache, whenever they could, liked to fight with a mountain to their backs. They could then keep their opponent in front of them and below them, which were tactical advantages. It made the Apache hard to approach, and they were pretty much impossible to catch running uphill.

LESSON: *Fight with a mountain at your back. Know your position relative to your opponent.*

But when daylight broke, the surprise attack had proved fatal for a dozen Apache warriors, and some twenty-five to thirty women had been abducted. Among the captured was Geronimo's beautiful second wife, Chee-hash-kish, whom he married in 1852, just after the massacre that killed his entire first family. She was the mother of his teenage son Chappo and daughter Dohn-say (nicknamed Lulu). He vowed to try to get her, and all the other Chiricahua captives, back from the Mexicans. Alas, he would never see her again, though he later heard rumors that she married another captive Chiricahua man.[6] Geronimo soon took another wife, named Zi-Yeh.

Juh was crazed with anger at the deceit and treachery, and he raged in his stutter that he would burn the

LESSON:
Effective leadership requires clearheadedness and an even temper. These must be learned and nurtured, especially in crisis.

THE NINE WIVES OF GERONIMO

Throughout his lifetime Geronimo had nine wives, though never more than three at one time. Exact dates of all his unions are not known, but here's an overview:

1840: Marries first wife, Alope. She and their two children slain in massacre, 1851. She was his first, true love.

1852: Marries second wife, Chee-hash-kish. Remains married to her for thirty years, until her capture by Mexicans in 1882.

1852: Marries third wife, Nana-tha-thtith. She and her child killed by Mexicans in a raid in 1855.

1860s–1870: Marries his fourth wife, She-gha, a relative of Cochise. Also marries fifth wife, Shtsha-she. Little is known about Shtsha-she, except that she was with Geronimo until 1884, when she was likely captured by whites and died in captivity.

1882: Marries his sixth wife, Zi-yeh, "a diminutive Nednai girl."

1885: Marries his seventh wife, Ih-tedda. A captured Mescalero Apache, Geronimo first offered her to Naiche, but he was well supplied so he deferred to Geronimo.

1905: Marries eighth wife, Sousche, a fifty-eight-year-old Apache widow with a grown son.

1907: Marries ninth (and last) wife, Azul (also called Sunsetso). She was a Chiricahua woman.

Sources: Magee, "The Many Wives of Geronimo," 18–21; Stout, *Geronimo*, xv–xvii.

Mexican leaders at the stake when he got the chance. Geronimo also sought revenge. Instead of retreating and licking their wounds, the two would attack aggressively. From various positions in the stronghold, both together and separately, the two launched vicious raids.

Geronimo and Juh then decided to split up for a while, partly so as not to imperil the tribe's leadership by being always together. Juh remained stationed in the high stronghold haunts with most of the people—some five hundred, including chiefs Loco and Nana. Geronimo took a smaller, more mobile fighting contingent of about thirty experienced warriors—as well as his son Chappo, who was an apprentice, and new apprentice Jason Betzinez.

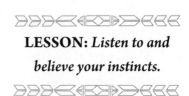

LESSON: *Listen to and believe your instincts.*

Lozen went too, entrusted by Geronimo to lead certain raids.[7]

Geronimo was bitter about the loss of his wife Chee-hash-kish and the other band members. For the next four months he took brutal warpath revenge across Sonora. His warriors prepared for their raids by "making extra pairs of moccasins, cleaning [their] hair, sharpening knives, and cleaning and greasing guns."[8] With his fast and stealthy force, he raided every Mexican pack train, ranch, or town he could. Mexican military forces tried to capture Geronimo, but he moved too fast and knew the land too well. Once, on a September evening in 1882 near a place called Oputo, Geronimo's Power came to him, according to Jason Betzinez:

> That night Geronimo told us that Mexican soldiers were on our trail. He prophesied as to the exact moment they would appear. The next morning . . .
>
> Sure enough, just as Geronimo had predicted Mexican soldiers appeared in the very place and at the exact time that Geronimo had foretold. The Mexicans went on to the creek, then retraced their steps toward Oputo. Our warriors followed and attacked them at about sunset. Our men captured all the enemy's horses and did considerable other damage.[9]

In October of that year, 1882, Geronimo led his small raiding force back to reunite with Juh at a place called Great Canyon, near Guaynopa.

When the good friends got back together, Juh told Geronimo stories of his own raids and exploits, for Juh had been busy too. He related one tale of a revenge raid in which they engaged Mexican troops for two days before finding themselves dangerously low on ammunition. So Juh hatched a plan, pretending to be in retreat and luring the Mexican troops to follow them. The Apache zigzagged up a sheer mountainside to a flat area just below the ridge-line. Juh ordered his strongest men to push large rocks to an overhang, poised for rolling when the time was right. Juh's warriors hid themselves behind the rocks, camouflaged by leaves, brush, and branches. They lay breathless as the Mexicans marched up the switchback trail. The Apache let them reach the summit, then leaped from their positions and attacked. As the Mexicans scattered and ran down the mountain, Juh gave the signal and his warriors sent the great boulders crashing down on them, the rocks so big that they splintered pine trees in their path. "Many soldiers were crushed by the tumbling boulders and falling trees," reported a participant. "Not many escaped."[10]

LESSON: *A great leadership strategy is to show a fake plan to the opposition—and then not implement it. It keeps the opposition always off guard and off balance.*

But Juh described horrible losses too. In one battle with Mexican cavalry, Juh's wife Ishton (Geronimo's sister, who he had saved with his Power when she almost died giving birth) was shot and killed. Juh's son Daklugie recalled, "I saw horsemen riding fast. They dashed through the camp firing as they came."[11] Juh's four-year-old daughter was hit and died instantly. Daklugie's sister Jacali took a bullet to the knee in that attack, and she limped on it for hundreds of miles. "Jacali had lost much blood and was very weak, but not once did she complain or make a sound. She was a true Apache," said

LESSON:

Suffer without complaint.

Daklugie. She eventually had to have the leg amputated. At the end of this attack, Juh's following of warriors was down to just four—and he would never recover from these losses.[12]

For many months Juh went about seemingly numb and broken. He also had a vision that shook him to his core. In the vision, Juh camped on a sacred mountain, at the edge of a great canyon. A cave he had never seen before appeared, and out of it came a great, never-ending stream of soldiers, some on horses and all carrying guns, and trains of pack mules loaded with ammunition.

LESSON:
Change is inevitable.
You must be ready for it
and even anticipate it.

"They came out of the cave without pause, like the lake that stretches to the horizon so that all the People could be lost in the sea of them without a trace." Juh knew then that they were doomed, that they were already *"Indeh*—the dead."[13]

Geronimo took charge. In the spring of 1883, with Chief Chihuahua, he led some eighty warriors on a rampage down the Sonora River to obtain more provisions and stock. It was a great success, and he lost not a single warrior. He also sent his trusted chiefs Bonito and Chatto on a dangerous raid all the way into southern Arizona because they needed American-made cartridges for their weapons. They swept into the United States under orders to kill anyone they came across. In less than a week they scorched across four hundred miles, leaving eleven dead whites in their wake. They returned with large quantities of stock, weapons, and ammunition. No one but their victims saw them coming or leaving. In its aftermath, this raid caught the attention of the U.S. military high brass, as well as the region's press, and the depredations were later reported:

> When the Chiricahua did break through into Arizona in the early days of March 1883, they numbered twenty-six, and were under the command of Chatto, a young chief of great

intelligence and daring. They committed great outrages and marked their line of travel with fire and blood; by stealing horses from every ranch they were enabled to cover not less than seventy-five miles a day, and by their complete familiarity with the country were able to dodge the troops and citizens sent in pursuit.[14]

Geronimo's raids were so successful that he called for celebrations in the mountains, dances and feasts and war victory ceremonies. Drum music thumped across the canyons and boomed into the night. They held a war dance, "the warriors dancing out into the firelight to show that they would go with Geronimo. . . . They danced in the old way; they danced the high steps and thrilled to the chanting of the women and the children and the sound of their names."[15]

Geronimo was content. They were safe in the mountains. The bellies of his people were filled with game and stolen meat. And as he chanted and sang and danced and laughed, Geronimo refused to believe that his world, his people's world, wouldn't stay this way forever.

Commentary

When Attacked, Counterattack. *Geronimo and Juh had been hit, and hit hard. They nearly lost their lives. But once back in the stronghold, they did not hesitate to counterattack—and that's often when your enemy or opponent least expects you to. They think they have you on your heels. That's the time to strike.*

Use Whatever Means Necessary—Even Trickery. *Geronimo and Juh resorted to trickery when they needed to—planning a ruse that convinced the Mexicans they were running away when they were really setting a booby-trap and planning to roll boulders down a mountain. Geronimo knew that sometimes you have to use subterfuge to your advantage, especially when you are on the defensive, or out of resources.*

CHAPTER TEN

>>>❮❮❯❯❯❮❮❮

Encountering an Old Adversary
(Rivalry)

MEANWHILE, AS GERONIMO clung to the old Chiricahua way of living in the stronghold, north of the border Juh's apocalyptic vision was coming to pass. It was the spring of 1883, and Geronimo was sixty years old.

Geronimo did not know it, but crucial developments north of the U.S.-Mexico boundary were taking place. The most important of these was the arrival back in San Carlos of General George Crook, or Nantan Lupan ("the Tan Wolf," as the Apache called him). Crook had left seven years earlier to head for the Black Hills to deal with the volatile Sioux situation, and he'd taken command of U.S. troops against Crazy Horse in the Battle of the Rosebud during the Great Sioux War of 1876. Crook, outnumbered three to one, got stymied and routed in a defeat that foreshadowed the disaster of Little Big Horn just eight days later. Except for Geronimo, Rosebud was the only major defeat Crook suffered in more than three decades of fighting Indians.[1] But the U.S. military persisted, and by the end of 1877 Crazy Horse had surrendered, and the Great Sioux War of 1876–1877 was over.

Now Crook was back in Arizona to deal with the Apache Problem. To appease anxious settlers, President Chester A. Arthur reinstated Crook in the region. Crook was, after all, the only general to date with any luck contending with these renegades, these "bad Indians."[2] Between 1872 and 1873 Crook had managed to subdue and round up all the Apache except the Chiricahua, and now it was time to finish the job. He was coming after Geronimo.

Crook returned still riding his favorite mule, Apache. He still dressed in drab khaki packer outfits rather than a military uniform, and he wore a pith helmet to shield his face from sun and bramble. He still carried a double-barrel shotgun slung over his saddle, ready to defend himself or shoot birds or game—whichever presented itself first. His mission was to root the Chiricahua Apache out of the Sierra Madre and bring them back to the reservation. The territorial press, inflamed by Chatto's recent and violent raid, called for nothing less than "the quick extermination of the Apache, both on and off the reservation."[3]

>>><<<>><<<
LESSON: *Don't fall for flashy uniforms (we can learn from Geronimo's adversaries too).*
>>><<<>><<<

Chatto's raids had caused a major stir for a couple of reasons. While pillaging between Silver City and Lordsburg, New Mexico, Chatto's raiders had encountered a buckboard driven by a federal judge, H. C. McComas. He had with him his lovely wife, Juanita, and their six-year-old son, Charley. The Apache rode the buckboard down, killed both McComas and his wife, and captured young Charley, taking him with them back to the stronghold on horseback. The killing of a well-known and respected judge made territorial headlines, but the mystery of what happened to little Charley consumed the nation for a short time and the incident achieved national fame.[4] The abduction spurred an intense search and investigation, and a call for Crook to find Charley, rescue him, and bring him home.

The Charley McComas incident became an unsolved mystery.

There are conflicting reports as to his fate. News accounts of the day reported that Geronimo had him and would ransom him in exchange for ammunition. A *Chicago Daily Tribune* article stated that Charley was living with Juh's wife, and that she had grown so fond of him she wouldn't release him. The Apache version of what happened to Charley is also conflicting and confusing. One account by Daklugie says that Charley died by gunshot during a raid by Mexicans;[5] another tale relates that an Apache named Speedy beat him to death with stones.[6] A few Mexican versions of what happened to him exist too, including a story that the boy wandered into the mountains and died from exposure. Probably we'll never know for sure—but most accounts agree that he died.

The abduction of Charley McComas by Chatto had another result: It prompted an agreement between the United States and Mexico that either side could cross into the other's country if they were "in hot pursuit" of the savage Chiricahua Apache.[7] This proved bad news for Geronimo. He was now an international fugitive, wanted on both sides of the border. Crook met with officials, who granted him permission to foray into Mexico to rescue Charley and bring in Geronimo once and for all. Crook's report to the secretary of the interior showed how serious he was and revealed his opinion of Geronimo and his band:

> The outrages reported have been committed by a small raiding party of the Chiricahua Apache, coming back from Mexico. . . . It is believed that they have killed not less than one thousand (1000) persons in this country and in Mexico [over the last ten years]. They are constantly trying to stir up mischief among Agency Indians and so long as they can run back and forth across the border this Territory and New Mexico must look out for trouble. They are the worst band of Indians in America.[8]

Crook knew that Geronimo and his followers were difficult quarry—the most cunning and fiercest warriors he'd ever faced.

Crook also believed that "only an Apache could catch an Apache,"[9] and he had been instrumental in organizing the scout system. He hired "conquered" Apache to track, interpret, spy, and otherwise gain intelligence. Crook praised the Apache fighting skill, tracking abilities, and general physical and mental toughness, saying, "In operating against the Apache, the only hope of success lies in using their own methods, and their own people with a mixed command."[10]

LESSON: *Innovation is someone doing things in a new and different way. Sometimes your adversary innovates. Learn from them too.*

Crook chose talented and enthusiastic junior officers to lead the scouts: These included Lieutenant Charles B. Gatewood at Fort Apache

GERONIMO'S ADVERSARIES:
EMMET CRAWFORD, ARMY OFFICER
(SEPTEMBER 6, 1844–JANUARY 18, 1886)

Born in Philadelphia, he enlisted in 1861 and took part in several major battles of the Civil War. In 1870 he transferred to the 3rd Cavalry for service in Arizona, and fought against the Sioux from 1872 to 1876, including in the Battle of the Rosebud, where Crook was also present. In 1882 Crawford became military commander of the San Carlos Apache reservation. His job included recruiting and training Apache scouts. In May of 1883, Crawford rode with Crook on the Sierra Madre expedition that breached the Apache stronghold. Crawford's role in the expedition was pivotal, though he rarely receives the credit he deserves. In 1885 Crawford was present after the final Geronimo outbreak, again chasing the hostiles deep into Mexico. On January 11, 1886, Crawford's camp took fire from Mexican irregulars and he was mortally wounded by a gunshot to the head. He was buried in Nacori, Mexico, but his body was later removed and reinterred at Kearney, Nebraska.

Sources: Thrapp, *Encyclopedia of Frontier Biography;* Lamar, *The New Encyclopedia of the American West;* PBS—*The West.*

going was so rough and brutal that even the mules struggled. Crook would need to send scout crews using axes and shovels to chop a trail and dislodge large rocks for the mule teams to pass. Some ten-hour days of this gained them only ten miles.[14]

Also along on the mission were Crook's aide-de-camp, Lieutenant John G. Bourke; Al Sieber, his chief of scouts; and interpreter Mickey Free (the controversial kid whom Lieutenant Bascom had accused Cochise of abducting, which resulted in the "Cut the Tent" affair and Cochise's ten-year war with the Americans). The mission into the heart of the Sierra Madre has been called "the most important and dangerous United States Army Operation against hostile Indians in the history of the American frontier,"[15] and none of those who embarked had any guarantee that they would return.

Peaches guided Crook and his force toward the towering heights of the Sierra Madre. The Apache scouts had all been outfitted with red scarves that they wore as headbands, so that Crook and his men could tell them apart from the hostile Chiricahua when and if they encountered them, thus avoiding shooting their own scouts.[16] Once they reached the mountains and the terrain steepened and became cliffs, the scouts were at their best, moving along at about four miles per hour, just fast enough to make a horse trot. They were able to keep up that speed day and night, sprinting up slopes that Crook's men could barely walk up.

As they ascended into the mountains, the Apache scouts seemed to get stronger while Crook's troops labored, drenched with sweat, gasping for air, their faces blistering in the sun. Even in the most sprawling canyon country, the scouts moved so much faster than the whites that they had time to hunt the scrub oak for antelope and deer, turkeys and quail, and to forage for wild acorns, walnuts, and sunflower seeds. In the evenings they still had enough energy to dance and sing.[17]

Peaches kept pointing higher and higher, and Crook drove his men and mules onward. The terrain was too steep even for some of the mules. They lost footing on the sheer slopes and fell, kicking and braying, to their deaths. The Apache scouts found signs of Chiricahua activity, including the sun-bleached bones of dead Mexican soldiers and slaughtered stock. Crook's men entered country more rugged and impenetrable than they'd ever seen: summit after summit towering one after the next; sheer, massive rock faces cut by chasms plunging five thousand feet; and knife-sharp ridges thickly covered with pine trees.[18] Crook realized he could not move the train of pack mules with sufficient speed and stealth to surprise the Chiricahua, so he sent Crawford and Sieber ahead with a hundred and fifty scouts.

On May 12, 1883—about two weeks after setting out, having traveled sometimes at night to avoid detection—Peaches brought Crook to an enormous natural amphitheater that was formidable and appeared to Crook "impregnable to attack."[19] The scouts and trackers agreed that the signs and tracks there were less than two days old. The Chiricahua had abandoned many items, as if leaving in a hurry. There was still meat drying on racks and tree branches, and stacks of horse and deer hides. Scouts from Crawford's party up ahead had come upon ninety-eight wickiups and large herds of horses and cattle. Most interesting, said the scouts—there did not seem to be any warriors around.

Crook feared a trap, so he advanced cautiously, establishing a base camp to await some of the straggling pack train. He sent Crawford on ahead. Just two days later some of Crawford's scouts came upon two Chiricahua, utterly surprising them and firing on them. The Chiricahua scattered, alerting others that they were under attack. Later that evening, just after dark, Crawford and his men descended on what turned out to be Chatto and Bonito's camp. Crawford attacked furiously, killing seven men and capturing two boys, one girl, and a young woman.

Crook had breached the stronghold. He had control of Bugatseka.

Remarkably, while this was happening, just as Crook was violating the most sacred inner sanctum of the Chiricahua, Chatto and Bonito were off hunting. Geronimo was about a hundred and twenty miles away on a raiding mission, abducting Mexican women he could exchange for those of his own people (including his wife) taken at Alisos Creek. Very few of the warriors were there to protect the stronghold.

When Your Power Speaks to You, Listen

CAMPED SOME THREE or four days' travel from the stronghold, Geronimo's Power revealed itself once more. According to Jason Betzinez, "We were sitting there eating. Geronimo was sitting next to me with a knife in one hand and a chunk of beef, which I had cooked for him, in the other. All at once he dropped the knife, saying, 'Men, our people whom we left at our base camp are now in the hands of U.S. troops!'"[20] Betzinez swore that Geronimo did not get this information from messengers, nor were there any smoke signals. Geronimo just knew—his Power told him.

Geronimo ordered them all to depart that evening, and they traveled all through the night and the next few days. Then Geronimo had another vision: "Tomorrow afternoon as we march along the north side of the mountains we will see a man standing on a hill to our left. He will howl to us and tell us that the troops have captured our base camp."[21]

Sure enough, the next afternoon a lone Apache appeared high in the rocks, on top of a hill to their left. He howled a warning, telling Geronimo that the main camp, fifteen miles away, was in the hands of General Crook and his Indian scouts. They had most of their people in custody. It was true; their stronghold had been breached. Geronimo's vision and Power had come to pass, as Betzinez put it, "as true as steel."[22]

Both Geronimo and Crook were in difficult spots, and both knew it. Crook had enough rations to remain in the mountains for a few weeks—maybe even a month. But he knew he had no chance of catching Geronimo and his warriors in this rugged country—it had been very bad luck for him that they were not in the camp when he'd found it. And he was also relying on his Apache scouts to remain in his camp: But what if they simply tossed their red headbands and mutinied, as most had done at Cibecue Creek? Crook and his men would be utterly outnumbered—and it would be a slaughter.

For Geronimo's part, he also had numerous problems. For one, Crook had many captives, including Bonito's daughter. Crook had been bribing the women and girls with food, telling them they would all be better off back at San Carlos. He had control of their most sacred of hideaways—and this was the worst thing. Neither Geronimo nor any of the chiefs still fighting had ever conceived that the U.S. military would invade their stronghold. Yet here they were. That the enemy had been led there by this Tzoe, this Peaches—one of their own—that was too great an insult to even speak of aloud.

So on the morning of May 20, 1883—five days after Geronimo saw his enemy in a vision—he and his warriors took offensive positions in the craggy outcrops a thousand feet above Crook's camp. Geronimo watched and waited. He was poised to attack, and yet he did not attack. He did not like the numbers—193 Apache scouts, almost twice the number of his warriors; and something about Crook's ability to even be there seemed to mesmerize Geronimo with superstition. That he had managed to get to this place made Geronimo wonder whether Crook also had supernatural powers. I think Geronimo may also have been hesitant because his best friend Juh was not with him. Juh had gone off with just a few of his followers after the death of his wife and had not returned. Hours passed, and finally Geronimo sent a messenger to say he wished to talk with Crook. If his messenger did not return within a certain time, Geronimo would attack. His best sharpshooters aimed their rifles, ready to begin firing.

Crook sent Peaches to tell Geronimo he would not ambush him and that Geronimo should come to Crook's camp—no harm would come to him or his people. Wary as a wolf, Geronimo still hung back, considering his options. Far below, he could see that some of the Chiricahua and some of Loco's band had been surrendering, coming in on their own by twos and threes. Disheartened, as evening approached Geronimo made his way down to Crook's camp and, through interpreter Mickey Free, said he wanted to speak to Crook. Crook looked up from his meal and told Geronimo he could surrender

ᗒᗒᗒᗕᗕᗕᗗᗕᗒᗕᗕᗕ

LESSON: *Don't fall for bluffs, but be an expert at bluffing yourself.*

ᗒᗒᗒᗕᗕᗕᗗᗕᗒᗕᗕᗕ

or fight it out, it was up to him. "You can choose peace or war as you please,"[23] said Crook.

It was a very bold bluff. Geronimo certainly had the ability to kill Crook where he sat on the log by his cookfire. But Crook said to Geronimo, "I'm not going to take your arms from you because I am not afraid of you."[24] Geronimo remained passive, confused, and even impressed by Crook's courage. He was showing great bravery and indifference toward Geronimo, traits Geronimo respected.

For the next two days, the two men had a series of talks, most of them interpreted by Mickey Free. What the two agreed upon, exactly, is unclear—but we do know that Geronimo never ordered any attack, and neither did Crook. Geronimo agreed, it seems, to return peacefully to San Carlos. But Geronimo did have one more scheme, one bit of trickery in mind. On May 22 or 23, he organized a Chiricahua dance and he even invited Crook's Apache scouts to participate. Geronimo's devious plan was to entice the scouts to dance with the most desirable of the Chiricahua women, then have his warriors surround them and kill them all. But Al Sieber, Crook's chief of scouts, forbade the Apache

LESSON: *Never make it easy on your opponent. Make them work for everything.*

scouts from participating in the dance. He'd seen scouts turn before: At Cibecue Creek two years before, when the U.S. army killed the ghost dance prophet Nock-ay-det-klinne, all but one of the scouts had mutinied. Sieber wanted no such repeat of that debacle. Geronimo's ruse was thwarted.

Still, Geronimo would not come easily. He watched, despondent, as most of the people came in and gave themselves up to Crook. Chiefs Nana, Loco, and Bonito surrendered, and at last Crook began the long march from the Bugatseka stronghold back north. He had some 325 Chiricahua, 52 men, and 273 women and children.[25]

But Crook did not quite have Geronimo. Geronimo at the last minute told Crook that he would come on his own eventually but that first he needed to round up the rest of his people—some hundred or so—scattered around the country. These included those still in Mexican captivity, as well as his lifelong friend and ally Juh. Geronimo said he could not abandon his people. Geronimo told Crook that he should be back at San Carlos within about two months. He even agreed to look for the missing McComas boy, Charley, and he would bring him along if he found him. Not wanting to start a blood bath, Crook had no real choice but to let Geronimo remain in the mountains. Crook rode north on his mule Apache, and Geronimo mounted his best war pony and rode off into the canyons to look for his wife and his best friend.

 | **Commentary** |

Trust Your Premonitions. *It's true that Geronimo was special—everyone agrees he had special powers and abilities. But premonitions, intuitions, feelings—these come to regular folk like us too. When they do, listen to them. Stop, pay attention, process, and act upon them.*

Don't Allow Your Adversary to Force You into Commitments. *Even though Crook had breached the stronghold, Geronimo was calm and shrewd and did not allow Crook to force him into anything. He agreed (tentatively) to return to San Carlos but only on his terms. He would come in if he deemed it the right thing to do, and only when he was good and ready. Geronimo had things he needed to do first, and he would take care of those obligations as necessary.*

There Are Some Things Beyond Your Control. *Who could have figured on a snitch nicknamed Peaches?*

CHAPTER ELEVEN

Honoring Commitments (Honor)

GERONIMO HAD SAID HE'D RETURN to San Carlos in two
months, but based on his actions he certainly had other priori-
ties and would honor his commitments to his friends and family first.
Crook he'd deal with later. Crook remained a perplexing adversary:
While Geronimo was glad to see him leave, he was shocked that Crook
had violated the stronghold. Geronimo now knew that the border
agreement between Mexico and the United States allowed each to
cross the border in "hot pursuit" of his band. That made things more
difficult. Plus he was now an international fugitive—wanted on both
sides of the border.

Then in late June 1883, while still processing the loss of Loco, Bonito, and all their people, Geronimo found Juh and his family. This was
great, and there was reason for optimism. Geronimo still had about
sixty able warriors and a total of almost two hundred Chiricahua.
Geronimo asked Juh and Chatto and the other chiefs (Chihuahua, and
Naiche) what they should do about their verbal agreement to return to
San Carlos. The chiefs said they needed to see about their people first
and that they needed horses and mules, since many of their animals had
been confiscated by Crook. They decided to do some raiding in Sonora

along the Sonora and Yacqui rivers. They waited out summer storms that swelled the rivers and drenched the cliff sides, then headed out. They split into two parties.

For the next few months Geronimo, at the head of one of the parties, roamed and raided violently across Sonoran villages and settlements, taking livestock and hostages to try to trade to the Mexicans for those Apaches captured at Casas Grandes, including his wife Chee-hash-kish. Although everyone agreed it was dangerous, in late August they camped some fifteen miles outside of Casas Grandes—the site of so many Chiricahua tragedies. They had determined to try to negotiate a prisoner exchange, and sent some of their women negotiators into the city to state that the main chiefs—Geronimo, Juh, and Chatto—wanted to talk about a deal. Certain women—like Lozen—were made messengers because they were excellent negotiators, had Power, were trustworthy, and, as women were less likely to be shot en route to delivering messages.

A Mexican official returned with Geronimo's messengers, flanked by armed soldiers. They talked. Juh demanded a large chunk of Mexican land and written permission to trade as he pleased in Casas Grandes. The Mexicans mulled it over, and negotiations went back and forth into September. Geronimo often spoke for the chiefs because of his skills in persuasion, reason, and passion. He demanded the return of their captured people. Things seemed to be moving along well, though in truth neither side trusted the other and there loomed the chance of ambush and slaughter at any moment. That's just how it had always been between the Chiricahua and the Mexicans.

Death of a Lifelong Friend and Fellow Warrior

JUH WAS A formidable warrior. He had multiple Powers, including foresight, a vision of the future. His name meant, literally, "He Sees Ahead." Riding, he appeared to others "a powerful figure on a sturdy warhorse."[1] He was a large man, just over six feet tall, thick and stocky but not fat. One of the white men who encountered him said he must have weighed 225 pounds, but that seems pretty unlikely given his exercise level. He was certainly muscular. He wore his heavy hair in braids that fell to his knees. He was Geronimo's best and lifelong friend.[2]

LESSON: *Learn to battle through life's adversities with friends by your side.*

Juh liked to drink, no question. And sometimes he went too hard; there is little question of that either.[3] During the negotiation period, Juh took to drinking the local mescal. On September 21, 1883, Juh rode his horse off a high, steep bank of the Casas Grandes River and died soon after. The details of what happened are sketchy and contradictory. Naiche—Cochise's son—was there and he offered this account:

> [Juh] got drunk one day in camp and got on a wild horse. The horse jumped on a high bank with him and threw him head forward into the river. I don't think there was enough water to drown him. I think in falling he hit his head and was killed. We found him lying with his head in the water dead.*[4]

News of Juh's death traveled fast. Geronimo mourned deeply. Juh was his boyhood friend, his brother in arms; impressively, Juh never did surrender to Crook. He had never even dignified Crook with a visit while the Tan Wolf was in the stronghold, returning only after

LESSON: *Don't drink and ride a horse.*

Crook had left. When he died, Juh was still roaming free. All the Chiricahua were shaken by his death. His two widows immediately cut their long locks short to show their mourning.

---

* Juh's relatives insist he was not drunk. So this one is a tough call and requires further review.

Juh's death also interrupted Geronimo's negotiations for the hostages. There was one final meeting in early October. The Mexican officers agreed to exchange three Chiricahua captives for three Mexican captives—and then they'd see where that led. But Geronimo sensed a trap, as did Naiche, who later reported, "We found that about sixty soldiers had changed from their uniforms and put on civilian clothes."[5] It was evident to Geronimo that the Mexicans were planning a double cross and a massacre. He said to his men, "We might as well go back. There are too many soldiers."[6] Geronimo signaled for his warriors to withdraw quickly, before they could be surrounded and attacked. Chatto said of the close call: "The way the Mexicans make a treaty is to get us all together and then kill us."[7] So any deal for a prisoner exchange was off. Geronimo might one day get his wife and people back, but not here, not now.

LESSON: *If you sense a double cross while negotiating, don't make the deal.*

Geronimo Takes His Time and Sends Chappo to San Carlos

GERONIMO HAD TOLD Crook that he'd return to San Carlos in a couple of months, but now he was in no hurry. With Juh's death, Geronimo, now sixty, was the unrivaled leader of the remaining Chiricahua. He would do what he thought best for his people. First he wanted to do some recon to find out if Cook had delivered on the conditions and treatment he had promised at San Carlos. Geronimo sent his eighteen-year-old son, Chappo, on a secret mission to go to San Carlos and see whether Crook was holding up his end of the bargain. Geronimo instructed Chappo to remain on the reservation for "three moons" and

LESSON: *As a leader, gather as much intelligence as you can.*

then return with a report—that would be in January 1884.[8] Until then, Geronimo planned to continue raiding in Mexico.

Chappo made his way to San Carlos and checked things out. He found that when Crook had returned to Arizona leading a few hundred surrendered Apache he received a hero's welcome, but that turned to suspicion and criticism when everyone realized he had failed to bring in Geronimo. The surrendered Chiricahua were told to camp near the army headquarters of the San Carlos reservation and await their fate. The officials running the reservation argued about whether to break them up into smaller groups, since if they were all together in one large group, according to Lieutenant Gatewood, "Lord knows how long we shall be able to hold them there."[9]

Crook's infiltration of the Sierra Madre was heralded in the nation's press as a brilliant achievement, and city dignitaries in Tucson hosted a grand banquet to honor him. But the praise died as soon as the press and the settlers realized that Geronimo was still out there, marauding. The papers called for action against the Chiricahua atrocities: "If the government fails now to hang these wretches by the wholesale, then Crook's campaign has been a failure."[10]

LESSON: *A good plan attacks as much of the opposition's organization as possible. You want to put severe pressure on the opposition while using space and numbers (personnel) to your advantage.*

Crook was in a bad spot. At Bugatseka, he'd told Geronimo that his people would be well treated if they came in. Now the press was calling for their execution. Crook was torn, and his own reports showed his conflicted mind. On the one hand, he agreed that the Chiricahua should be punished for "the atrocities of which they had been guilty."[11] Yet he cautioned his superiors that Geronimo and the others should not be punished for "violations of a code of war he has never learned,"[12] and that to punish them after they had surrendered in good faith would be dishonorable and lead only to further war and bloodshed.

Crook was a tough and even ruthless Indian fighter, but he was sympathetic to the Apache plight. He even supported granting the Apache the right to vote. He wrote to his superiors in Washington, stating that corruption on the reservations and "greed . . . on the part of the whites"[13] was responsible for nearly all of the Indian troubles. Crook had learned of graft and fraud on the reservation. Food rations promised the Apache were being sold instead to nearby settlers and miners; the meat the Apache were given was "skin and bone," and their weekly rations "were almost negligible when issued and frequently not issued at all."[14] Crook did his best to improve these conditions.

APACHE NAMES AND NICKNAMES

The Chiricahua had a fascinating relationship with names and nicknames. Early in a child's life he or she was given a descriptive name, like "One Who Smiles," or, like Geronimo, "One Who Yawns." Their names could change as they grew into other characteristics. It was considered impolite to call someone by their name in person—though it was semi-acceptable to refer to them by name when they weren't around. To avoid using real names, the Apache created nicknames to identify people. Some of these nicknames suggest personal characteristics of the person in question—but not always. Anyway, Juh was called "He Sees Ahead" for his ability to foresee the future, as well as "He Brings Many Things" for his abilities at raiding.

Some of the Apache made up nicknames for the American military who were chasing them. These are pretty telling and pretty amusing. They called Britton Davis "Fat Boy." They called Lieutenant Gatewood "Long Nose." One sergeant they called "He Consistently Places His Life in Danger." Another man who clearly got lost all the time was called "For Him They Search." Another sergeant was nicknamed "Flattened Penis." I don't even want to speculate on that one.

Sources: Goodwin, *Western Apache Raiding and Warfare*, 149; Opler, *An Apache Life-Way*, 429–430; Mails, *The People Called Apache*, 60.

Several months passed and there was still no sign of Geronimo. Crook had to do something. In October 1883 he sent a trusted second lieutenant named Britton Davis of the 3rd Cavalry and some Apache scouts to the border to try to locate Geronimo and the remaining renegades. Davis was a bright young officer fresh out of West Point. The Apache scouts called him Nantan Enchau ("Stout Chief" or "Fat Boy"), which I find amusing since he was stocky or fleshy compared to Gatewood and Crawford, who were lanky.[15] At the border, Davis sent three scouts into Mexico on reconnaissance and to encourage Geronimo—if they found him—to come in soon. They did not find him.

But Davis's mission was not a complete failure. After a few weeks, small groups of Chiricahua—who had told Crook they would come in—began to arrive near Davis's camp. Naiche showed up with nine other warriors and about twenty women and children; then, in mid-November, Chihuahua and Mangas arrived with about ninety people. They were all still armed, and Davis was impressed by their appearance and the way they could move on foot forty or fifty miles a day:

> Chests broad, deep, and full . . . from generations of mountain dwelling . . . they moved along the trail with a smooth, effortless stride that seemed as tireless as a machine and as rhythmical. The thought of attempting to catch one of them in the mountains gave me a queer feeling of helplessness, but I enjoyed a sensation of the beautiful in watching them.[16]

In February, even Chatto turned up, along with nineteen other Chiricahua.

Davis escorted all these Chiricahua to San Carlos under armed protection, taking remote routes to avoid any encounters with trigger-happy settlers or miners. Then he hurried back to the border to see about Geronimo.

GERONIMO'S ADVERSARIES:
BRITTON DAVIS, ARMY OFFICER
(JUNE 4, 1860–JANUARY 23, 1930)

Born at Brownsville, Texas, Davis graduated from West Point in 1881. He joined the 3rd Cavalry and was sent to Arizona. Crook put Davis in charge of Apache scouts, a job Davis performed well. From 1881 until 1885, Davis tried to keep the peace with the hostile Apache, like Geronimo, who kept leaving and returning to the reservations of the Arizona territory. In 1885 Davis and Al Sieber, Crook's chief of scouts, embarked on a perilous and grueling expedition into the Sierra Madre of Sonora, Mexico, after Geronimo and his rogue Chiricahua band. Davis chronicled his experiences in the book *The Truth about Geronimo*. After failing to bring in Geronimo, Davis resigned from the army in 1886. For the next two decades he managed the Corralitos Mining and Cattle Company in western Chihuahua, Mexico, amassing a fortune of nearly a million dollars. He lost his entire fortune, however, in the Mexican Revolution. He moved to San Diego, California, in 1924, where he wrote his book about his time chasing Geronimo. He died in 1930.

Sources: Thrapp, *Encyclopedia of Frontier Biography;* Lamar, *The New Encyclopedia of the American West;* PBS—*The West.*

"Reverend Doctor" Predicts Geronimo's Arrival

AFTER MANY WEEKS of waiting for Geronimo with no news, Davis was desperate. The following anecdote is great. It shows that even adversaries can learn from and use the resources of their opponents. Davis enlisted one of the Apache scouts, who was a medicine man, to see if he could locate Geronimo or at least divine some information as to his whereabouts.

The medicine man, whom Davis referred to as "Reverend Doctor," built a canvas hut some ways from the camp and entered it with his pouch of herbs. He stayed in the hut all that day and long into the evening, "uttering incantations and from time to time burning a pungent powder."[17] Around nine or ten o'clock that night he came out of the hut twirling a "thin buckskin thong to the end of which was attached a small, flat piece of wood with a hole in it. Twirling this around his head it gave out a shrill, whistling noise, not unlike the call of a night-bird."[18]

The medicine man moved around the hut, circling it as he swung his call above his head and sang incantations. Finally he came to a stop at the scouts' campfire, tossed powder onto the fire, raised his face skyward, and with a "singsong chant made many gestures with his arms; then suddenly he ceased and, bathed in sweat, tottering a little with weakness, announced that he had found Geronimo."[19] He said that Geronimo was three days away, riding on a white mule and leading many horses.

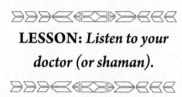

LESSON: *Listen to your doctor (or shaman).*

Four days later Geronimo arrived. (Okay, so the medicine man missed it by one day.) Geronimo rode a white pony, and behind him trailed a herd of horses so large that they sent a huge cloud of dust into the sky. Davis could not comprehend how the shaman had nailed his prediction so accurately; he was amazed by it, saying that he'd seen no smoke signals or messengers. And yet, here was Geronimo.

He looked like a man you did not want to mess with. A scar from a bullet wound slashed across his forehead, and he rode with a bullet still lodged in his left thigh that stayed there until the end of his life. The third finger of his right hand was twisted backward, also from taking a bullet. He looked vicious.[20] He came fully armed, riding with seven men and twenty-two women and children. The warriors included his son Chappo, who'd returned to report the conditions at San Carlos as "not unhealthy like it had been before."[21]

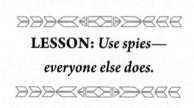

LESSON: *Use spies— everyone else does.*

When Geronimo rode up to the camp in the Animas Valley, just east of Skeleton Canyon (right over the Sonoran border in Arizona), he was in a foul mood. He rammed his horse into Davis's mule and demanded to know why he needed an army escort when he'd said he would come in peaceably. Davis told him (and this was at least partly true) that it was for his own protection. There were nervous and angry settlers demanding retribution for Geronimo's past violence against them; fueled by whiskey, these folks might take potshots at him. Geronimo said no more about it but simply demanded a three-day halt so that his 135 cattle could rest and graze, since they'd been driven hard to get here after he'd stolen them from the Mexicans.[22] He also had a large herd of horses and mules. They too needed rest.

Davis was now in a fix himself. Geronimo was planning to do what he always did—which was whatever he wanted. He'd driven a large herd of stolen cattle illegally across an international border—and now he was being escorted by the U.S. army. It was an international incident, and if the Mexican government caught wind of this there'd be hell to pay. But there was little Davis could do.

Finally, Davis suggested that they should not stop so close to the border but should press on ahead another thirty or forty miles to Sulphur Springs, where there was also good grazing. He added that he was worried the Mexicans were chasing Geronimo and would attack them if they delayed. This touched a chord. "Mexicans!" Geronimo hissed. "Mexicans! My squaws can whip all the Mexicans in Chihuahua." Davis pointed out, rightly, that the Mexicans had plenty of cartridges, while Geronimo and his warriors were running out of ammo. Geronimo's response was cocky and arrogant. "We don't fight Mexicans with cartridges," he said, smiling. "Cartridges cost too much. We keep them to fight your white soldiers. We fight Mexicans with rocks."[23]

LESSON: *Compromise is sometimes the best option you have. But compromise wisely, and in your favor.*

In the end they compromised. Geronimo agreed to press the herd to Sulphur Springs, but at a slow enough pace to not "run the fat off the cattle so they would not be fit for trading"[24] when they reached the reservation. They moved, more slowly than Davis wanted, across broken prairie scrub, the dry arroyos filled with hundreds of small wild hogs called peccaries, which the army men shot at for target practice. Wind hurtled across the parched ground and the herd raised dust as it went. Geronimo led his herd to a watering hole, the women set up wickiups, and Davis pitched his tents.

The U.S. Marshal and the Customs Agent

JUST THEN TWO white men rode up: a U.S. marshal named Clark and a customs agent named Howland, both out of Tombstone. The marshal wanted Geronimo for murder in Arizona, and the customs agent wanted to confiscate the illegal cattle. The marshal pulled out his badge and said to Davis, "I order you to arrest them and take them with their smuggled stock to Tucson for trial."[25] The marshal added that if Davis did not cooperate, he'd head over to the nearby town of Willcox and round up his own posse. But Davis had orders from General Crook to safely escort Geronimo to San Carlos. He had no intention of ignoring that order—U.S. marshal or not. Davis was in a bind. If Geronimo reacted badly, they'd likely all be dead. He needed to act fast.

Davis took Geronimo aside and carefully explained the situation to him. Geronimo grew angry, adamant that he would not give up his stock without a fight. Davis then took the marshal and the customs agent over to his camp and offered them some good Scotch whiskey. Perhaps a drink and some camaraderie would allow cooler heads to prevail (though usually with drink the opposite occurs). Finally, Davis turned to them and laid down a challenge, saying that if they thought they could take Geronimo's cattle from him, then they should go for it; give it a try the next day. With that, he told them he was going to bed.

They drank themselves to sleep.

When they awoke, the marshal and the customs agent discovered smoldering cook fires, jerked meat still hanging on wood racks, and wickiups still standing. But Geronimo, his people, and every single one of his horses, mules, and cattle had vanished in the night. Both men scanned the vast horizon with field glasses. Not a sign of Geronimo, his band, or his stock as far as they could see—not even a dust cloud hung over the prairie. They said they were giving up and heading back to Tombstone. As they packed their saddle bags, Clark admitted to Davis that Geronimo had pulled off "a mighty slick trick. . . . I would never have believed it possible if I had not seen it."[26]

LESSON: *Be brilliant. Leave your adversaries scratching their heads, wondering how in the world you pulled that off.*

Geronimo finally arrived at San Carlos in mid-March, 1884—more than eight months after he'd parted ways with Crook at Bugatseka and half a year after he said he'd be there. When pressed about what had taken him so long, he said he'd needed to get enough cattle that he could raise them at San Carlos, then sell them and make some money for his people. That was true. Plus, he'd been trying to trade hostages with the Mexicans to rescue his stolen wife and other tribe members. The other reason was that Geronimo had been waiting for Chappo's return and his report about San Carlos. If the report had been unfavorable, Geronimo would definitely have stayed in Mexico. But Chappo had told him that the reservation Apache were camped closer to the main agency and not on the low, bug-infested bog where they'd been before. Chappo told him that from what he'd seen, conditions were better than before, and the Indians were being treated fairly.

LESSON: *As a leader you must sometimes be elusive.*

However, the first thing General Crook did when Geronimo arrived was to confiscate his cattle. He ordered that the stock be slaughtered and added to the inventory of agency beef, and he made sure to pay the Mexican ranch owners generously for the loss of their herd animals. Crook saw this as a way to maintain smooth relations with the Mexican government. Geronimo fumed.

He saw it as one more reason not to trust the white man. He would never forget this act of treachery:

> Soon after we arrived at San Carlos . . . General Crook took the horses and cattle away from us. I told him that these were not the white man's cattle, but belonged to us, for we had taken them from the Mexicans during our wars. I also told him that we did not intend to kill these animals but wished to keep them and raise stock on our range. He would not listen to me, but took the stock.[27]

Geronimo and nearly all of the remaining Chiricahua in existence, about 520 Indians, were now camped at San Carlos. Geronimo had honored his promise, although on his own time and own terms. With Crook's first move being the confiscation of his herd, Geronimo had to wonder whether Crook—or any of the White Eyes—would honor their side of the bargain to let the Chiricahua live in peace. It wouldn't take very long for him to find out.

Commentary

Honor Your End of a Bargain. *It's important to do what you say you are going to do, otherwise people will never believe you. Geronimo took his own sweet time coming in, and why wouldn't he? He didn't really WANT to go to San Carlos—he hated it there. Even though he came in late, he did come in as he said he would.*

Send a Message of Strength to Your People. *By coming in on his own terms and on his own time, Geronimo sent a message of strength and leadership to his band: He might do what the whites asked of him, but he'd do it the way he wanted to, on his terms.*

CHAPTER TWELVE

Turkey Creek and Tiswin (Resolve)

I N THE SPRING OF 1884, once all the Chiricahua were camped at San Carlos, Geronimo made a formal statement to Lieutenant Crawford, to be relayed to Crook, laying out some of the terms or demands for his cooperation. First among these was the return of his wife and the other captives. "We want all our captives here," Geronimo said. "They are in Mexico and we believe that General Crook can get them for us."[1] Also, if Geronimo and his people must remain on a reservation and make another attempt at farming and ranching, he wanted suitable land, and he wanted his Chiricahua people separate from the other Apache tribes, since there was bad blood between them. "We

LESSON: *As a leader, always negotiate better terms for your people, your unit, your team, or your family. Okay, and for yourself too.*

don't want any of these Indians around here with us. We want to be alone, and have no Indians but Chiricahuas with us."[2]

For his part, Crook must have been feeling pretty good. With Geronimo now finally on the reservation, at least some of the heat was off of him—both from the press and from his superiors at the faraway Indian Office in Washington. But he had made certain promises to Geronimo back at Bugatseka (only he and Geronimo would ever know, for certain, exactly what they agreed to), and now he needed to at least attempt to honor those.

Crook knew that Geronimo was right—that tensions between the various Apache factions (the scouts whom Geronimo believed turn-coats, the more assimilated Indians who had always stayed on the reser-vation and who even feared Geronimo) might escalate into bloodshed. Crook agreed that the Chiricahua should live apart. He suggested some-thing radical: Not only would he give the Chiricahua their own area, he'd give them a choice of where they wanted to live. They could choose anywhere, so long as it was within the boundaries of the San Carlos res-ervation. Seemed like a fair deal, the downside being that most of what good land there was on the reservation had already been taken by the other surrendered tribes. Geronimo and the leaders mulled it over in council, and they settled on Turkey Creek, an area about forty miles northeast of San Carlos and seventeen miles east of Fort Apache.

Turkey Creek is a tributary of the Black River, fed from the White Mountains and adjacent to where Crook had some of the White Moun-tain bands settled. The place made sense to Geronimo because it was in the vicinity of his birthplace, and the place of one's birth was really im-portant to the Chiricahua. It mattered so much to them that whenever they returned near their birthplace they'd roll around four times on the ground and cover themselves with the dirt to celebrate the homecom-ing. Also, some of Geronimo's people were married to or closely con-nected to members of the White Mountain Apache. There were towering pines, flowing streams filled with deer, and some decent arable land—though not enough on which to really feed themselves without U.S. government rations. Once there, the Chiricahua Kaywaykla com-mented, "There was an abundance of good water, wood, and game. There was good grazing. There were no mosquitoes, few rattlesnakes, and no cavalry."[3]

No cavalry, but Geronimo and his Chiricahua were not to be left without constant surveillance. Geronimo watched as Second Lieutenant Britton Davis set up his camp in a pine glade on the stream, erecting his living quarters as well as a larger storage tent for rations. His headquarters was several miles away from where Geronimo and his people chose to camp, but Geronimo knew he was being watched. The worst part was that Davis had along with him, as his interpreter, Mickey Free, because he spoke Apache, English, and Spanish. All the Chiricahua—and especially Geronimo—regarded him with deep distrust and suspicion, forever connecting him with Cochise's difficulties and ultimately with his demise. He'd been there with Crook when he infiltrated Bugatseka too. They referred to Mickey Free as "the coyote whose kidnapping had brought war to the Chiricahuas."[4] He was a bit creepy—he'd lost sight in his left eye and it was glazy and gray and made him look sinister. One army official who knew him well said, "Mickey is . . . the most curious and interesting combination of good humor and sullenness, generosity, craft, and bloodthirsty cruelty to be found in America."[5]

Geronimo also discovered that Crook had employed the turncoat Tzoe—"Peaches" to the whites—as a messenger between San Carlos and Fort Apache. Geronimo would never forgive Tzoe for leading Crook to the stronghold—and he did not trust him. So it was with uneasiness and guarded suspicion that Geronimo and his 520 Chiricahua pitched their wickiups along Turkey Creek. It was in a valley that was shaded and cool in summer and caught the southern sun in winter.

As Geronimo tried begrudgingly to change from a nomad to a farmer, he had some other suspicions. He learned from his own informants that Lieutenant Davis ("Fat Boy") had recruited three "secret agents" or spies from among his scouts. These spies kept a close watch on Geronimo and would come to Davis's tent at night and toss a pebble against the canvas to alert him that there was something to report. None of the Chiricahua knew exactly who these spies were, so they remained wary of all the scouts. Nobody trusted anybody.

But Geronimo was clever enough to make some moves of his own. Davis organized a unit of thirty Chiricahua scouts, appointing Chief

Chatto as his first sergeant. Chatto was now a turncoat; that was clear. I get the feeling that Geronimo would have killed Chatto if he could have after that, but on Turkey Creek there was too much military presence and it probably would have landed Geronimo in prison.

Chief Chihuahua then enlisted as a scout too, though he would quit very soon—suggesting that he was likely planted by Geronimo to gather intelligence. And Chappo—loyal son to Geronimo, just twenty years old, who had just recently been on a recon mission for him—signed on as Davis's "striker," a kind of personal servant. Chappo insisted on this position because it paid an extra five dollars. As close as Geronimo was to Chappo, I'm quite sure Geronimo encouraged Chappo to take the position, since it would keep him near Davis and allow Chappo to secure plenty of intelligence. After all, Geronimo had very recently used his own son as a spy.[6] Geronimo knew that the army used spies, and so he would engage in counterintelligence.

LESSON: *As a leader, show deep loyalty to your people, and that loyalty will be returned.*

The Return of the Women

ONE DAY AFTER they'd settled on Turkey Creek, something remarkable happened. Soldiers arrived at Davis's tent driving a wagon carrying five Chiricahua women. They had disappeared after a Mexican massacre at Tres Castillos* more than four years before, believed forever lost either to slavery or death. Now here they were. Among them was Huera, wife of Mangas (youngest son of Mangas Coloradas), a very special woman with healing Powers, an expert tiswin maker who also served as a messenger for the warriors. The story is quite amazing. It's called "The Return of the Women" in Apache lore. After the Tres Castillos massacre,

---

* During this massacre the great Chihenne chief Victorio, Lozen's brother, was killed.

the women were sold into slavery and taken far south to Mexico City. There they worked on a large hacienda for a prominent family, toiling for years in the farm fields and as caretakers for the hacienda owner's children.

Throughout their time in captivity the women used secret signals to communicate with each other, always planning an escape, until at last they were able to gather together and sneak away into the night. They walked north, following the stars, sharing a single blanket and one knife among them. Sometimes they used the knife to kill a stray calf; they'd cut the meat and wrap it in their blanket. Sometimes, to avoid detection by the Mexican army, they'd separate and reunite days later. They traveled mostly at night, always cautious to avoid villages. Using their skill and guile, they survived mainly on prickly pear cactus until they reached southern Chihuahua. Here they recognized the mountains and found some of the caves they remembered as food-storage sites for Apache bands. They finally crossed the border into the United States. They had walked well over one thousand miles when they were picked up by U.S. soldiers and brought to Turkey Creek. It was an epic journey of courage, toughness, and survival.[7]

Interestingly, the U.S. officers immediately tried to enlist Huera as an interpreter because she was now fluent in Spanish, but she refused to serve the White Eyes.

The return of the women was cause for celebration among the Chiricahua, who were also able to learn how the Mexicans were treating Chiricahua captives. The treatment of captives by the different groups was really interesting. The Mexican practice with captives was to take women and children and sell them into slavery, often to the homes of wealthy hacienda owners, as had been done with Huera. The women would then be put to work in various jobs, in the fields but also as caregivers for the landowner's children. Unless for immediate ransom, the Mexicans typically killed Chiricahua warriors rather than take them captive.[8]

As for the Chiricahua, their approach with adult male captives was to interrogate them, and then, as a kind of privilege, they'd hand them over to the women, who'd kill them. Usually the women were relatives or widows of an Apache warrior whose death was being avenged. Letting the women do the killing offered them some satisfaction and compensation for their slain kin.[9] The women were merciless and brutal. They stabbed the captives with knives or spears, and sometimes even pounded them with rocks. Grown men were never kept to integrate into the tribe; they were thought too dangerous. The Chiricahua rarely took women captives, but when they did, they refrained from sex with them—there was a taboo of bad luck for such behavior. Young boys, when taken, would be integrated into the band, adopted by an Apache mother, and raised as an accepted member of the tribe. There didn't seem to be any negative stigma against young male captives once they were integrated into the group.

The American military had its own practices, of course. Captives were called, simply, "prisoners." That could mean one of a number of things, depending on who got you and where. An Apache might be brought in to the reservation—then, depending on the perceived offenses, he would stand trial and either be sentenced to hang or spend hard labor in prison at places like Alcatraz. In all cases, it was better not to get caught.

No More Tiswin—Again

FOR JUST OVER a year, Geronimo tried to be a "good" reservation Indian. Or at least that's the impression he gave to Davis at Turkey Creek, to Gatewood now running nearby Fort Apache, and Crook, who was overseeing the entire reservation. The Chiricahua had raised crops and continued to forage for wild berries and herbs; they killed many deer and jerked the meat and tanned the hides for their clothing and for their wickiup walls and covers; they ground corn and acorns for meal, which they mixed with the jerked meat and deer fat to make meatballs that would keep all winter.[10]

Geronimo went along as if things were tolerable and as if he was changing, even saying at one point, "I am now in a new country. I am hunting for a new world. I think that the world is mother to us all, and that God wants us all to be brothers."[11] I suspect that Geronimo was playing smart politics here, getting on the government's good side.

Geronimo also reminded Crook of their conversation and compromises back at Bugatseka, that Geronimo would come in if he and his people were treated fairly. "I have put away in my head all that you then told me," he said, "and I hold it tight."[12] Crook thought

LESSON: *Confuse your opponent as to the nature of your true intentions.*

things were going well, writing to Washington that "for the first time in the history of that fierce people, every member of the Apache tribe is at peace."[13] Well, not exactly, and not for long.

Crook always had the burden of answering to the higher authorities in Washington. He began to demand compliance with restrictions he'd formally imposed when he first returned to Arizona in 1882, restrictions that the Chiricahua had been ignoring. It was time to crack down on tiswin once and for all. Crook enforced the ban on the making and drinking of tiswin—anyone who made it or drank it would be thrown in jail.

For Geronimo and the rest of the Chiricahua, tiswin was more than just a way to get drunk. It was an important ceremonial aspect of their way of life, an integral part of their social fabric. So while Geronimo and his people tried to uphold their end of the bargain, to farm and run some cattle and not leave to go on raids, they continued to make and drink tiswin. To give up tiswin was asking too much. Before coming here they'd agreed to live on the reservation and give up war against whites and Mexicans, but they had never agreed to give up their tiswin. Geronimo and the other leaders pointed out that Davis himself loved his whiskey, so it wasn't fair that they should be told what to do regarding tiswin. They couldn't be swayed.

So the peace on Turkey Creek started to break down. Huera's tiswin was the best and strongest, so it was highly sought after, and she kept making it. Davis learned through his spies and Mickey Free that a Chiricahua chief named Kaytennae was drunk on tiswin and stirring up trouble among the other Apache, as well as making threats against Davis. At least that's what the spies told him.

Davis acted fast, sending for Kaytennae. Still drunk, Kaytennae came along, armed, with some of his men. He stopped just a few feet from Davis, his hands shaking with rage, and angrily demanded to know what the officer wanted from him. Davis, with armed scouts flanking him, told Kaytennae that he was under arrest and would be taken into custody and tried by Captain Crawford at San Carlos. Kaytennae then "wheeled in his tracks and started for his men [who] spread out, leveled their guns . . . their breech locks clicking as they came on."[14] It looked like there would be blood, perhaps even another Cibecue Creek disaster. Tension hung over Turkey Creek as everyone waited for what would happen next.

But no one fired a shot. Davis took a great chance then. He stepped forward and disarmed Chief Kaytennae, taking both his revolver and his cartridge belt. The crisis, for the moment, was over. Davis had Kaytennae escorted to San Carlos, where he was shackled and imprisoned to await trial for inducing the Chiricahua and Warm Springs Apache to go on the warpath, and for inciting a widespread Apache outbreak. But really, his only offense seems to have been getting drunk on tiswin.[15] The U.S. army was trying to make an example of him.

Kaytennae was convicted and Crawford recommended a sentence of three years' hard labor on Alcatraz. Crook read the sentence, thought it too harsh, and reduced it, calling for Kaytennae to be shackled in leg irons for one month of hard labor on Alcatraz, after which he could be released on good behavior.

When You Get Pushed Too Far, Push Back

GERONIMO HAD BEEN trying to live peacefully (or at least he'd been giving that appearance), but Kaytennae's arrest showed him once again that he must be ever wary of the white man. Geronimo remembered the feeling of being chained and nearly hanged—he now knew that the white man would never let his people live in their traditional ways. What rights they'd been granted were being stripped from them one at a time. Though they were allowed to move to their winter camps in lower country near Fort Apache when the snows came, this was done with a heavily armed military escort. "Fat Boy" Davis seemed bloated with his own authority. In May of 1885 he convicted a Chiricahua man of domestic abuse and sentenced him to prison. He also arrested men from Geronimo's and Mangas's bands for tiswin violations.

Davis's spies were always about, informing on any of the Chiricahua making or drinking tiswin. Huera heard a rumor that Geronimo was going to be arrested any day. It got so bad around the camps that Chief Chihuahua, who had become a scout with some of the others when he arrived in 1884, stormed into Davis's tent and declared, "I am quit!"[16] Davis tried to intimidate him with military logic, replying, "But you're in the army; you can't quit." Chihuahua threw down his army scout uniform and equipment and simply said, "Give them to your spies. I won't scout any longer."[17] He returned to Geronimo's side.

In mid-May 1885, Geronimo and Bonito organized a feast, dance, and tiswin party and enlisted Huera to create her special brew. All the Chiricahua chiefs except Chatto (still a hated turncoat, who had fully bought into the white ways) drank and celebrated. By the end of the day some eighty or ninety members of the hundred and twenty men in the tribe were reeling drunk. They'd had enough of the prohibition and decided to confront Davis the next morning.

When Davis awoke on Friday, May 15, there were thirty prominent Chiricahua warriors stationed outside his tent, and Chiricahua sentry warriors stood atop a high knoll in the distance. Geronimo and the Chiricahua chiefs—including Chihuahua, Naiche, Mangas, Nana, Loco, and Bonito—were all armed with knives and revolvers. Geronimo and Chihuahua were still drunk, and the rest were badly hung over. All were in foul moods. They said they wanted to talk. Davis had Chatto and some of his other scouts stand guard and invited the chiefs and Geronimo into his tent. They all squatted around Davis in a semicircle. Mickey Free was there to translate. Geronimo sat silent, brooding.

Loco started to talk, but his words were too slow for the impatient Chihuahua, who interrupted him and blurted out, "What I have to say can be said in a few words. Then Loco can take the rest of the day to talk if he wishes to do so."[18] Chihuahua vigorously protested the tiswin ban, arguing that they'd never agreed to it with General Crook and that they had drunk tiswin all of their lives. So had their ancestors. The government had no right to advise them in this matter. They were not children who should be told what they could or could not eat or drink. He added, "The white man drank wine and whiskey, even the soldiers of the posts."[19] All the chiefs believed they had complied with their promises to Crook—Nantan Lupan, the "Tan Wolf"—in the Sierra Madre. They had kept at peace and harmed no one.

Davis listened, and then he began to counter with the army's reasons for the sanctions. Old chief Nana didn't let him finish. He stood up angrily and said to Mickey Free, "He can't advise me. . . . I killed men before he was born." Then he stormed out of the tent.

Chihuahua continued his rant, growing bolder. "We all drank tiswin last night, all of us in the tent and those outside . . . and many more. What are you going to do about it? Are you going to put us all in jail? You have no jail big enough even if you could put us all in jail."[20]

Davis thought about it. He was surrounded by armed Chiricahua chiefs. To avert disaster, he replied calmly that the situation with the tiswin was too serious for him to decide. He would have to telegram General Crook and ask his opinion on the situation. That was the best he could do. He said it might take some time for Crook to receive the telegram and respond. Geronimo and the chiefs left the tent and returned to their camps.

Davis did as he had told them, immediately rifling off a telegram to Crook explaining the volatile situation at Turkey Creek. But Crook was gone from the post, and the newly arrived captain who received the telegram simply handed it over to Al Sieber, the chief of scouts. Ironically, Sieber was himself in bed nursing a terrible whiskey hangover, and he was short-tempered when he woke up to read it. "It's nothing more than a tiswin drunk," he said. "Don't pay any attention to it. Davis will handle it." With that, Sieber fell back to sleep. The captain then filed the telegram away. Crook would not get that telegram for four more months. Too late, it turned out.

Over the next few days, Geronimo considered what to do. He prayed and consulted his Power, his guardian spirit, for guidance. He felt hemmed in once again, surrounded. He did not trust Crook to make the right decision about the tiswin: It was Crook, after all, who had imposed the ban. Davis had overstepped his authority and was dangerous. Then there was Chatto, turncoat scout, who had started making the sign of throat slitting by passing his finger across his neck at Chiricahua minding their own business. The Chiricahua now regarded Chatto as a traitor: He'd gone over to the other side because he had lost the leadership of his band, and he craved the recognition he now got with his new position.[21] Geronimo wanted to kill him. Finally, the double-dealing Mickey Free was always around, spying and conniving.

LESSON: *Observe the nuances of mannerisms, body language, and behavior of your adversaries. Study them, then act accordingly.*

Then a White Mountain man arrived at camp to inform Geronimo that he'd heard a rumor that Crook had ordered scouts to come and arrest him and Mangas. Mangas's wife Huera confirmed the rumor, and she suggested that they leave, calling out to them, "If you are warriors, you will take to the warpath and then the Tan Wolf must catch you before you are punished."[22]

That was all Geronimo needed to hear. In the predawn light of May 17, 1885, some thirty-five or forty-five warriors (including three or four scouts who'd mutinied and joined Geronimo) and about a hundred women and children rose from their wickiups and stole away from Turkey Creek. Geronimo led the outbreak along with Mangas, Chihuahua,

Naiche, Nana, and Lozen, the warrior woman.[23] It was the third time he'd escaped the reservation.

Geronimo and Naiche commanded the rear guard, while Mangas commanded the women and children fleeing at the front. As they departed, Nana sent young boys shimmying up trees to cut telegraph wires. They cleverly cut the wires, then spliced them back together with buckskin thongs to conceal the locations of the breaks and slow down their detection, buying them some time.[24] They did this in numerous places—wherever they found wires attached to trees. The band ran and rode hard and fast, runners and riders swapping mounts, stopping only to cut wire.

LESSON: *A good leader anticipates the opposition's next move, but he remains focused on the goal at hand and his people's own abilities.*

That day, Davis was still waiting for a telegram response from General Crook, which he would not get since the original telegram was stuffed in some desk compartment. To pass some time, Davis agreed to umpire a baseball game between two of the army posts at nearby Fort Apache. He was standing in the dust calling balls and strikes when Mickey Free and Chatto rushed up to him to tell him that a bunch of Indians—including Geronimo—had broken out and were hightailing it for Mexico, disappearing in their own cloud of dust.[25]

Commentary

Disguise Your Intentions. *Geronimo used the element of surprise in his final breakout. Davis was so unsuspecting that he was off umpiring a baseball game when Geronimo rallied his band and fled once more. But this was only possible because Geronimo had analyzed his opponent and the situation and then acted in an unexpected way. It allowed him to escape.*

As a Leader, Try to Anticipate What the Opposition Is Going to Do, but Remain Focused on Your Own Abilities and Your Own Actions. *Geronimo believed that he was about to be arrested, so he acted. He'd already seen what his opposition (Davis, in this case) had done, and he was not about to sit around and wait for his opponent's next move. Instead, he acted.*

People Will Take Advantage of You if They Want to and Have the Power to Do So. Right or Wrong May Not Have any Bearing on Their Decisions. *Geronimo understood this. He believed he was fulfilling his obligations at Turkey Creek, but the government continued to renege on the bargain.*

Succeed and Win in Hostile Environments. *Succeeding and winning in safe, familiar environments is one thing—never easy, but not as hard as doing so in hostile environments. San Carlos, Turkey Creek, reservations with armed guards—those were hostile environments. Geronimo managed to succeed despite hostile environments and circumstances.*

CHAPTER THIRTEEN

Speed and Endurance (Fluidity)

GERONIMO WAS A SPRY AND SAVVY SIXTY-TWO as he led his people to safety and freedom once more. It was late May 1885. He knew that scouts would soon trail them, so he headed for the most difficult terrain he could find. They crisscrossed every creek bed and canyon possible, cutting over high mesas and ridges, the group splitting up and reuniting to thin and scatter their trail. The Chiricahua had a saying that described their approach to traveling over landscapes versus the whites: "The Indian follows the mountains and the white man the streams."[1] The Apache just moved with ease over tougher terrain, whereas the whites often took the lower, easier river routes. In the first full night and day the Chiricahua traveled an amazing ninety-five miles.

After crossing the Black River, they climbed high into the Mogollon Mountains and hid. Warriors went to known caves where they'd stashed provisions. Geronimo had for years organized an elaborate storage program, storing tons of food, gear, ammunition, and guns in secret caves that stretched all the way from New Mexico to Sonora, Mexico. Inside these caves his people had cached everything they'd need in their flight: dried venison, jerked beef, cactus fruit, piñon nuts, mesquite beans, and baked mescal, as well as cooking pots and pans, tanned hides, extra clothing, and moccasins.[2] It was a brilliant preplanned strategy that allowed him to move fast and light.

Geronimo knew it would take time for the army to rally its troops, and he was right. By the time Davis had gathered Gatewood and various divisions of cavalry and scouts (including Mickey Free and Chatto), Geronimo was well ahead and it was nearing dark. Davis sent scouts in pursuit, but the going was slow and they feared an ambush as the skies darkened. They did find places where the Chiricahua boys had cut the telegraph wires, and they came to places where Geronimo had set brushfires in an attempt to hinder pursuit. The ground was rough and rocky, and in the darkness many riders fell from their bucking mounts going up and down steep canyons. The soldiers had to halt and regroup. When they did, they found that one trooper had broken his leg, and a number of horses were so lame and injured they could not continue.[3] The U.S. cavalry had fine riders, but they were certainly no match for the Chiricahua, whose training started when they were very young—as soon as they were strong enough and brave enough to grab a mane and sling themselves onto the back of a horse.

LESSON: *Proper execution requires months and even years of practice and preparation.*

At this point, Davis realized that "further pursuit by troops was useless and that we were in for a long campaign in Mexico."[4] He returned to Fort Apache to wire General Crook (once the telegraph was repaired) to ask for instructions and to handpick only the finest and most trustworthy scouts—especially those who would not mutiny. This was the first Crook was hearing of the breakout, and he was obviously angry. Crook responded quickly. He told Davis to take only the best scouts and to try to make contact with the renegades to see if diplomacy would still work.

Crook dashed off telegrams to the Mexican governors of Chihuahua and Sonora, alerting them that Geronimo was once again heading their way. He also notified local newspapers to warn ranchers, farmers, and citizens, and he reported the situation to the War Department in

Washington.[5] Then he contemplated a number of possible routes Geronimo might take into Mexico, and he stationed cavalry at all posts between Geronimo's suspected location and the border. Maybe, just maybe, he could intercept the veteran warrior before he got there. Crook called on troops and cavalry from almost every military post in New Mexico and Arizona to cut off the fugitives or hunt them down at all costs. Before long, he had more than twenty troops of cavalry and some two hundred scouts out of five separate forts, with a total of two thousand men chasing Geronimo.[6]

Speed: Being Fast Helps

BUT GERONIMO BLAZED across the desert at an unbelievable clip. At one point early in the chase, Gatewood and his scouts got within ten miles of the Chiricahua—they could see them through their field glasses sprinting over high ridges in the distance. But then Geronimo notched up his speed, traveling another hundred and twenty miles, stopping only to raid ranches for horses, weapons, and ammunition.[7] It was as if Gatewood and the scouts were chasing dust devils. Cleverly, Geronimo split into separate smaller and faster groups. Geronimo and Mangas pressed hard for Mexico, bearing

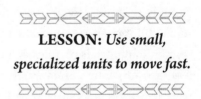

LESSON: *Use small, specialized units to move fast.*

east and then south, simultaneously avoiding the military as well as settlements, flourishing mining towns, even schools. Chihuahua swung north to hide in the mountains above the border until the military presence died a bit and he could sneak his people south.

Geronimo and Mangas were first to Mexico, followed by Naiche and then Chihuahua. Somewhere along the way Chappo, Geronimo's son, had caught up too. He was definitely on his father's side and would be to the end. By mid-June, all of the renegades were tucked away in their familiar haunts back in the Sierra Madre. They left a trail of carnage in their wake: seventeen dead civilians and some hundred and fifty horses and mules ridden to death and killed or abandoned.[8] And I'm sure they ate some of their stock too.

Geronimo Is Headline News—Again

WORD OF GERONIMO'S run from Turkey Creek terrified the frontier, and again he was headline news. The May 22, 1885, issue of the *Silver City Enterprise* warned that there were "Fifty Bloodthirsty Red Devils . . . on the Warpath, under the leadership of that Murderous devil Geronimo."[9] The press and citizens were deeply critical of the whole handling of the reservation system, and Crook was taking serious heat. One editorial fumed: "The truth is, there is no more room in this territory for the Apache. FOR HIM THE RESERVATION SYSTEM IS NONSENSE. These braves . . . massacre, rob, torture, burn, pillage."[10]

Hysteria flamed like wildfire. Citizens wrote desperate pleas to President Grover Cleveland, begging for help. Here's a part of one addressed to the White House that expresses the fear—whether warranted or not: "I am a pioneer living on the Mexican line, in South Eastern Arizona. We are surrounded by the Apache. We have many small children and women with us. We are poorly armed, there is not a soldier in hundreds of miles of us."[11] Well, not exactly. In fact, there were less than fifty Chiricahua warriors on the warpath. Geronimo's Apache were really the ones surrounded, and there were soldiers everywhere. It was a case of finite real estate, and Geronimo was running out of it. He was caught smack in the crosshairs of Manifest Destiny. The mass terror Geronimo caused gave him the reputation of a bloodthirsty killer, but he believed in his cause. He believed he was protecting the rights of his people and their way of life.[12]

Catch Me if You Can—If You Can't, Then Quit

FOR CROOK, GERONIMO'S escape meant another trip to Mexico, another foray into the stronghold. He was sure that's where Geronimo would go, and he was right. Crook set up his headquarters at Fort Bowie.

He "sealed" the border with twenty-four-hour patrols from the Rio Grande to the mouth of the Colorado, and he employed Britton Davis, Wirt Davis (no relation to Britton), and Emmet Crawford for the mission, each with experienced soldiers and scouts. Throughout the blazing summer of 1885, Wirt Davis and Crawford tried to find Geronimo in his Mexican haunts, but always he eluded them. Heat and thirst nearly broke Davis and his men. Davis reported temperatures up to 128 degrees in the shade, and one of his packers told of their frustration: "The Indians lured us more deeply into the mountains. Our maps were worthless. The cavalry horses and men were worn out, and the clothing of all was in tatters."[13]

LESSON: *Develop better systems and techniques than your adversaries.*

Geronimo could evade the army in part because of his intimate knowledge of the mountains. He did not need maps or a compass; his routes were in his head. But he also knew where springs were, knew where to find water from memory and topographical clues, and he could go much, much longer without water because of certain techniques the Chiricahua had mastered. They'd put a dry stick or stone in their mouths, and that created a saliva response, which helps with thirst. They also found snow in the mountains and either melted it or ate it. In the scorching desert they ate the inner parts of cactus leaves, which are cool and contain fluid. There is one plant, named the barrel cactus, that has water inside, like watermelon—they'd squeeze the pulp to wring fluid out of it. And then there was the mescal cactus—so useful to them. The Chiricahua had for generations watched deer chew and then drink from the inside of the leaves, which hold water. For drinking out of big ones, Geronimo's people carried long hollow reeds they used as straws.[14] These techniques allowed them to carry less and move faster.

The Apache had great planning and problem-solving strategies. There were a few other practices they used that helped them stay ahead of both Davises and Crawford that summer of 1885. They ran or rode on hard, rocky ground as much as possible, avoiding soft ground that left tracks. They also jumped from rock to rock, boulder to boulder, to leave no trace of their route, and broomed their tracks clear behind them with tufts of grasses. When they dispersed into small groups, they left barely noticeable signs and signals for other Apache: sticks or stones left on animal trails pointing in the direction to go; pieces of fabric or leather tied in trees at prearranged places. They even had mirrors once these were introduced, and they flashed directions and instructions to each other. Flashing a beam of sunlight downward meant "come on." Flashing left or right meant "go left" or "go right."[15]

LESSON: *Teach effective communication and coded language known only by your people.*

Geronimo didn't have to be wary only of the U.S. army, because thanks to Crook's urgent telegrams, the Mexican troops were searching for him too. But he remained undetected in the early summer. Then in June, Chatto led his scouts to Chihuahua's camp and attacked, capturing fifteen women and children—and all of Chihuhua's family. One woman died in this attack. Then in July, a U.S. detachment, with scouts, found and attacked part of Geronimo's camp. They killed a woman and a young boy and captured fifteen members of his group, including one of Geronimo's wives and some of his children—along with other family members and relatives. But Geronimo got away.

Crawford sent his A team of Chatto, Al Sieber, Mickey Free, and forty of the finest scouts, all under the command of Britton Davis, after Geronimo. Then, as usual, Geronimo did the unexpected. And it remains one of the most impressive feats he ever accomplished. For twenty-four days Geronimo led his small band more than five hundred

LESSON: *Find ways to get your opponent to second-guess themselves. Wear your opponent out.*

miles over some of the steepest, roughest terrain in the world, zigzagging, dropping down into deep caverns and ascending massive peaks, always changing directions to confuse Davis. Geronimo went far east, into the state of Chihuahua, then shot north. Davis's A team, his hand-chosen squad of the finest scouts and most experienced Indian fighters, never even caught so much as a glimpse of Geronimo. Finally, Geronimo's trail vanished, and Davis gave up the hunt.[16] Davis was broken and discouraged—his men in tatters, busted and limping. Britton Davis resigned from the army and agreed to run a friend's ranch in northern Chihuahua—ironically, right smack in the middle of Geronimo's raiding territory.[17] Geronimo had driven him to resignation.

Geronimo's Secret Mission to Rescue His Wife and Child

THEN GERONIMO OUTDID even himself. He'd vowed to retrieve his family and relatives, even if they were north of the border. Despite Crook's dragnet of patrols and scouts and military detachments, Geronimo and just four warriors—as if invisible—passed through Crook's defenses and made their way to Fort Apache, where all the Chiricahua had been moved after the Turkey Creek breakout so they could be closely guarded. How Geronimo knew this—and knew exactly where they were—remains a mystery. Probably he consulted his Power. He also often used runners to gather intelligence. At any rate, on September 22, 1885, Geronimo and his four warriors crept into Fort Apache, right under the noses of scouts and soldiers, went straight to the correct wickiup, and retrieved his wife and a daughter, age three. Then he vanished into the darkness and returned to Mexico, via a bold and unexpected detour through New Mexico, where he raided for ammunition, which he needed. Mexican bullets didn't always work in his American-made Winchesters and Springfields.

But if Geronimo hoped to hold out, he'd need even more ammunition. In November a trusted warrior named Ulzana—Chihuahua's older brother—offered to lead an ammunition raid. Ulzana had raided and run with old Nana, from whom he'd learned much. Taking just a dozen men, Ulzana rode and raided at lightning speed for two months, travel-ing twelve hundred miles, killing thirty-eight whites, and stealing two hundred and fifty horses and mules (and a lot of ammo). He lost only a single warrior.[18] But Ulzana's epic raid had serious consequences. The heat on Crook reached a fever pitch, with newspaper editorials branding him a "liar, a coward, and a murderer"[19] for failing to bring in Geronimo and calling for his job. It hardly mattered that of the 5,000 Apache rounded up and contained at Fort Apache and San Carlos, only 144 rogue Chiricahua had escaped and were at large. To the press and the public, it was all Crook's fault.

Geronimo was also implicated by association, blamed for many of the attacks and murders, including some of Ulzana's. That was a cost of his fame.

Geronimo's incredible skills and tactics forced Crook to adapt. Now that Davis had resigned, Crook would rely on Emmet Crawford, the best man remaining for the job. Crook's new plan this time had an inge-nious wrinkle: He'd send Crawford with a much smaller command of only fresh scouts, and he'd keep his army presence behind, hopefully lulling the Chiricahua into a false confidence that they were winning. In many ways, they were.

While Crawford and his second-in-command, Lieutenant Marion Maus, mustered scouts and prepared to launch them into Mexico, Geronimo remained free in the Sierra Madre. The highest brass in Washington was at wit's end. Pressure from angry citizens and local government was so great that the Departments of War and the Interior met to discuss the Apache Problem. The meetings included famed Union Civil War general Philip Sheridan, who had chased down Robert E. Lee to help force his surrender at Appomattox. Now Sheridan met with Secretary of War William Endicott to consider permanently re-moving the entire Chiricahua tribe to Florida. They discussed trans-porting not just Geronimo and his bands in Mexico (if they could ever catch them), but even those living peacefully on the reservations. The terms and length of the removal they'd make up as they went along.

In early December 1885 Crawford crossed back into Mexico for a last-ditch attempt to catch Geronimo. His fresh scouts moved well, but after three weeks in Sonora they had nothing but blisters and empty stomachs. From a high base camp near Nacori, Crawford sent out small scouting forays. Finally, early in the new year of 1886, a scouting party returned from the Aros River to report the location of a Chiricahua trail. They thought the trail led straight to Geronimo's steep-walled hideout in the brutally rough region called the Devil's Backbone. Crawford and his scouts climbed upward for two days, rarely stopping, until on January 9 they came within twelve miles of Geronimo. They crept through the night and got to within a few hundred yards of Geronimo's camp at first light.[20]

Geronimo and his warriors sensed something and scattered up into the rocks. Not a warrior, woman, or child got caught—but once again Geronimo's hideout was breached, and he'd lost his horses. From a hiding place in the rocks, Geronimo sent Lozen down to talk to Crawford. Scouts recognized her and they did not shoot. She told Crawford that Geronimo and Naiche wanted to talk to him the next day. Crawford readily agreed.

But Crawford would never get to talk to Geronimo. The next morning, a group of Mexican irregulars (volunteers who served for plunder, not pay) who had been trailing Geronimo attacked the camp. They thought that Crawford's scouts were the hostile Chiricahua, and they opened fire. Crawford yelled out for his scouts to cease fire, then moved to higher ground where he might communicate with the Mexicans. He waved a truce flag and called out that he was an American, but a shot ricocheted off the rocks, sending Crawford tumbling down the hillside. His scouts returned fire.

Lieutenant Maus hurried to aid Crawford amid the shooting, but when he got to him he found Crawford shot through the forehead and his head split open on the rocks. After about an hour the Mexicans gave up, having suffered four dead and five wounded. Maus and a field surgeon tended to Crawford, but he fell into a coma. The scouts made a stretcher and with a mule dragged him down out of the mountains for a week, but he died on January 18, 1886.

By this point, Geronimo had driven Britton Davis to resign and Emmet Crawford to his death. And he wasn't done yet.

Geronimo had watched the entire episode from the safety of the steep hillsides above the Aros River, and after a few days he decided to honor his pledge to talk. Although the Mexicans had left, it didn't look like Maus and the scouts were going anywhere. He sent a messenger to tell Maus that he'd talk only if the lieutenant came unarmed. Geronimo's trust was pretty well used up, and he knew how badly the U.S. authorities wanted him. Maus agreed to parley.

Geronimo and Naiche came fully armed to "their" camp, now occupied by Maus, who had assumed command. Geronimo said he'd meet only with Crook, and only at a spot of his choosing. Also, Crook must come without a bunch of soldiers. Geronimo, as he'd done before, said he'd come "in two moons."[21] As assurance, Geronimo agreed to turn over old Nana, who was tired of running and fighting, one other warrior, and seven women and children. These included one of Geronimo's wives and daughters and one wife and son of Naiche.

With his numbers dwindling and the knowledge that he was running out of places to hide, Geronimo turned his back and disappeared into the mountains.

Commentary

Practice Endurance and Physical Fitness. *I know it's hard to believe, but Geronimo could run up to ninety miles a day in his sixties. At first I wondered if this was even possible, but I looked into it. The current male record holder of the Western States 100-Miler, a trail run from Squaw Valley to Auburn, California, did it in just under 15 hours. The 60–69 age-group men's record holder did it in 20.5 hours.[22] So I believe the distances Geronimo covered, no question. And his are even more impressive when you consider that he was carrying gear, guns, water, and NOT following a trail. Plus he was getting shot at.*

Geronimo and the other Chiricahua learned from a very early age that tremendous physical fitness was essential to survival—it would allow them to catch game and to outrun opponents during raids. During childhood they practiced hand-to-hand combat, wrestling, tug-of-war, and running, always running. Their training demanded that they could run for two days without eating or sleeping, and to stave off hunger they tied a leather strap around their waist and cinched it tight.[23]It's unclear whether this offered any physical appetite-reducing effectiveness, but they believed it reduced the discomfort psychologically, and that was enough.

Hone Special Skills and Creativity. *All Apache men were skilled in making moccasins and could repair or replace them quickly, even on the run. Each warrior carried a bone awl and some animal-sinew thread and hand-selected pieces of sole leather and soft buckskin for the upper leggings. They designed different moccasins for different types of terrain—some had plain toes and some had toes upturned an inch or two, which protected the toes from stubbing in extremely rocky terrain. They also knew how to fashion moccasins quickly from plants in an emergency; if they had no time to make proper ones, they wrapped thick strands of matted grasses around their feet and tied them secure with strips of yucca.[24] Then off they ran.*

As a shaman, Geronimo also possessed the skills of medicinal practices. He knew how to use curative herbs on wounds and for illnesses. He treated sore mouths by mixing the juice from milkweed leaves with pine and cottonwood sap to make a soothing chewing gum. Sore throats were treated with wild mint juice, and he knew how to break a fever with aspen or willow-leaf tea. Geronimo possessed steady hands too. He was able to perform surgical procedures in the field, cutting arrowheads, spear points, or bullets from the flesh of his wounded warriors, and heal them quickly.

CHAPTER FOURTEEN

>>>><<>><<<

Once He Moved Like the Wind
(Resistance)

The Canyon of the Funnels

AFTER THE MEETING with Lieutenant Maus in the Devil's Backbone, Geronimo wondered what to do. His people were now divided. Nana, once a defiant warrior, had turned himself in. In Geronimo's group there remained only Geronimo, Naiche, Chihuahua, Ulzana, and about twenty-five other warriors. The women and children brought the total of his group to just over fifty. Although they were expert at it, running forever was not what they wanted to do, and Geronimo had grown weary, despondent even. This was no way for his people to live.

For the first few months of 1886, Geronimo raided while considering his situation, always consulting his Power. Then, after two months, Geronimo showed up near the border as he'd said he would. He sent smoke signals to Lieutenant Maus, now in charge. Geronimo sent word that he'd meet Crook at a place called Cañon de los Embudos (Funnel Canyon, or Canyon of the Funnels), some twenty-five miles south of the border, in Mexico. He'd meet on his terms, at a place of his choosing.

Geronimo chose the place for its fortification. He camped on top of a cone-shaped hill, on a large brushy lava bed cut with deep funnels and ravines that were difficult to navigate. From the elevated position Geronimo's sentries had a long view of an enemy's approach, as well as of Maus's camp half a mile away. A series of deep gulches separated the two camps. As the Chiricahua preferred, there were mountains to escape to nearby, at their backs.

LESSON: *A good leader dictates the terms of engagement.*

Crook traveled the eighty-four miles from Fort Bowie without a large contingent of troops. Geronimo was glad to see he'd honored that demand. But Crook did bring along a couple of surprises. First among those was Kaytennae, whom you'll remember was tried by Crawford for tiswin violations and sentenced to hard labor on Alcatraz by Crook. I guess Crook brought him along to illustrate to the "hostiles" what a "civilized" Indian looked like, since Kaytennae had been taught English and he'd even toured San Francisco to see the sights. But this backfired, as Geronimo saw instead a compliant, broken-down man, a former warrior who now bowed to Crook's command.

Crook also had with him Tombstone photographer C. S. Fly, who'd either bribed or talked his way along. Good thing too. His amazing photographs are like no others, documenting for the historical record armed American Indian warriors in the field. Geronimo actually took the time to arrange family groups for the photos. In many of these Geronimo is center stage—sometimes mounted and sometimes standing, but always armed and dangerous. He looks like a man you wouldn't want to mess with.[1]

The meeting took place on March 25, 1886, in the shade of some large cottonwood and sycamore trees. Recording the talks was Crook's aide, John G. Bourke, who would call the Chiricahua "the shrewdest and most ferocious of all the tribes encountered by the white man."[2] There were a number of interpreters present—though *not* Mickey Free.

Crook knew better than to bring him along. Geronimo didn't trust him and it would hurt any negotiations. Crook came with only about a dozen men so as not to unnerve Geronimo.

Let's Make a Deal

Geronimo (squatting, third from left) parleys with George Crook (second from right) at Canyon des los Embudos, March 25, 1886.

ONCE THEY WERE all together, they sat in a circle on the ground next to a stream and Geronimo spoke. First he explained his reasons for breaking away from Turkey Creek, noting that he'd feared he was about to be arrested. He reminded Crook of his treatment by Chatto, by Mickey Free, and even by Britton Davis—the arrests of his people. He complained of the treatment by the agents running the reservation. After a time Geronimo said, "I think I am a good man; but all the papers in the world say I am a bad man; but it is a bad thing to say about me. I never do wrong without a cause."[3]

Crook played his cards close to the vest. He would not even make eye contact with Geronimo. He used a negotiation strategy of indifference. He did not show Geronimo any reverence at all, and he certainly did not show any fear. That was important, since courage was respected. Geronimo reminded Crook of the promises he had made before, at Bugatseka: "I have not forgotten what you told me, although a long time has passed."[4] (He was referring to the fact that none of his people had ever agreed to a tiswin ban.)

Geronimo understood the gravity of the situation—he could see the aide Bourke recording every word with pen and paper. I think he understood that this moment was part of history, part of his destiny. He said then, "There is one God looking down on us all. We are all children of one God. God is listening to me. The sun, the darkness, the winds, all are listening to what we now say."[5]

Then Geronimo thought of his people and tried to make a deal for them should they surrender: "There are very few of my men left now. They have done some bad things but I want them all rubbed out now and let us never speak of them again."[6] He wanted their past offenses to go unpunished.

LESSON: *Never assume that your enemy or adversary thinks the same way you do.*

Crook listened for a long time and finally he cut in. They argued back and forth at length, going in a circle. But Crook had not come here to argue—he'd come to get Geronimo to surrender. At last he said, boldly, "Your mouth talks too many ways. . . . You must make up your mind whether you will stay out on the warpath or surrender unconditionally. If you stay out, I'll keep after you and kill the last one, if it takes fifty years."[7] In his heart, Crook knew this was asking too much—that Geronimo was too wily and proud to agree to unconditional surrender. But this is what Sheridan had ordered Crook to demand, so he'd demanded it. In truth he knew he'd have to offer them something, but not yet.

It was a stalemate. The two leaders agreed to resume talks the next day, but it ended up being two days before they reconvened. During the break Geronimo and his men talked among themselves back at their camp, always watchful and suspicious. The sentries had orders to shoot any White Eyes that approached, then scatter into the mountains. Crook sent Kaytennae to mingle among the Chiricahua and try to divide them, which he did. He came and went a few times, passing messages back and forth with Crook. The Chiricahua wanted to be able to return to Turkey Creek and live as they had before, but Crook sent word back that no, that would not be enough punishment. They would have to pay some price for their crimes.

LESSON: *Some cliché adages are actually true. If a deal sounds too good to be true, it probably is.*

In the end Crook promised a deal: All the warriors (except Nana, thought too old to travel) would spend jail time in the east for two years, and then they'd be returned to their homeland after serving out their sentences.[8] It was a deal he hoped he'd be able to keep. He made the deal based on a February 1 letter he had from U.S. army headquarters mandating that he "make no promises at all to the hostiles, unless it is necessary to secure their surrender."[9] At that time, Crook felt he had to dangle some carrot, and he thought he had the power to negotiate on behalf of the United States. He felt the two-year promise was necessary to secure their surrender. He only hoped that the president would go for it.

Chihuahua bit on the carrot first—he even sent a note to Crook saying he'd surrender no matter what Geronimo decided. He offered to come right then, but Crook suggested he stay and try to convince the others, especially Geronimo, who was the key to the entire negotiation.

At high noon on March 27, 1886, the talks resumed. Chihuahua was first to surrender. Next came Naiche, tall and handsome, the youngest son of Cochise. He said, "When I was out in the mountains I thought I should never see you again. . . . I think now it is best for us to surrender and not remain out in the mountains."[10] I'm sure he'd hoped he would never see him again. Naiche then shook hands with Crook, as Chihuahua had done.

At last Geronimo spoke. He sat solemnly under a mulberry tree, his face ceremonially rubbed black with pounded galena. Many tribes, like the Comanche, wore black because it symbolized death,[11] and I think Geronimo was making a statement that he was experiencing a kind of death: He and his people were experiencing the death of their way of life. He said simply, "Two or three words are enough. I have little to say. I surrender myself to you." He reached for Crook's hand, shook it, and then he went on, "Once I moved about like the wind. Now I surrender to you and that is all."[12]

Another Premonition

BUT OF COURSE this is Geronimo we're talking about, and with Geronimo the story doesn't ever end quite like you'd think. That, as it turned out, was not all. Geronimo's Power had brought him another premonition: Crook's "deal" was a lie; Geronimo knew in his heart that the terms he'd agreed to would be broken.

That night Geronimo, Naiche, and Chihuahua returned to their camp on the funnels. Before long a man named Tribolet visited them, a man they knew well, for he'd been selling whiskey and mescal to them for some time. He was a Swiss-American beef broker and bootlegger who ran a makeshift saloon just a few hundred yards over the Mexican side of the border. I guess Geronimo and the boys needed some cheering up, having just surrendered again, but anyway they bought five gallons of booze from Tribolet and had a big night. Hooting and gunfire kept Maus awake much of the night, and the next morning Bourke reported the Chiricahua unfit to travel: They were riding around two to a mule, "drunk as lords," is how he described them. Knowing what they knew about the tiswin ban, and quite uncertain of the fate that awaited them in the unknown world of "back east," I guess they just wanted one last hurrah.[13]

Crook decided to head back to Fort Bowie to telegraph Sheridan the terms he'd made. He left the job of herding in the renegades to Maus and his scouts. It was a decision he'd soon regret. With their late start and the drunken condition of the Apache, Maus didn't get them very far the first day. Spring rains came down throughout the day and the Chiricahua stopped to camp well before the border. Maus camped nearby. He heard arguing among them but knew better than to mess with them and went to sleep. He'd get them across the border first thing in the morning.

But Geronimo had yet another premonition. In the middle of the night, Geronimo and Naiche took eighteen warriors and about twenty women and children across the funnel canyons and disappeared through the lava flows and into the scrub. They'd had time to take only two horses and one mule, so nearly all of them were on foot. Geronimo's explanation for his decision to leave was this: "We started with all our tribe to go with General Crook back to the United States, but I feared treachery and decided to remain in Mexico."[14]

Given what happened to his people, and finally to him, Geronimo had every reason to fear treachery, because they were about to be dealt one of the biggest double crosses in U.S. history. On top of the government's double dealings (which we'll see), the civil and political climate in Arizona was not favorable toward Geronimo, and he knew it. When on the reservation, he'd read the papers (or had them read to him), and English-reading scouts like Mickey Free told him what they said about him. One article from the *L.A. Times* (the city then had nearly a hundred thousand residents) speculated as to what would happen to Geronimo and the other leaders if they were brought in: "It is believed that [General Crook] will make a requisition for Geronimo and the other ring-leaders to be turned over to the civil authorities for trial . . . the general belief is that the ring-leaders will be executed."[15]

Maybe Geronimo believed he could run forever. Maybe he only wanted one last run at freedom, one last look at Apache country, the land of his ancestors that was his

LESSON: *Have the courage to do what others will not do.*

home and his birthright. He knew to keep going when the choice to stay meant death: Better to die in the company of friends than to live in the company of enemies.[16]

Geronimo, Naiche, and their small band once more moved like the wind, sprinting into the mountains for sixty miles without once stopping to camp. Rarely running in a straight line, they switched directions, doubled back, and at Fronteras, Sonora, they split into two, to regroup later at a chosen mountain haunt. Maus chased after the fugitives with scouts, but, finding the terrain nearly impossible and losing the trail, he turned back.

Officers and scouts took Chihuahua and the rest of the seventy-six surrendered Chiricahua to Fort Bowie to await their fates. Interestingly, two warriors who'd bolted with Geronimo changed their minds and turned around, and they returned with Maus's scouts.

Resignation of the Tan Wolf

FOR CROOK, BAD news got worse in a hurry. Arriving at Fort Bowie, he got a telegram from Sheridan that denied and revoked the terms of surrender. Under NO circumstances would President Cleveland consent to the two-year terms Crook had given Geronimo.

Sheridan and the president ordered him to renegotiate with Geronimo, offering nothing less than UNCONDITIONAL SURRENDER OR COMPLETE DESTRUCTION OF THE HOSTILES unless they agreed to terms. The telegram went on to say (and this next part must have killed Crook to read) that he must TAKE EVERY PRECAUTION AGAINST THE ESCAPE OF THE HOSTILES.[17] Whoops. Crook now had to tell the president of the United States and the commanding general of the U.S. army (Sheridan) that Geronimo had already escaped! Talk about an awkward telegram to have to send. He had to tell them it was going to be pretty difficult to negotiate with Geronimo now. Crook was in a really tough spot. Washington thought him incompetent. The press was calling for his head. And now the Chiricahua would call him a liar. Crook's honor was at stake.

Crook was out of options. To Sheridan and President Cleveland, he tried to explain his choices, his decisions, and the realities of dealing with Geronimo, but Washington wouldn't listen or didn't understand. So on April 1, 1886, with Geronimo and his band of thirty-eight still running free, Crook sent a telegram respectfully requesting to be relieved of his command. He was immediately reassigned to the Department of the Platte, which ended eight years of living with, overseeing, and chasing the Apache for hundreds, even thousands of miles. In the end, Geronimo had driven him to quit.[18]

But I'll say this: Crook's intuitions about his policies were sound. In his resignation telegram Crook wrote, "I believe the plan on which I have conducted operations is the one most likely to prove successful in the end."[19] His "plan" meant using Apache scouts, small detachments of cavalry, and mules. He'd been able to breach the stronghold this way not once, but twice. Why he did not personally escort Geronimo to Fort Bowie is a question I wondered about. But when you think about it, Crook never really *had* him. Geronimo certainly wasn't going to let anyone cuff and shackle him again, as Clum had once done long ago at Ojo Caliente. Crook must have figured that if he'd

GERONIMO'S ADVERSARIES: NELSON A. MILES, ARMY OFFICER (AUGUST 8, 1839–MAY 25, 1925)

Born near Westminster, Massachusetts, Miles was commissioned as first lieutenant of the 22nd Massachusetts Infantry in 1861. He served with great distinction in the Civil War, being wounded four times and earning the distinguished Medal of Honor. After the Civil War, Miles spent fifteen years fighting various Indian tribes on the Plains and the far West, including the Comanche, the Kiowa, and the Cheyenne. In 1876–1877 Miles took part in the last of the Sioux resistance on the North Plains, and he chased Sitting Bull all the way to the Canadian border. In 1880 Miles became a brigadier general, and he commanded the Department of the Platte until 1886, when he succeeded George Crook as commander of the Department of Arizona. Crook had stepped down and requested reassignment after Geronimo's final escape. Miles took credit for Crook's successes, and a bitter feud lasted until the end of Crook's life, in 1890. In 1886 Miles accepted Geronimo's surrender and took credit for it, despite the fact that it had been orchestrated by Charles Gatewood. In 1890 Miles was named major general, and he would rise to commander in chief of the army in 1895, and then lieutenant general in 1900. Teddy Roosevelt called him a "brave peacock" because he wore gaudy military-dress uniforms bedecked with medals. He was pompous and vain and insecure about his lack of a West Point education and training, but he certainly served his country ably and with distinction for over four decades. He retired in 1903 and died in Washington, D.C., in 1925.

Sources: Thrapp, *Encyclopedia of Frontier Biography;* Lamar, *The New Encyclopedia of the American West;* PBS—*The West.*

tried something like that, Geronimo would have reacted violently and maybe even killed him.

Enter Civil War Hero General Nelson A. Miles

CROOK'S REPLACEMENT WAS General Nelson A. Miles. Miles wasn't a West Point–groomed soldier. Born on a farm in Massachusetts in 1839, he was a clerk working in a dry goods store when the Civil War broke out. He volunteered and was wounded four times, once in the neck, and another time from musketfire to the gut and hip that was nearly fatal. He survived and went on to rise through the military ranks faster than any officer other than Custer, eventually achieving lieutenant general. Part of his rise might be attributed to his marriage to the daughter of a judge related to William Tecumseh Sherman, commanding general of the U.S. army. So he was clearly good at playing the games that needed to be played.[20]

Miles was a strapping, muscular man, with intense blue eyes and a knack for getting into beefs with his associates. He bore long grudges too and was known to take credit for the exploits of others. In 1877 he

drove his troops in a forced march across Montana to intercept the fleeing Chief Joseph. Later, he took credit for Joseph's capture despite the
fact that General Oliver O. Howard
and his troops had been chasing
the Nez Perce for fifteen hundred
miles and many months. They argued about it for the rest of their
careers. Miles was also prone to exaggeration, inflating the numbers
of Apache his men shot in battles.

Miles took over the Department of Arizona from Crook less
than two weeks after the latter requested reassignment. Crook had
spent eight full years in Arizona
and knew the Apache as well or
better than any other white man.
He could never have imparted all
of his knowledge to Miles even had
he wanted to. He'd developed real
personal relationships with many
of the Chiricahua, knew them by
name, knew their families and their
stories.

General Nelson A. Miles, whom
Teddy Roosevelt called a "brave peacock"
for his tendency to show off his medals,
dressed in all his splendor.

Before he left, Crook visited some of the recently surrendered, including Chihuahua. He felt obliged to tell them that he was leaving and
would be replaced by a new man named Miles. The Chiricahua were
rightly concerned that the deal they'd struck was still in place—and
Crook didn't have the heart to tell them that no, it was not. The two-
year prison sentence was now "indefinite," a term to be determined only
by the president of the United States. Crook feared, for one thing, that if
Geronimo learned this he'd never come in. Perhaps Crook also couldn't
bear to see their faces as he broke his promise—or, more accurately, as
President Cleveland broke his promise.

U.S. PRESIDENTS, THE APACHE PROBLEM, AND GERONIMO

It's pretty remarkable when you think that Geronimo's life spanned the terms of twenty-two U.S. presidents. Initially just a nuisance and an inconvenience in the settling of the West, the Chiricahua Apache involved presidents quite directly beginning with Ulysses S. Grant and all the rest through Theodore Roosevelt, to varying degrees and at varying levels, directly and indirectly, in Geronimo's lifetime. By 1869, President Grant was directly involved. He developed something called "Grant's Peace Policy," attempting to conquer through more humane means, say, than Andrew Jackson's 1830 Indian Removal Act—or that was Grant's intention, anyway. Grant and Congress authorized a Board of Indian Commissioners to advise the Department of the Interior on funding for reservations and policy. Additionally, Protestant religious organizations (including the Dutch Reformed Church) were called on to "civilize" and convert those Indians on the reservations. From that time on the Apache Problem went all the way to the president.

Sources: Utley, *Geronimo*, 64; Sweeney, *Cochise to Geronimo*, 39; Debo, *Geronimo*, 80.

Instead, Crook went around and said goodbye to many of the Apache he'd known. He spoke to Chihuahua like a father to a son, urging him to stop the tiswin drinking. But Crook also cared what they thought of him. He asked Chihuahua, after they separated, to judge him by his acts and not by what others had to say about him, since talk was cheap.[21] Chihuahua thanked Crook and said, "I believe every word you tell me. Wherever you send me is all right."[22]

Of course, Chihuahua believed he was going away for two years, not for the rest of his life.

On April 7, 1886, Chihuahua and the other seventy-six Chiricahua were loaded onto a rail car at Bowie Station, a Southern Pacific railroad stop just ten miles from Fort Bowie. They were to be shipped to Fort Marion, in Florida, where they'd be imprisoned in tight quarters in tents on a low-lying bog. One of Chihuahua's sons boarded too, and he later recalled, "The day they put us on that train at Bowie, Arizona, would have been a good day to die. Banishment from our land and the bones of our ancestors was worse than death. . . . We knew we were facing two years of slavery and degradation, but my father was willing to endure that for the sake of the future when we were to be free again."[23]

But the future they'd been promised wasn't the future they got.

| Commentary |

Trust but Verify. *The dealings between Geronimo and Crook remind me of the dealings between Reagan and Gorbachev during the Cold War. The catch phrase, which Reagan borrowed from a Russian proverb, was "Trust but verify." The idea was that even if information from your adversary seemed reliable, you'd better verify that it was accurate.*

That's what Geronimo needed to do in dealing with bureaucracies. Bureaucracies are inefficient and dishonest—maybe not intentionally, sometimes, but because there are too many moving parts. Deliberately or otherwise, by design they can't get all the moving parts on the same page. This is what ultimately led to a lot of bloodshed and a worse fate for the Apache. A workable situation was never achieved because the U.S. government was repeatedly dishonest and corrupt to the Apache. The lack of credibility on the part of the United States made it impossible for the Apache to trust them and consistently agree to anything. The result was more bloodshed and a refusal to surrender. In the end, no truly amicable solution was ever achieved.

Manage Time, Space, and Numbers (Personnel). *Geronimo understood intuitively three keys to success: managing time, space, and numbers (personnel). His space had become severely limited or compromised in the crowded Southwest, now filled with ranches and mines and mining communities. It's remarkable to think what was going on in his traditional tribal grounds while he was running and raiding, and how his space was shrinking. Nearby Tombstone swelled to nearly fourteen thousand residents, and it had a bowling alley, three newspapers, and a hundred and ten saloons. Geronimo understood that*

Mexico offered more space in which to move, so he made that his base of operations. With space, it's about figuring out how to use all the available area, because if your strategy becomes restricted (by lack of space), then the opponent has a clear advantage. With time, it's about determining how fast you can get where you need to go. With numbers (personnel), it's important to have everyone contributing. And of course, Geronimo's smaller numbers allowed him to move through constricted space faster, buying him time.

CHAPTER FIFTEEN

"Until the Stone Should Crumble to Dust" (Surrender)

THE FIRST THING that General Miles did after Crook rode away in April 1886 was fire all the scouts and request additional U.S. troops and cavalry. They'd tried Crook's way. Now Miles would throw manpower and money at the Apache Problem. In my experience that's not a great strategy, but that's what Miles did. Miles didn't think Apache scouts were a good idea, even though Crook had proven them to work. Miles (and Sheridan) thought that having to use Indian scouts was an embarrassment that reflected poorly on the abilities of the U.S. cavalry. Miles requested more troops, employing five thousand U.S. soldiers—a full one-fourth of the entire U.S. military at that time—to go after Geronimo, sev-

LESSON: *Great leaders are almost always overachievers.*

enteen fugitive warriors, and a handful of women and children.[1] He'd get the support of thousands of Mexican soldiers also stalking Geronimo. Geronimo was outnumbered 263–1. (For comparison, a quarter of today's active military would be around 200,000 soldiers going after Geronimo).

General Miles put soldiers and cavalry at all the known water holes and ranches in Arizona. They'd finally figured out that was a good idea. Then he got creative and installed a pricey heliograph system. Heliographs were big, portable mirrors that he pointed toward the sun to flash Morse code signals across the desert and mountains. He split the region into distinct "districts of observation" and placed these mirrors on top of mountain peaks in Arizona, New Mexico, and Sonora. The plan was to use the glaring sun and clear skies to communicate rapidly and over long distances the movements of Geronimo and his band.[2] It looked good on paper, but it didn't really work. I mean, it worked in that they sent messages—some 2,264 of them that Miles bragged about. But none of these messages helped him find Geronimo; they simply reported the movement of his own troops.[3] The heliograph wasn't much more than a costly, time-wasting gadget.

Besides, Geronimo was one step ahead of the army, as usual. For a long time he'd used a similar, if more basic, system. Warriors ascended mountaintops at night and waved torches to signal their location to other groups far away. It worked great, allowing them to organize their movements and reunite whenever they wanted to. It was a lot cheaper and simpler and more effective than a heliograph system.

LESSON: *Take risks.*

Most great achievements throughout history are the result of taking a risk.

Meanwhile, as Miles marched large troops of infantry and cavalry around, Geronimo, Naiche, Lozen, and their gang went on a half-year raiding tear and killing spree that remains one of the most risky and daring military operations in history. Geronimo felt like the entire world was against them—and it practically was. "We were reckless with our lives," the shaman said, "because we felt that every man's hand was against us. If we returned to the reservation we would be put in prison and killed; if we stayed in Mexico they would continue to send soldiers to fight us. So we gave no quarter to anyone and asked no favors."[4]

Geronimo's Guerilla-Style Tactics

WHAT THEY DID is run and raid and kill. Using all of the skills honed over his lifetime, Geronimo cut west through the mountains of Sonora, then sped hundreds of miles south, to the Rio Yaqui near Ures, then north again all the way back to near the Arizona/New Mexico/Mexico border. Pursued by Mexican and U.S. soldiers, Geronimo and Naiche split up.

Geronimo took just six warriors and four women and slid through the heavily patrolled border area, killing ranchers, herders, and a doctor in southern Arizona. The raids were for ammunition, and they took him as far north as Ojo Caliente in New Mexico—the sight of that showdown and arrest by Agent John Clum many years before that nearly ended with him being hanged. His last raids north of the border left some twenty dead settlers in his dust and continued spreading fear across the land. The *Silver City Enterprise* now ran ads offering $250 for any Apache scalp and $500 for Geronimo, dead or alive.[5] Journalists from all over the country traveled to the Southwest to tell the story of Geronimo's run, producing stories that fanned the flames of his growing legend. Like Butch Cassidy and Billy the Kid, Geronimo was establishing himself as a big part of western lore, even while he was still alive.

To Geronimo and Naiche, the killing was justified: It was their lives or those of the settlers. Naiche said, "It was war. Anybody who saw us would kill us, and we did the same thing. We had to if we wanted to stay alive."[6] Geronimo thought only of his family and of his people. Said one warrior who was with him: "Geronimo was a great fighting man. Geronimo had to obtain food for his men, and for his women and children. When we were hungry, Geronimo got food. When we were cold, he provided blankets and clothing. When we were afoot, he stole horses. When we had no bullets, he got ammunition. He was a good man."[7]

For months Geronimo used all his craft, guile, leadership skills, and toughness to remain nearly invisible to the army. Even for the Chiricahua it was a brutal time. Geronimo remembered, "We frequently suffered greatly for water. At one time

LESSON: *Improvisation is key. Don't spend a lot of time thinking about what you don't have. Think about the resources you DO have and how you can best use them.*

we had no water for two days and nights, and our horses almost died of thirst."[8] When they did find water, they fashioned horseshoes from cut pieces of cowhide softened in water, fitting these over the hooves like low boots that protected the animals from cactus thorns and sharp stones to keep them running.[9] For food, in an emergency, the women followed packrat trails to their dens and stole their piñon nuts, then ran on.[10] They were remarkably industrious under pressure.

The soldiers trailing them suffered even more. Miles's troops followed Geronimo for nearly five months, traveling over three thousand miles through landscapes and conditions that finally broke them. Their feet blistered and swelled, their rifle-barrels got too hot to touch, and they found scorched canyons full of rattlesnakes and cactus, but no Chiricahua. Men sagged on the trail with dysentery, some losing nearly fifty pounds. Miles claimed (though he was prone to exaggeration) that his men's thirst was so great that they sliced their veins and drank their own blood![11] They hadn't learned, as Geronimo had, to suck on sticks and chew on cactus pulp.

Working sometimes in tandem and sometimes separately, Geronimo, Naiche, Lozen, fifteen other warriors, and twenty women and children achieved what one historian calls "the most remarkable campaign of guerrilla warfare ever witnessed on the North American continent."[12] It's hard to argue with that. During the entire campaign, with five thousand U.S. troops and nearly the same number of Mexican soldiers and mercenaries, not one single Chiricahua was captured or killed. Zero. As a tactician and war leader, Geronimo was unrivaled. His strategic defiance against overwhelming odds has never been surpassed or even equaled, and I doubt it ever will be.

Lieutenant Charles B. Gatewood and Another Pair of Aces

DESPERATE, FRUSTRATED, AND embarrassed, Miles was forced to make some changes. First, he recommended sending *all* the Apache away as prisoners of war. Not just the Chiricahua who had caused so much trouble—but every last Apache, even those who'd lived peacefully and served in the army as scouts. Even all those who'd voluntarily surrendered. This took some politicking and convincing. They were mountain people and desert people unlikely to fare well in Florida's humidity.

But in the end Sheridan and Cleveland accepted the plan to send the Apache to Florida. The idea was to move them as far away from Arizona as possible. There was an initial proposal to send them to Fort Leavenworth, Kansas, but in the end they decided on Florida, which was even farther away.[13] It was a raw deal for the many Apache who'd never run off like Geronimo and his Chiricahua, but the government justified the move as a way of controlling the reservation Indians who might potentially become hostile and bolt like Geronimo. Both Chatto and Kaytennae, former scouts, pleaded to allow the non-hostile Apache to remain on the White Mountain reservation in their traditional lands, but the plan was already in motion and they would all soon be designated "prisoners of war."[14] It was dirty dealing, the worst form of treachery. The U.S. authorities would continue to prove that Geronimo was right about them all along.

Next, Miles was forced to admit that Crook's theory was correct: "Only an Apache can catch an Apache." Miles's heliograph system and bloated army had failed. He simply had to use Apache scouts if he wanted to get close to Geronimo. His best bet was to use only Chiricahua Apache scouts. So before Miles sent all the Apache away (and before he told any of them their fate), he enlisted two Chiricahua who knew Geronimo well and had relatives still running with him. Their names were Martine and Kayitah. Miles convinced them (the scouts said he promised to pay them three thousand dollars apiece) that they could help hunt down Geronimo and bring their relatives home safely.[15] (As it turned out, they were never given the three grand, but each did receive a pension, so it looks like Miles did bribe them).

Then in July 1886, Miles played his other ace in the hole. He called on Lieutenant Charles B. Gatewood, then stationed in New Mexico. Gatewood knew the scouts, knew Geronimo, and knew the terrain. Besides, with Emmet Crawford dead and Britton Davis now running a ranch, Gatewood was the most experienced officer left, and he could speak some Apache. Gatewood didn't like being brought back out on Geronimo's trail—Geronimo had already run him ragged. He also had a wife and family to think of, he was in poor health and had lost a bunch of weight due to his rheumatism, and he had no desire to eat Geronimo's dust again. Geronimo had pretty much proven his point: You couldn't catch him if he didn't want to get caught. But Miles dangled a carrot for Gatewood: He'd make him aide-de-camp if he successfully completed the mission. Thinking it might lead to better duty assignments, Gatewood agreed.[16]

Gatewood's mission: take the two guides and an interpreter named George Wratten*[17] deep into Mexico, find Geronimo without getting killed, and demand his surrender by promising him a free railroad trip to Florida, to await the president's decision on his fate. Then, after he had him in custody, Gatewood was supposed to inform Geronimo that, by the way, he was a prisoner of war. It's no wonder Gatewood thought this a fool's errand. But off he went, crossing the border mounted on mules, trailing just a three-mule pack train.

By mid-August Gatewood met up with Captain Henry H. Lawton, who was aimlessly tromping around the mountains near the Aros River looking for Geronimo. Lawton's force was tattered and broken, beaten

---

* George Wratten (or *Wrattan*—it's spelled both ways) had worked at a trading post on the San Carlos Indian reservation as a teenager, and he became fluent in the Apache language. The Apache said that he understood their language better than any other White Eye. He learned Chokonen, Chihenne, and White Mountain dialects. Interesting fact: Wratten ended up marrying a Chokonen/Chihenne Apache girl named Annie when she was just seventeen, and they had two daughters together—Amy and Blossom.

by the heat, the impenetrable terrain, and by Geronimo's speed and stealth and guile.

Just after his arrival at the Aros River, Gatewood got an amazing break. Word came from Mexican officials in Fronteras that only days before, two Chiricahua women (one of whom was said to be Lozen, the woman warrior) had come into town to trade. Geronimo and Naiche were holed up in the mountains near Fronteras, and Geronimo had sent the women under the flag of peace to trade for horses, mescal, and food. The Mexicans complied, sending the women back with the goods and then quickly assembling two hundred soldiers. They planned to lure Geronimo's band back for a wholesale slaughter.

Gatewood hurried to the area and the scouts soon found signs of a Chiricahua trail. Gatewood sent his guides Martine and Kayitah up front, while he, Wratten, and a handful of soldiers crept fearfully behind, trailing the two women for three days up a narrow box canyon high into the Torres Mountains. One of Gatewood's soldiers held a stick with a white flour sack on top as a peace flag, but that didn't make them feel any better. As Gatewood put it, a white flag "don't make a man bullet proof."[18]

Gatewood should have been worried. High above on the mountaintop, Geronimo's sentry Kanseah, just eleven years old, was hidden among the rocks, watching them through army-issue field glasses. Gatewood sent the two Chiricahua scouts up ahead to try to make contact. When Kanseah recognized their Chiricahua relatives in his binoculars, he told Geronimo who they were.

Geronimo wanted to shoot them for their treachery. Other band members convinced him not to, since they were relatives. Uncocking his rifle, Geronimo let them come. The two Chiricahua scouts arrived, believing they'd be killed at any moment. They sat down with Geronimo and explained his grim odds. With ten thousand chasing so few, it was only a matter of time before they would be caught. Troops were everywhere, they said, spread across their lands and coming from all over the United States. Kayitah made a plea for Geronimo to stop, saying, "All of you are my friends, and some of you are my brothers-in-law. . . . I don't want you to get killed. At night you do not rest. . . . If you are awake at night and a rock rolls down the mountain or a stick breaks, you will be running. You even eat your meals running."[19]

Geronimo looked at the women and children. As much as he hated to admit it, Kayitah was right. This was no way to live. Being always on the move was the Chiricahua way, yes, but being always *forced* to move was not. At one point during an escape they'd had to strike camp so fast they'd been forced to leave two infants to die or else they all would have been caught. The women just couldn't move fast enough carrying them. This pained Geronimo deeply. The children were tired, undernourished, dehydrated most of the time. They were gaunt from eating and drinking on the run. He had to do what was right for his people.

LESSON: *As a leader, you have to think about all of the people, not just one. And certainly not just yourself.*

Geronimo thought for a long time. Then he reached for some mescal hearts the women had baked and formed in his hands a lump of the mescal flesh the size of a man's heart. He wrapped it in cloth and handed it to Martine, telling him to take it to Gatewood as a symbol (speaking honestly, from the heart) that he was ready to talk. He kept Kayitah as insurance, in case of a double cross.[20] Geronimo had learned long before not to trust the army's "deals." His suspicions were well founded. Ironically, on that very day President Cleveland sent a telegraph to the War Department, making it clear that Geronimo was to be treated as a prisoner of war—"if we cannot hang him, which I would much prefer."[21]

The next day Geronimo sent messengers instructing Gatewood to meet him on a bend of the Bavispe River of Geronimo's choosing. The fugitives came in at their own pace, in pairs and threes. Geronimo arrived at last. He set down his rifle, shook hands with Gatewood, and then teased the lieutenant about his thin and sickly appearance. They sat on a downed log. Gatewood offered horsemeat jerky and rolled tobacco* and they ate and smoked. It was too quiet. Both Gatewood and his interpreter Wratten wondered if they were about to die.

Geronimo broke the silence. He wanted to know Miles's terms.

Gatewood delivered the deal: Surrender now and join all of your people in Florida. The president would make a final decision. Accept these terms or fight it out to the end; Miles would chase him for fifty years if he had to.

Geronimo looked Gatewood straight in the eye. "Take us to the [San Carlos] reservation or fight,"[22] he said. He was defiant.

Gatewood broke Geronimo the grim news: There was no more reservation to take them to. He told him that all of the Apache had been sent to Florida to join Chihuahua and the rest. The truth was that the final mass removal had not happened yet, but Gatewood did not know this since he had no communication in the mountains. He thought what he said was true, but it wasn't. This news was a deciding blow to Geronimo and the others. With their families gone, what was left to fight for?

Geronimo, Naiche, and two other leaders split off to talk about it.

The Chiricahua way was to have a council and try for consensus, but in the end every man could do what was in his heart. Geronimo's cousin Perico decided to give up. "I am going to surrender," he said. "My wife and children have been captured. I love them and want to be with them."[23] One after another, all the warriors agreed with Perico. They should give up.

Geronimo thought for a while. Finally he stood up. "I have been depending heavily on you three men. You have been great fighters in battle. If you are going to surrender, there is no use my going without you. I will give up with you."[24]

LESSON:

Make lasting commitments that are solid as rock.

---

* The Apache smoked rolled tobacco and not a "peace pipe."

Skeleton Canyon: "Until the Stone Shall Crumble to Dust"

ON SEPTEMBER 5, 1886, Geronimo, his son Chappo, Lozen, fifteen warriors, and twenty women and children met General Miles at Skeleton Canyon, thirty-five miles north of Mexico on the Arizona–New Mexico border. Geronimo rode up the stream that wound from the Peloncillo Mountains, dismounted, and shook the hand of General Miles. It was the first time they'd ever met. Through an interpreter, Miles assured Geronimo he was his friend. Geronimo smiled and told the interpreter that he'd never seen Miles before, but he sure could use some friends. He joked, why doesn't Miles ride off with him, come over to his side? They all laughed.

Miles found Geronimo impressive: "He was one of the brightest, most resolute, determined-looking men that I have ever encountered. He had the clearest, sharpest, dark eyes that I think I have ever seen. . . . Every movement indicated power, energy, and determination. In everything he did, he had a purpose."[25]

LESSON: *Have a purpose in everything you do.*

Geronimo and Miles sat near the stream bank under a sycamore tree.

Miles restated the terms. "Lay down your arms and come with me to Fort Bowie, and in five days you will see your families now in Florida, and no harm will be done to you."[26] He promised Geronimo his own house to live in, horses, mules, and cattle to raise. There would be plenty of timber, water, and grazing land. He told Geronimo that his past deeds would be wiped out and that he could start a new life.[27] Geronimo had heard such promises before. He had no good reason to

LESSON: *Abraham Lincoln said, "No man has a good enough memory to be a successful liar." He's right.*

believe Miles, but with everyone else surrendering, what else was there to do?

Geronimo said of his surrender: "We stood between his troopers and my warriors. We placed a large stone on the blanket before us. Our treaty was made by this stone, and it was to last until the stone should crumble to dust. So we made the treaty, and bound each other with an oath."[28]

Geronimo, his face creased by years of wind and weather and battle, his body riddled with bullet holes, had at last given up. He handed over his rifle. With this act, Geronimo came to symbolize the last American Indian to hand over his gun to the white men.

 | **Commentary** |

Know When to Compromise. *From his first contact with white settlers in 1852, Geronimo's lifestyle had been encroached upon, and he and the Chiricahua had been on the run periodically for more than thirty years. Geronimo didn't so much give up as give in. He compromised and struck what he thought was the best deal for his people. If it had been only about him, he would have kept on running. I'm sure of it. But he saw that his people could take the pace no longer, and he stopped running only for them. To be the last American Indian to hand over his gun is valiant and heroic—though in the end, he'd wish he hadn't done it.*

Know Your Terrain Better Than Your Opponent. *The Apache managed to always remain ahead of their pursuers, in large part because of their intimate knowledge of the terrain and their abilities to hide almost anywhere, virtually disappearing behind rocks, knolls, and even yucca trees. The Chiricahua were unbelievably skilled at hiding. One soldier described their technique: "Chase them and they slink into the ground and somehow vanish. Look behind and they are peeping over a hill at you."[29] They moved in almost complete silence, their moccasins lightly padding the ground. Because they often stripped down to just their loincloths in battle (even in the dead-cold winter), they blended* in with the rocks and hillsides. Perhaps worst of all for those chasing them, their arrows arrived silently, hitting soldiers without the loud report of a rifle. Also, because they knew where mountain and valley springs were, and could even dig for water with their bare hands in dry stream and creek beds, they did not have to carry much water with them, allowing them to move faster.

Practice Stealth. *It's much more efficient to move thirty-eight people around than it is ten thousand. By traveling light and fast, with very little excess baggage and no bureaucracy or chain of command, Geronimo and his smaller team were fast and furious. They were able to strike camp in minutes and leave virtually no trace of having been there. Geronimo's efficient, well-trained team is still considered the most successful light cavalry force in military history.*

CHAPTER SIXTEEN

>>>><<<<>>><<<<

Prisoners of War (Patriotism)

Geronimo, Naiche, and the last of the renegade Chiricahua band, waiting for the train to take them to Florida as POWs, September 8, 1886. (Naiche is front and center, Geronimo directly to his left.)

WELL, SO MUCH FOR TREATIES. On September 8, 1886, Geronimo and his band were lined up like cattle and loaded onto heavily guarded wagons and transported to the Bowie railroad stop. So were the scouts Martine and Kayitah, who had just risked their lives in service to the United States and made the contact with Geronimo that spurred his surrender. Before they'd left, Miles had allowed Geronimo to get fresh footwear and clothes, but he confiscated Geronimo's rifle as a souvenir.[1] Geronimo even posed for a few photos in his new duds.

LESSON: *It's disappointing and discouraging, but some people have no intention of honoring their agreements. Don't be one of these people.*

The citizens of Arizona and New Mexico wanted all the Apache hanged or shot (as did President Cleveland), but in the end the president and the War Department realized that turning them over to the civil authorities would create a mob lynching and a political and public relations nightmare. Whether they wanted to or not, the government (and especially the president) couldn't allow the very kinds of vigilantism for which they were supposedly arresting the Chiricahua.

Instead, they shipped them by train, bound for a military prison in Florida.

The train windows were bolted shut to prevent escape; an attempt would have been likely had Geronimo known where he was headed. Most of his people didn't think they had long to live. Kanseah, Geronimo's eleven-year-old nephew, said, "Nobody thought we'd get far before they'd stop and kill us."[2] But they arrived at San Antonio unharmed. Under heavy guard, the prisoners were led to nearby Fort Sam Houston, where they pitched tepees and waited for what came next.

They waited for weeks, most of them expecting to be killed any day. What was going on? The president and the War Department were trying to decide what to do with them. But no one told the prisoners anything.

While Geronimo and his band sat there in San Antonio, all the rest of the Chiricahua—434 of them—were on a separate train headed for Fort Marion, on the shore near St. Augustine, Florida. All of the Chiricahua had been led by caravan to the special eighteen-car tourist train. Their twelve hundred horses were confiscated and sold, and they had to leave all of their personal belongings behind. Some three thousand dogs followed them to the train, and the soldiers shot hundreds of these animals as the Indians boarded. There were too many dogs to shoot them all, and once the train pulled away some of the loyal dogs chased their owners for twenty miles before giving up.[3]

Nearly all of the Chiricahua were on a train for the first time in their lives, and the weeklong ordeal terrified them. They had seats but could only lie on the floor to sleep. When a train entered a dark tunnel, many screamed, thinking they were plunging down into the earth. Soldiers rode in the first and last cars.

The windows were barred and shuttered to prevent Indian escape, and the Chiricahua had no toilets. Only a few times during the weeklong trip did they let the prisoners out to go to the bathroom next to the tracks. The rest of the time they simply had to go on the floor of the cars. At stops the Chiricahua would be let out, and soldiers hosed out each train car with water. That was how they went to Florida.[4]

After six weeks President Cleveland finally made a decision for the prisoner distribution. The Chiricahua would be split up. The women and children were shipped to Fort Marion, along with the 434 others on a separate train. Geronimo and the renegade warriors were sent to Fort Pickens, on Santa Rosa Island near Pensacola, on the Gulf Coast. Geronimo received the highest level of security. He'd escaped countless times; they could not let him escape again. He was kept in some of the stone forts there, put to work five days a week cleaning up the fort grounds. President Cleveland and the War Department's justification for Florida as the final destination was that "these Indians had been guilty of the worst crimes known to the law," and it was for reasons of "public safety" to send them far from their crimes against humanity.[5]

Being separated from their families crushed Geronimo and all the Chiricahua. The promise of reuniting with them had been the main reason they'd surrendered. Now they had no idea when, or if, they would ever see them again. Through interpreters Geronimo dictated letters to his wives and children at Fort Marion. Coming from the man whom the press was calling "the wickedest Indian that ever lived," they are pretty poetic and sensitive. Because he was a national curiosity, one letter was intercepted and published in the newspapers with the title "A Love Letter from Geronimo." It read, in part, "My dear wives, and my son and daughter. Are you at Fort Marion? Have you plenty to eat and do you sleep and drink well? . . . As sure as the trees bud and bloom in the spring, so sure is my hope of seeing you again. Talking by paper is good, but when you see one's lips move, and hear their voice, it is much better. . . . Do what is right, no matter how you may suffer. . . . Your husband, GERONIMO."[6]

LESSON: *Be utterly devoted to the people you love, especially family.*

Geronimo was right to worry about his family, for at Fort Marion the Apache were suffering, dying from malaria and tuberculosis, for which they had no immunity. The army gave them tepees that they pitched all around the fort area, even on the roof. Other quarters were below, in the basement, where the Spaniards had originally built dungeons. The quarters were severely cramped—only about sixty-five square feet per prisoner, a space of merely eight feet by eight feet.[7] By the end of the first year eighteen Apache had died, including Geronimo's four-year-old daughter. Within a few years, 119 of his people died, about one-fourth of their entire population. They suffered greatly in Florida.

Then, to make things worse, the War Department sent all of the school-age children to the special Carlisle Indian Industrial School in Pennsylvania. The parents wailed and clung to their kids as officials dragged the crying children away. The terrified Indian kids traveled by ocean steamer up the coast to Pennsylvania. (Interesting note: The famous Jim Thorpe, arguably the greatest athlete in American history, enrolled at Carlisle at age sixteen in 1904, during the same time period that Geronimo's people were there. Thorpe was of mixed-blood descent—his father was an Oklahoma farmer and his mother was a Sauk and Fox Indian descendant from their great chief Black Hawk. Thorpe was raised as an Indian and his athletic talents were discovered at Carlisle by Pop Warner, who coached Thorpe. Thorpe gained national attention when—in a football game against Harvard—Thorpe played running back, defensive back, place-kicker, and punter. Carlisle beat Harvard 18–15. Harvard was at the time a top-ranked team in the early days of the NCAA. Thorpe went on to win two gold medals in the 1912 Stockholm Olympics, competing in the decathlon and pentathlon. He also played fifty-two games in the NFL and played six seasons of Major League Baseball.)

The idea at the Carlisle school was to forcefully educate and assimilate the Indians. Administrators cropped the boys' hair short (ironically, a traditional sign of mourning), forbid them to speak Apache, and replaced their religion with Christianity. The school's motto was: "To civilize the Indian, get him into civilization. To keep him civilized, let him stay." School officials took their traditional clothes and dressed them in conventional uniforms. Then they lined them up by height and renamed them alphabetically, assigning them arbitrary names and pinning estimated birth dates to

LESSON: *No matter what happens to you, always have an acute awareness about yourself and your identity. Know who you are, no matter what others choose to call you.*

their jackets. Juh's son Daklugie became Asa Daklugie, Nah-delthy Batsinas became Jason Betzinez, and Geronimo's nephew Kanseah became Jasper.[8] Geronimo's son Chappo got sent there too, but for some reason they let him keep his name, calling him Chappo Geronimo.

But much worse than being renamed, at Carlisle some thirty Apache children got tuberculosis and died, further devastating the Chiricahua people.

After a half year of Chiricahua separation, disease, and death, in late April of 1887 President Cleveland—as a result of public pressure for more humane treatment—began to move all of the prisoners at Fort Marion and Fort Pickens to the Mount Vernon military post near Mobile, Alabama. Mount Vernon was 2,160 acres of low-lying swamp, bayous, creeks, and pines. It was better than Fort Marion but worthless for agriculture. There was little for the Apache to do but cut logs and build the cabins they'd live in. Geronimo reunited with his wives, and his young daughter Dohn-say ran to him, leaped into his arms, and wept. Then he got a great surprise: His seventh wife, Ih-tedda, came forward and handed him his daughter Lenna, born in captivity as a prisoner of war. It was the first time he had seen her.[9] His time with her was short, though. In 1889 the government allowed the Mescalero Apache to return to New Mexico. It was the Chiricahua who kept escaping, so they would be the ones punished most.

Geronimo saw an opportunity to save some of his family. His wife Ih-tedda was Mescalero, so he suggested that she return to New Mexico with Lenna. He could see his people dying in droves, and he hoped to spare their lives. Ih-tedda was pregnant at the time too. "We were not healthy in this place," said Geronimo. "So many of our people died that I consented to let Ih-tedda go to the Mescalero Agency in New Mexico to live."[10] (It was similar to what happened to the Aztec when the Spaniards brought smallpox to the Americas: The native people had no immunity to the disease and it decimated their population.) Ih-tedda begged to stay, but Geronimo insisted she go, for the sake of her health and their children's. It was a difficult choice but a good one. In New Mexico, Ih-tedda gave birth to their son, Robert, remarried, and lived on. Robert and Lenna were the only two of Geronimo's children to survive. All of his other children who were forced to stay died while prisoners of war, including Chappo, who contracted tuberculosis at Carlisle.[11]

Geronimo and the remainder of his people lived poorly at Mount Vernon for six years. Geronimo was right—they were not healthy in that place. His people continued to get sick and die. Lozen was among them. While at Mount Vernon the great woman warrior who rode with Geronimo, sister of the famous Chief Victorio, succumbed to tuberculosis. Her age was estimated to be about fifty. She was buried in an unmarked grave.[12]

The post surgeon, Walter Reed, treated those he could, the ones who did not die. He would go on to become famous for proving that yellow fever was transmitted by mosquitoes, and he ended up having many medical schools and hospitals named after him, including the Walter Reed National Military Medical Center and Walter Reed General Hospital.

In January 1890, Geronimo's nemesis General Crook came to visit the Chiricahua at Mount Vernon. Crook had been sent there officially, under orders from the secretary of war.[13] Although his techniques (the use of Apache scouts, smaller forces, the use of mules) had ultimately led to their capture, he was always an advocate for their better treatment. Crook assessed the conditions at Mount Vernon and heard the prisoners' grievances. He wrote to Washington, criticizing sending the children to the Carlisle Indian School, and he went so far as to suggest that the Chiricahua be granted their own reservation in Oklahoma.[14]

A number of the Apache chatted with Crook, the man who'd been their main adversary, including Chatto, who greeted him warmly. But not Geronimo. Geronimo and Crook had bad blood to the very end. The Chiricahua believed that Crook hated Geronimo because he never defeated him. Geronimo, to the end, believed that Crook lied to him. Crook finished his inspection, wrote and sent his report recommending their transfer to Fort Sill, and within two months he died abruptly of a heart attack at age sixty-one.

Geronimo didn't mourn Crook's passing. He only said, "I think that the General's death was sent by the Almighty as punishment for the many evil deeds he committed."[15] Geronimo would never forgive Crook for relocating his people and for his broken promise of the two-year sentence that became, for him, a life sentence.

Finally, in 1894, Geronimo and his band got to go west. Not all the way west, but at least closer to home: to Fort Sill, Oklahoma. Though it took time, Crook's suggestion had been influential. The Chiricahua boarded a special train, stopping at New Orleans, Fort Worth, and finally Rush Springs, Oklahoma. Along the route something incredible happened. Crowds came to get a glimpse of Geronimo, the famous warrior, and they cheered for him at every stop. It was an uncanny shift.

When he'd first arrived at Fort Pickens in Florida eight years before, tour groups had come to view him like a caged animal in his stone quarters, taunting him. Newspapers called him evil and diabolical. At that time the president himself had wanted to hang him. Now he was an American cult hero, getting standing ovations as he waved and smiled and signed autographs.[16]

How did this change happen? I don't think Geronimo ever changed, but public sentiment toward him did. While imprisoned he had tons of visitors who told his story. There were even societies of so-called "Friends of the Indians" who came to see and report on the Apache plight and living conditions. Word spread of the raw deal given the Apache, and the winds of public opinion shifted in Geronimo's favor.[17] And I think, also, Americans believe in second chances.

His final surrender ended the bloody Indian Wars that marred the country for decades. The country was ready to start fresh. The "bloodthirsty Apache" was now viewed as a freedom fighter, a patriot who'd defended his home, his people, and his honor.[18] He was a patriot. And there was always something special about Geronimo himself—his Power, his charisma, a kind of greatness—and people were drawn to him. As the prison train carried him

LESSON: *Develop the innate ability to connect with people. It's true that some people are born with it, but it can be practiced and developed.*

to Oklahoma, fans reached out to see him and touch him, and he cleverly sold his autograph for a quarter. He'd rip buttons off his coat and sell them for a quarter, then sew more on and sell those at the next stop. His hats went for five bucks.[19] This was 1894. Geronimo was seventy-one years old and about to become an international celebrity, the most famous Indian in the world.

Geronimo began to symbolize the core ideals that the revolutionary patriots stood for and fought for and died for. He stood for freedom.

| Commentary |

Embrace Patriotism. *Geronimo was as patriotic as any American who ever lived. He fought for his rights, his family, his land, his convictions, and his belief, and he never wavered in their defense. He understood at a core moral level that he was there first, that the land was NOT the land of the encroaching white Americans (international and federal laws and boundaries notwithstanding), and that the U.S. army certainly did not OWN him and should not be able to tell him where he could or could not go. In his autobiography, when reflecting on the coming of the white men, Geronimo mused, "I do not think that I ever belonged to those soldiers, or that I should have asked them where I might go." All he ever wanted was "life, liberty, and the pursuit of happiness," and he was willing to fight and kill for those inalienable rights, just as our founders were.*

Live with Honor. *In negotiations with the U.S. government, Geronimo and his people were not dealt with honorably. The feds broke every treaty they made with the Chiricahua, most within minutes of their making them. Even the Apache scouts (turncoats, yes, but still) got cheated. Had Geronimo known he was being lied to, and that families were going to be separated, and that surrender would lead to permanent banishment from his homeland—not just for him but also for all Apache—Geronimo NEVER would have agreed to the terms. He believed one's word was binding and true, as if written in blood. In his many dealings with the U.S. government, he learned an important lesson—though he may have learned it too late: If they lie to you in negotiations, then they will lie to you when you start working with them. If you move through life with HONOR, you can hold your head high, but you might still get a raw deal. Honor is more important than the deal made.*

CHAPTER SEVENTEEN

Fame

O N OCTOBER 4, 1896, Geronimo and the remaining 295 Chiricahuas arrived at their new "home," a prisoner compound at Fort Sill,
Oklahoma. The area was a small section of a reservation that the Comanche and Kiowa now shared. Hundreds of Comanche and Kiowa,
defeated and rounded up years earlier, came to see the Apache prisoners.
Though they'd been bitter enemies in the eighteenth century (there was
some overlap in their traditional ranges), now the Kiowa and Comanche
sympathized with Geronimo and his people and they tried to speak with
them through Plains Indian sign language. But the mountain Apache
had never learned their sign language, so both sides brought out some
of their Carlisle-educated young men to translate and communicate
through English, and they talked of their shared stories and situations.[1]

The Chiricahua built wickiups along the cottonwood-lined creeks
and bluffs of the nearly fifty thousand acres at Fort Sill. Their wickiups
would be replaced by log- and timber-framed houses over the next few
years. The terrain for them was way better than the Florida and Alabama
swamps and bayous. Sagebrush grew on the land, and on the western
horizon Geronimo could see the slopes of White Wolf and Signal
Mountains; but these rose less than two thousand feet toward the sky,

mere foothills for the Chiricahua. Still, at night his people heard the distant yips and howls of coyotes, making them feel better and homesick at the same time.[2]

At Fort Sill the Chiricahua had more rights and freedoms than they'd had in eight years of confinement. They rode horses, raised cattle, and each family got some ground to cultivate and farm. Whether they liked it or not, these seminomadic people were being turned into farmers and ranchers. Geronimo and Naiche worked as cowboys, herding and branding, ironically employed in the very range industry that had brought thousands of settlers to their homeland and disrupted their lifestyle. Adding insult to this injury, Geronimo wasn't happy that he and Naiche, the ones doing the work, didn't get all the proceeds from selling the cattle they raised. A percentage of their earnings went through an agent to a mysterious "Apache Fund" created by the government, but Geronimo never trusted the agent who divvied up the money.[3]

When the Chiricahua first got to Fort Sill they learned that mesquite trees grew in Oklahoma; the nearest grove was only forty-five miles away. Mesquite was a big part of their culture. They convinced their captors to let them harvest the beans, a favorite food. Under military supervision, the Chiricahua ran and trotted the ninety-mile round trip, gathering three hundred bushels of beans in two days. The beans tasted like home.[4]

One of their new perks was the freedom to walk or ride a horse to the town of Lawton, four miles from the military compound. This proved both good and bad, as it lured Geronimo to seek whiskey, which remained forbidden. Twice he got arrested and thrown into the guardhouse for getting caught drinking whiskey. For him it was worth it. To his credit, at no time making treaties did he ever say he'd give up drinking tiswin or whiskey.[5]

LESSON: *Don't make promises that you can't keep.*

But despite being allowed to roam and ride on the compound, make no mistake, the Chiricahua remained prisoners. They'd remain classified as prisoners of war for twenty-seven years—to this day the longest kept POWs in our nation's history.

Geronimo remained a shaman and a leader of his people. During his imprisonment people came to him for his Power, his ability to treat various illnesses. An elderly man showed up with "coyote sickness," a disease contracted by contact with a fox, wolf, or coyote—even through encountering their tracks. His symptoms included severe leg and hand cramps. In front of his house, Geronimo laid the man out in front of him while silent family members watched. The shaman took out his ceremonial tray with a bag of pollen, an eagle feather, and an abalone shell. He rolled a cigarette and blew smoke to the four directions, then rubbed pollen over the man, praying and singing to Coyote while beating a drum. The ceremony went on for four nights, and the man was cured.[6]

Another time the people brought him a woman whose body shook with violent seizures, like epilepsy. Her face was contorted, her eyes crossed. Geronimo sang over her and cured her too.

But despite Geronimo's curing Power, and treatment by military doctors, his people continued to die in shocking numbers. The dead and buried at Fort Sill included three of Geronimo's children; Juh's widow; Chatto's relatives; two daughters and six sons of Naiche; Nana; and also Loco, the chief so reluctant to rebel—the one Geronimo "rescued" from San Carlos and brought to the stronghold in the Sierra Madre. All of them perished at Fort Sill along with nearly three hundred others, about half the tribe. There is a sign at the cemetery identifying the place as a "roll call . . . of the most famous names in Apache history." Buried far from their tribal homes are the sons and grandsons of Mangas Coloradas, Victorio, and Cochise.[7]

Geronimo believed they died because they'd been taken from their homeland. "In the beginning," he said, "the Apache and their homes were created for each other by Ussen himself. When they are taken away from these homes they sicken and die. We are vanishing from the earth. . . . How long will it be until it is said, there are no Apache."[8]

Fortunately, his grim vision has not yet come to pass, for some of their descendants live on. Recent census reports show that about three hundred Chiricahua Apache descendants live in Oklahoma, and there are roughly another three hundred and seventy-five living around the United States.[9]

Celebrity

GERONIMO'S FAME REACHED across the country, and it didn't take long for his captors and clever promoters to begin using him as a PR tool. Already the most famous Indian in America, Geronimo's name and story would soon go international.

LESSON: *Ask yourself this question every day: Why not me?*

In 1898 Geronimo and Naiche were brought by train to Omaha to appear for more than a month as exhibits in the Trans-Mississippi and International Exposition. It was a world's fair to showcase the settling and development of the West. Even by today's standards, it was a big deal: Over four months, 2.5 million visitors came to see four thousand exhibits, and Geronimo proved a main attraction.[10] Smart enough not to let the promoters* alone gain from his appearance, Geronimo sold autographed photos of himself and turned a tidy profit.

There's a great story from the Omaha World's Fair. It shows that Geronimo's legend could still create fear. The performers got Sundays off, and one time Geronimo and Naiche hired some horses to ride around the countryside and check it out. Security on the two former public enemies was apparently pretty lax by now—after all, Geronimo was seventy-five, how dangerous could he be? One overcast Sunday afternoon Geronimo and Naiche rode miles into the Nebraska farmland. What they saw wasn't too impressive. "No mountains," said Geronimo, "nothing but corn."[11]

---

* Naiche, incidentally, became a fine artist in captivity. His paintings on deerskin are world class and ended up in museums.

The two were supposed to return before nightfall, but without stars or mountains for navigation, they got lost and missed their curfew. Once they were reported missing, the entire area around Omaha went into a panic. The Omaha press jumped on the story. Newsboys cried out, "Extra! Extra! Wild Apache Escape!!" and sold hot-off-the-press papers with this headline:

GERONIMO AND NAICHE ESCAPE. APACHE MURDERERS
THOUGHT TO BE ON THEIR WAY BACK TO ARIZONA.[12]

Mass panic and hysteria broke out. Farm folks grabbed their guns, barred their doors, and waited nervously throughout the night. Police detectives went after the renegades. Telegraph warnings shot across the country: Be on the lookout for Geronimo. Before daylight, the military officer in charge of Geronimo and Naiche managed to locate them twenty miles from town, and he brought them back in to the fair grounds. The power of his reputation and legend was amazing. Even the thought of him being on the warpath again, at seventy-five, still caused widespread panic.[13]

LESSON: *Always keep your opponent off balance.*

Geronimo's exposure at the Omaha World's Fair vaulted his fame to a new level, a fame that would continue to rise for the rest of his life and continue beyond the grave. The Omaha World's Fair launched a late-life career as a traveling celebrity; he was the main attraction at any fair he attended, and he milked his celebrity for all it was worth—both for personal profit (at the end of his life he supposedly had more than ten thousand dollars in the bank) and to try to get himself and his people back home to Arizona.

Geronimo diversified his money-making ventures, selling handmade bows and arrows in addition to his autograph and signed pictures. He rode horseback in many parades, and then in 1901 he agreed to appear at the Pan-American Exposition in Buffalo, New York, for forty-five dollars a month. To earn his pay he wore a traditional head-dress and Apache clothing and participated in shows and staged reen-actments of battles between Apache warriors and U.S. cavalry.[14] Playing Indian clearly wasn't Geronimo's first choice. He'd rather have been living with those he loved, in the place he loved. But as a prisoner of war he figured it was better than tending a melon patch at Fort Sill, and he compromised. That's what leaders sometimes have to do.

Geronimo played mock war games for large audiences. Tragically, though, the Buffalo exposition became most known for President William McKinley's assassination. He was assassinated by a radical anarchist named Leon Czolgosz, who shot McKinley while the president was greeting the public at the Temple of Music inside the fairgrounds. (Czolgosz's explanation for pulling the trigger was that McKinley was an enemy of the good working people and had too much power.) The assassin got the electric chair, and the assassination led to legislation requiring the Secret Service to protect future presidents. Geronimo went back to Fort Sill as the nation mourned.

Wild West Shows, World Expos, and Inaugural Parades

WILD WEST SHOWS had gained popularity more than a decade earlier, when Buffalo Bill Cody created his famous entertainment extravaganza that exploited and glamorized frontier life. Staged Indian attacks on settlers' wagon trains, shooting demonstrations (with pistol, rifle, shotgun, bow and arrow), and depictions of Indian life would culminate in a dramatic battle reenactment.

Cody's show first toured around the United States in 1883 and eventually went overseas, entertaining Queen Victoria and her subjects at her Golden Jubilee (celebrating fifty years of the monarch's reign) in London in 1887. Copycats followed, of course, and one imitator was Pawnee Bill, whose own Wild West show featured Geronimo as a buffalo hunter. This show was pretty absurd, since it featured Geronimo shooting the buffalo out of an automobile. That fact didn't keep an estimated sixty-five thousand spectators from paying to watch him, billed as "the Apache Terror," shoot a buffalo and then run up to it and finish it off with a knife.[15]

In 1904, now eighty-one, Geronimo took part in the Louisiana Purchase Exposition (also called the St. Louis World's Fair), where he lived for many months in a replica "Apache Village" as part of the Ethnology Exhibit inside the fairgrounds. It was (at the time) the largest world's fair ever, attracting 20 million visitors over its run and hosting the 1904 Summer Olympics. Lots of famous people were there, including Helen Keller, who gave a lecture in the main auditorium.[16]

At the St. Louis fair, Geronimo now commanded a hundred dollars a month, and his price for an autograph was up to two bucks. One of the promoters admitted that he was pretty expensive, but then conceded, "He *is* the only Geronimo."[17] To bolster his image and fearsome reputation, false rumors were circulated: One was that he kept a vest made of the hair of all the white people he had killed. Another was that he had nearly one hundred white scalps. Neither was true. Still, awed onlookers watched him perform tricks with a rope and demonstrate his healing powers, complete with gyrations, chants, and songs.[18] Lots of people say that Geronimo was being exploited, but I don't see it that way. He was exploiting his opportunities too. He was earning money, capitalizing on his growing fame. Not only that, the shows and fairs gave him a chance to escape the reservation for a time and to see and experience other parts of America.

LESSON: *Be interested in how things work and in everything that you don't understand.*

He had an incredibly curious mind, and through his journeys he learned and witnessed much.

Geronimo visited many of the other exhibits and shows himself, but after the debacle and false alarm of his Omaha "escape," he now had guards with him. He watched a magician slice a woman in half with a knife and tried to figure out how he'd done it, saw a polar bear trained to do tricks, and rode the Ferris wheel. Always interested in learning, he was fascinated by the Igorots, Philippine mountain people from the island of northern Luzon. The word *Igorot* means "mountain people." Ironically, like the Apache, the Igorot were being displayed as "primitive people."

He was most impressed by a sword fight performed by two Turkish men. "They tried to hit each other over the head with these swords," he said, "and I expected both to be wounded or perhaps killed, but neither one was harmed. They would be hard people to kill in a hand-to-hand fight."[19] I love it: Even in his eighties he was sizing other men up, wondering whether or not he could take them out with his bare hands.

By 1905 Geronimo's fame was such that he was invited to ride in President Theodore Roosevelt's inaugural parade. Roosevelt personally requested him. On his way to Washington, fans crowded the platforms at every stop, cheering and applauding him. He sold autographs as fast as he could sign them. When he changed trains, the crowds were so large that his handlers had to surround him and shuttle him from one train to the next, like modern-day celebrities ducking the paparazzi.[20]

At the inaugural parade Geronimo rode his favorite black pony, shipped from Oklahoma. A massive crowd witnessed the event, and thirty-five thousand people participated.[21] Geronimo rode down Pennsylvania Avenue beside the great Comanche chief Quanah Parker, whose fearsome tribe had finally surrendered in 1875.[22] (These two great warriors knew each other. They were neighbors while Geronimo was incarcerated at Fort Sill, and apparently they had dinner together at least once. No record exists of their conversation, but I sure would like to have heard what they said to each other.) Geronimo stood out mounted on his black horse, wearing a broad-brimmed hat, black jacket, and pants. The chiefs flanking him both rode white horses. As Geronimo rode along, upright and severe-looking in the saddle, thousands of onlookers applauded and hooted, tossed their hats in the air, and cheered "Hooray for Geronimo!"[23] He stole the show. The ovations for him were bested only by those for President Roosevelt himself. As one journalist said, "When old Geronimo, as if carried away by the cheers . . . brandished his spear and gave a wild whoop, the President acknowledged by waving his hat."[24]

Geronimo wanted to use his celebrity for more than public adulation and profit. Four days after the inauguration he was granted permission to speak with President Roosevelt on his own behalf, and for his people. His great desire was that the Apache be allowed to return to their home in Arizona. His appeal was heartfelt. "Great father," he addressed the president, "I and my people have no homes . . . my hands are tied as with a rope. My heart is no longer bad. I pray you cut the ropes and make me free. Let me die in my own country."[25]

Roosevelt seemed moved by the old warrior's request. He replied, "I have no anger in my heart against you." But he explained that the people of Arizona still feared him, and that his return might yet, almost twenty years later, result in more war and bloodshed. "It is best for you to stay where you are. That is all I can say, Geronimo, except that I am sorry, and have no feeling against you."[26]

Geronimo felt that they'd suffered enough. For him and the Chiricahua, banishment was the worst form of punishment—worse than death. Yet banishment is what they received. Geronimo had personally appealed to the most powerful chief in the land to end their banishment, and he had been denied. But even that did not stop him. He returned to Fort Sill dejected but not deterred. He had a new plan: He

LESSON: *Be a great storyteller so that audiences hang on every word.*

would write a book about his life and struggle. Perhaps his written words would convince the president to let him and his people return to die where they were born.

| Commentary |

Know Fame Will Get You Only So Far—and Don't Trust Politicians.
Geronimo had more than served his time, and Roosevelt should have allowed him to return home. It's true that Geronimo used his celebrity for financial gain, but he also tried to use it to help his people. Geronimo's autobiography, which he dictated while incarcerated at Fort Sill in 1905–1906, was in part a plea to President Roosevelt to listen to Geronimo's side of the story, to explain that none of the treaties he had ever agreed to had been upheld by the U.S. government. The plan did not work, but at least he got to air his side of the story. As for the fame—sure, Geronimo got paraded around the east as a celebrity, he got to hobnob with high-ranking politicians, he even got to drive a car. But all he really wanted was to die in the place he was born, in Apache country. So, clearly, fame is valuable only as long as they need you. Then they will move on.

EPILOGUE

Immortality

GERONIMO'S FINAL YEARS represented how he lived his entire life. He was a devoted husband, father, and family man; he fought for the rights of his people; he was defiant and competitive and independent. He pursued spiritual questions and answers to the end.

When he returned from Teddy Roosevelt's inauguration in 1905 he dictated the story of his life to S. M. Barrett, the Lawton, Oklahoma, superintendent of education. The two had met in Lawton in 1904, when Geronimo needed an interpreter to help him sell a war bonnet to a cus-

The legendary warrior Geronimo, defiant to the end. "Once I moved about like the wind; now I surrender to you and that is all."

tomer. They got to talking, and Barrett mentioned that he'd once been wounded by a Mexican. That really got Geronimo fired up, and they became friends, visiting each other's homes to exchange stories. Barrett loved listening to Geronimo's tales and recollections, and he eventually asked the Chiricahua warrior if he might record and publish his memoirs. Geronimo at first said no. He worried that his words would not be recorded accurately—or, worse, that what he said might be used against him. He was a prisoner; they could still hang him if they wanted to, after all. But after a time he agreed. Since Geronimo remained a prisoner of war, the army initially denied Barrett's request to pursue the book. Barrett wrote directly to President Roosevelt, who approved the project.[1] The Rough Rider would let Geronimo speak his mind.

From the beginning, Geronimo's reason for writing the book was clear:

> Because he has given me permission to tell my story; because he has read that story and knows I try to speak the truth; because I believe he is fair-minded and will cause my people to receive justice in the future; and because he is chief of a great people, I dedicate the story of my life to Theodore Roosevelt, President of the United States.[2]

Barrett, sympathetic to the Chiricahua, believed the book would "give the reading public an authentic record of the private life of the Apache Indians . . . and extend to Geronimo . . . the courtesy due any captive, i.e., the right to state the causes which impelled him in his opposition to our civilization and laws."[3] (Geronimo's book was in many ways his personal declaration of independence. He had been denied those "inalienable rights" to which we are all entitled: life, liberty, and the pursuit of happiness. In his book, among other things, Geronimo declared the causes that had led him to separation. Just like Geronimo, the founding fathers were breaking their ruler's laws, committing treason. Had they been caught, they would have been hanged for their offenses. It's clearer than ever to me how much of a patriot Geronimo was.)

To translate Geronimo's Apache to English, Barrett and Geronimo agreed on Juh's son Asa Daklugie, who'd returned from eight years at the Carlisle Indian school. Geronimo had in fact encouraged Daklugie to learn as much as he could about the ways of the White Eyes while he was there—Geronimo understood the importance of knowing one's adversary.

LESSON:

Be curious about everything.

Daklugie proved the perfect interpreter: Second cousin to Geronimo, he was an assimilated Indian but one who stayed true to his Apache heritage and traditions. Geronimo trusted him.[4]

The short book is remarkable, told with the guile and savvy of a man who had an agenda. The warrior-shaman's voice comes through each page. He relates his early life, his cultural traditions, the importance of family, his spiritual upbringing, raids and wars, and he finally restates what he wants and what he thinks his people deserve after nineteen years:

> It is my land, my home, my father's land, to which I now ask to be allowed to return. I want to spend my last days there, to be buried among those mountains. If this could be I might die in peace, feeling that my people, placed in their native homes, would increase in numbers, rather than diminish as at present, and that our name would not become extinct. . . .
>
> If this cannot be done during my lifetime—if I must die in bondage—I hope that the remnant of the Apache tribe may, when I am gone, be granted the one privilege which they request—to return to Arizona.[5]

It was an eloquent plea—but it was ignored. While Geronimo waited for an answer, he worked bailing hay, herding cattle, and farming. "Although I am old," he

LESSON: *Fight for the rights and future of your people— always, and to the end.*

said, "I like to work and help my people as much as I am able."[6] But he had never wanted to be a farmer. It was against his nature and he never took to it. There's a picture of him at Fort Sill standing in a melon patch with his wife Zi-yeh, his daughter Eva, and his son Fenton. Geronimo holds a large pumpkin. His face shows what he appears to have been thinking: "There, I'm a melon farmer, are you happy now?"

He stayed vigorous throughout his captivity and despite his advanced years. During his dictation of the book Geronimo's wife Zi-Yeh died from tubercular lupus. He mourned her passing, but he was not one for bachelorhood; he married again on Christmas Day, 1905. He was eighty-three. His eighth wife was a fifty-eight-year-old Apache woman named Sousche. The marriage didn't last long—less than two years. Geronimo only said of the union, "We could not live happily and separated. She went home to her people—that is an Apache divorce."[7] Amazingly, after he split up with Sousche he married again for the ninth and last time in 1907—at the age of eighty-four! This final wife was named Azul.

Always spiritual, in his final years he questioned his faith, and especially why Ussen had put him on this earth and what Ussen intended for his people. Geronimo even converted to Christianity for a time. He got baptized and joined the Dutch Reformed Church, which had been tasked by President Grant way back in the early 1870s to educate, "civilize," and Christianize the Apache. He taught Sunday school until the church kicked him out for "incessant gambling,"[8] which was prohibited. But always he returned to his traditional beliefs, always he returned to Ussen. Geronimo felt he was being watched over: "I have always prayed, and I believe that the Almighty has always protected me."[9] Still, he feared for his people, and in his darkest thoughts he envisioned their passing from this earth, forgotten: "The sun rises and shines for a while and then it goes down, sinking out of sight and it is lost. So it will be with the Indians."[10]

Despite these doubts, Geronimo's belief in his own Power never faltered. It even grew. Once an artist named Burbank, commissioned by the Field Museum of Chicago, came to Fort Sill to paint a portrait of the fearsome warrior Geronimo. As he sat for the portrait, Geronimo flatly told the artist that no one could kill him. To prove his point, he stripped off his shirt. Burbank was stunned by the number of bullet wounds in Geronimo's body. The old warrior-shaman put small stones in some of them, pretending they were bullets hitting him. He made loud gunshot sounds, and then he dropped the stones to the ground as if they'd bounced off. Burbank was skeptical. He argued that the shots had proba- bly all been fired at such great range that the bullets had failed to pene-

LESSON: *Use intimidation to your advantage, especially if you are bulletproof.*

trate him—if any of the shooters had been closer they would have killed him. Geronimo just looked at him and shouted, "No, no. Bullets cannot kill me!"[11]

But Geronimo wasn't immortal. By late 1908 he'd become frail and forgetful. On a freezing February day in 1909, he rode his horse into Lawton to sell some of his bows and arrows. He talked a friend into buying him some whiskey, though it was illegal. He had a good night, then mounted up and rode off into the darkness. Almost home, he fell off his horse into a creek bottom. He lay there, half submerged, until morning, when locals found his horse standing near him, still saddled. They pulled Geronimo from the creek and brought him home. He lapsed in and out of delirium for three days. While conscious, he whis- pered his dreams and regrets to Daklugie. He asked for them to tie his horse to a certain tree and hang his belongings from the tree; in three days he'd come get them. He died of pneumonia on February 17, 1908. He was eighty-five.[12]

Geronimo, Goyahkla ("One Who Yawns"), was buried by his peo- ple in the Apache cemetery at Fort Sill, next to Cache Creek. Naiche spoke at the funeral, praising the shaman-warrior's skill as a war leader. He told stories of the warpath and of his loyalty to his people. His widow Azul, for whatever reason, did not honor Geronimo's dying request about the horse, and she buried his belongings with

YALE'S SKULL AND BONES . . .
AND GERONIMO'S SKULL AND BONES

Rumors first arose in the 1980s that Yale University's famous and famously secretive Skull and Bones society had Geronimo's skull, other bones, and relics they'd taken from his gravesite at Fort Sill, Oklahoma. A document surfaced, written by a literary critic named F. O. Matthiessen. He was a club member of the Class of 1923. The document discussed a "mad expedition" in 1918 to Fort Sill, and a logbook of that year revealed that four men, including Prescott Bush (father of George Herbert Walker Bush and grandfather of George W. Bush), robbed Geronimo's grave. The logbook declared it the society's "most spectacular" heist.

Then in 2006, the *Yale Alumni Magazine* printed a newly discovered letter from one Skull and Bones member ("Bonesmen," as they call themselves) to another that referenced the "skull of the worthy Geronimo the Terrible, exhumed from its tomb at Fort Sill."

In February of 2009, Harlyn Geronimo, Geronimo's great-grandson,* filed a lawsuit in federal district court in Washington, D.C., to "free Geronimo, his remains, funerary objects and spirit, from one hundred years of imprisonment at Ft. Sill, Oklahoma, the Yale University campus at New Haven, Connecticut, and wherever else they may be found." Yale University was only one of the defendants; the first-named defendants were President Barack Obama and the secretaries of defense and the army.

Harlyn Geronimo's desire is the same as Geronimo's. Harlyn made this statement at a press conference when he filed the lawsuit: "If remains are not properly buried, in our tradition, the spirit is just wandering, wandering, until a proper burial has been performed." Harlyn's goal is to gather all of Geronimo's remains and perform a proper burial at the place of his birth, at the headwaters of the Gila River in New Mexico.

The Skull and Bones society is, as always, secretive. It neither confirms nor denies possession of Geronimo. In 2010 a federal judge dismissed Harlyn's lawsuit on technicalities. When a former U.S. attorney general was asked if he thought the Bonesmen had Geronimo's skull and bones, he replied: "We don't know. There's been enough commentary about it over enough time that you can't ignore it."

Sources: Wortman, "The Skull—and the Bones"; Bass, "Apaches Sue to Recover Geronimo's Skull"; Reitz, "Geronimo's Descendants Sue Yale's Skull and Bones over Remains."
* Lariat Geronimo, a great-grandson of Geronimo from Mescalero, NM, disputes Harlyn's ties to Geronimo. It's complicated.

him. Geronimo's grave is marked by a large pyramid of round rocks. A carved stone eagle perches on top, its wings outstretched, guarding over him.[13]

Geronimo was complex, and imperfect as the rest of us. It's true that he killed a good many people. Sometimes it was for revenge. "I have killed many," he said. "I do not know how many, for frequently I did not count them. Some of them were not worth counting."[14] That's vengeful, sure, but vengeance was an Apache trait, and blood grudges die hard. Sometimes he killed because he had to in order to survive. His enemies, after all, were trying to exterminate him and his people. There was a religious aspect too. Geronimo believed that his god Ussen had created the Chiricahua lands, and Geronimo was certainly spiritual enough to fight to the end in defense of those god-given lands. We can't lose sight of the responsibility he felt as a leader. There were large armies chasing the Chiricahua and trying to kill every last one of them. The truth is that Geronimo had a fighting spirit and the courage to hold out longer than all the rest. He was able to hold out longer than the rest because of his courage, his spiritual Power, and his supreme knowledge of and intimacy with his landscape.

Geronimo was extraordinary and unique, an unparalleled leader. He was better conditioned, better trained, wiser and tougher and braver than his adversaries. He could run farther—even in his late sixties—than anyone will ever know. He was a medicine man, a shaman skilled in cutting bullets, arrowheads, and knife points from his fellow warriors. He was a patriot,

LESSON: *If you lead and act with honor and nobility, you should not fear the opinions of others.*

and he tried to do what was right by his people. Those who fought and raided with him saw and understood his greatness and his tenacity. Said Daklugie, "There was only one leader who did not give up and that was Geronimo."[15]

Despite Geronimo's intense patriotism, not all Apache today revere him as a hero. Some believe his defiance caused all of the Apache bands to be imprisoned, not only the ones who resisted. For this resistance he will always remain controversial. While some Apache bands (like the Mescalero) were allowed to return to their tribal homeland, the Chiricahua were exiled, banished from Arizona. In 1913 the federal government finally did free the Chiricahua, but the state of Arizona refused to let them return. The Chiricahua were forced to live on the Mescalero reservation in New Mexico. After twenty-seven years as prisoners of war they'd made it close to home, but never all the way home. They paid the ultimate price for the Chiricahua resistance—banishment, their worst form of punishment.[16]

Yet because he resisted, Geronimo has become a legend and an American icon. Against overwhelming odds he left his mark on American history, a lasting imprint on the American memory and consciousness. His life and his lessons we should never forget. In recalling his long life, he cataloged his many battle wounds and scars: "I was shot in the right leg above the knee, and still carry the bullet; shot through the left forearm; wounded in the right leg below the knee with a saber; wounded on the top of the head with the butt of a musket; shot just below the outer corner of the left eye; shot in the left side; shot in the back."[17]

But no bullet ever killed him.

Like the many battle scars he endured, he too left a scar on the American conscience, a scar that will always remind us what he stood for. As one observer put it, "No tougher, smarter, or more perfectly formed warrior ever fought."[18]

Geronimo never stopped fighting. In his final days, as he mused about his life, he reflected: "I am old now and shall never go on the warpath again, but if I were young, and followed the warpath, it would lead into Old Mexico."[19]

In his final hours, Geronimo was haunted by that moment when he had given up to General Crook. On his deathbed he drew his nephew Daklugie close to him.

"I should never have surrendered," he whispered. "I should have fought until I was the last man alive."[20]

In many ways, he did. In many ways, he was.

| Commentary |

Become a Legend. *Not through talk, through deeds. Geronimo became a legend through actions—through a lifetime of unwavering belief in his convictions and a steadfast commitment to live in pursuit of and as an example of those convictions.*

Acquire Battle Scars. *The eight wounds and scars Geronimo references are only those he received in fights with the Mexicans. He doesn't even mention all those received in his skirmishes with settlers, miners, and other Indian tribes.*

Live Your Dreams—or Try To. *Geronimo devoted his life to living out the dream of freedom. He gave it his best shot. It was a worthy aspiration, one he was willing to kill for and to die for.*

Never Give Up. *If you do, it will haunt you to your grave, as it did Geronimo.*

ACKNOWLEDGMENTS

From Mike Leach:

For me, this book came together through a series of strange coincidences. I am not a big "it was meant to be" guy, but maybe this book was meant to be.

I was living in Key West, Florida, and was as busy as could be. I was on Sirius/XM radio three hours a day, five days a week. Then in my spare time I was flying all over the country doing book signings for *Swing Your Sword*, which I wrote with Bruce Feldman.

It was some time in October 2011 that Scott Waxman called me. Bruce and I self-published *Swing Your Sword*, but Scott helped us bring all the pieces together and print it through his publishing company Diversion. Scott is a literary agent, and he told me that he represented a writer, Buddy Levy, who was interested in writing a book with me. He said that Buddy was one of the historians on the History TV show *Decoded*, and had written *American Legend: The Real-Life Adventures of David Crockett* and *Conquistador*. Scott said that like me, Buddy was very interested in Geronimo. He said that we would hit it off and that we ought to write a book together on this subject. I've had an interest in Geronimo since I was in second grade. I'd read about him extensively and had pictures of him hanging in my office for years. I'd even referred to him in press conferences for football games. Geronimo is the ultimate in resourceful competitors. When I was a child and at my request my mom, Sandra Leach, read me books about Geronimo. My interest in him steadily blossomed from there.

Soon I got a call from Buddy Levy. We did hit it off, but I was so busy with *Swing Your Sword* that I never realistically thought that we would ever meet. All I knew is that I had a good conversation with a guy who said he was going to send me his Davy Crockett book, *American Legend,* and maybe we would talk some time in the future. Scott Waxman said that Buddy was a college professor somewhere in the Northwest.

I received Buddy's book on Davy Crockett, *American Legend,* and began reading it. I thought it was excellent. Instead of a bunch of boring facts, dates, and events, it was a very human, colorful story written from the perspective of a regular guy. It talked about stories and anecdotes, and as you finished each chapter, you felt like you knew Davy Crockett better and better.

Several months later, my life became even busier. In December, jobs began opening up in Division I college football. I got several calls. Bill Moos, the athletic director from Washington State University, came down to Key West to interview me. I rode my bike to his hotel for the interview. Things really happened fast after that. He hired me. I uprooted my whole family and we temporarily moved into the Holiday Inn Express in Pullman, Washington.

I can't describe how incredibly hectic a time this was. I was moving my family, hiring a staff, putting together an entire recruiting class in a month, learning my way around Washington State, doing PR events, et cetera.

I had been on the job for about a week when our secretary said that there was a professor in the office who wanted to see me. It was Buddy Levy. I was stunned. It turns out Buddy is a professor at Washington State! So in the midst of everything else that I had going on, he says, "Let's write this book on Geronimo."

We had to finesse our schedules to get it done. We met for hours in the Café Moro coffee shop, spent even more hours on the phone, emailed incessantly, and spent most of the spring and summer of 2012 writing this book.

In the end, we wanted to not just help people know who Geronimo was, but how he accomplished the incredible feats that he did. Our process was, that as we had questions about Geronimo and how and why he did what he did, we tried to answer them. I hope for the most part we did that.

First, I want to thank Buddy Levy. This book would not have been possible without him. He is an incredible researcher and writer. As I would dream up obscure questions, somehow he would find the answers. Our dialogue was incredible and I think we both expanded each other's thinking.

My wife, Sharon, has believed in me unconditionally for thirty-one years. When I think about doubting or going soft, she never lets me flinch. She has ushered me through some impossible adversities. Also, I'm thankful for my four children, all overachievers—Janeen, Kim, Cody, and Kiersten. I love and value them more than they can ever know.

My parents, Frank and Sandra Leach, taught me that anything is possible, and I believed them. Thanks to my mom, who read books to me about Geronimo when I was eight years old and patiently explained them to me.

Sam Gwynne graciously wrote the foreword. He is a great writer and can create visuals of his characters like none other. I learn about writing every time I read his work.

Bruce Feldman, CBS Sports reporter and my coauthor for *Swing Your Sword*, taught me how to put a book together, and we learned a lot along the way. Bruce is a true and loyal friend who has the courage to do what is right when it isn't easy. People like him make us all better individuals.

I'd like to thank Ferhat Guven, who cowrote *Sports for Dorks: College Football* with me. He's an expert on nearly everything and a great resource every time I have a question on almost any subject.

Bestselling author Michael Lewis has been a brilliant resource and taught me the value of constantly remaining curious.

I also want to thank my current employers, Dr. Elson Floyd, president of Washington State University, and our athletic director, Bill

Moos. These are easily two of the most visionary men in college athletics. I am proud to have the opportunity to work for them.

I want to thank the coaches and players that I have had the honor to work with. They are all warriors in their own way.

My agent at IMG, Gary O'Hagan, as well as Scott Waxman were instrumental in putting two of my books together. They were key in encouraging me to write books in the first place.

Finally, I want to thank Geronimo for providing the inspiration for this book. I hope that somewhere in his happy hunting ground, Geronimo is smiling.

From Buddy Levy:

Books are creative collaborations and come to life only as a result of many people sharing a common goal. First off, I owe great thanks to Mike Leach for the time, effort, and care he put into the writing of *Geronimo*. Mike's energies are unbounded, and he's taught me a lot about what achievement really is. I'll always remember those long conversations at Café Moro in Pullman. The discussions were so wide-ranging and fascinating, illustrating to me the incredible breadth of Mike Leach's knowledge and interests.

As always, I'd also like to express deep gratitude to my literary agent, Scott Waxman, of Waxman Leavell Agency. Scott has been a champion and an ally of mine since 2003, and he was instrumental in making *Geronimo* happen. I am continually amazed by Scott's vision of what a book might be, and by his tireless contributions from a book project's first origins to its final form.

We are appreciative that Jeremie Ruby-Strauss, our editor at Gallery Books/Simon & Schuster, had the vision and confidence to take on the project. He's a great editor and has been terrific to work with, as have all the gang at Simon & Schuster.

A special shout-out to the writer and journalist Sharon Magee, who generously gave her time to read our *Geronimo* manuscript in its entirety and offer comments. Sharon is a fine scholar, writer, and journalist, and her article on Geronimo's wives, plus her own book, *Geronimo! Stories of an American Legend*, were inspirational and extremely helpful. I look forward to many years of continued exchange about various aspects of the American Southwest, from the demise of the buffalo to marital practices of the Chiricahua Apache!

Sam Gwynne, whose profound and monumental book *Empire of the Summer Moon* is one of the best books ever written on American Indian history, offered insight and fielded questions during the research process and also wrote a fine foreword to our book, and I'm grateful for his contributions.

As always, the Free Range Writers—Kim Barnes, Collin Hughes, Lisa Norris, and Jane Varley—provided support both literary and spiritual. Love ya'll. And also as always, John Larkin and Melissa Rockwood—the Larkwoods—have been there every step and sentence of the way; they are a support team, and dear friends, who are unrivaled.

Thanks to the Washington State University Department of English, and especially Todd Butler, for always supporting my research and creative endeavors over the years.

And finally, as Geronimo knew so well—nothing in this world has much meaning or worth without family. Thanks to every member of mine, but especially to my dear wife, Camie, and my remarkable children, Logan and Hunter, who nurture me every day and help me fulfill my wildest dreams.

A NOTE ON THE TEXT AND SOURCES

THE AUTHORS HAVE BEEN AIDED AND GUIDED by the many
Chiricahua Apache and Geronimo scholars who have so ably and
comprehensively chronicled his amazing life and times. We are deeply
indebted to a number of key historians and writers. The source material for *Geronimo: Leadership Lessons of an American Warrior* is rich and
varied. For those readers wishing to further explore particular areas of
interest, please see the works discussed below and the extensive bibliog-
raphy that follows the notes in this book; many of these works have been
cited, quoted directly, or used as references in our book.

All serious Geronimo research and inquiry must begin with his own
book, *Geronimo, His Own Story: The Autobiography of a Great Patriot
Warrior*, as told to S. M. Barrett. Through this fascinating (and at times
heartbreaking) book, readers get real insight into the mind, character,
personality, and worldview of the great warrior-shaman. Sure, it con-
tains some errors—and sometimes Geronimo's memory is faulty—but
as a whole the book is an indispensable work for understanding many
aspects of Geronimo's era, and to hear his own voice resonate through
history.

The go-to biography for all Geronimo scholars and enthusiasts is
Angie Debo's *Geronimo: The Man, His Time, His Place*. Born in 1890,
Angie Debo moved to Oklahoma Territory in a covered wagon when
she was nine years old, so she knows what she's talking about. Debo
wrote more than a dozen books and hundreds of articles on American

Indian history and life, and her biography of Geronimo remains, to this day, the gold standard. Like Geronimo, Debo was tenacious, vibrant, and highly productive even as her years advanced. Her Geronimo biography came out in 1976, when she was eighty-six years old.

It would be nearly impossible to tap into the complex and fascinating social, spiritual, and cultural life of the Chiricahua Apache were it not for American anthropologist Morris Opler's classic work *An Apache Life-Way*, which was published in 1941. Opler spent years in the field compiling notes from scores of Chiricahua Apache informants to write his monumental (and definitive) ethnographic study, covering every conceivable aspect of Chiricahua Apache life. We are greatly indebted to his work.

The works of scholar Edwin R. Sweeney have been invaluable resources. Three of his books in the Civilization of the American Indian Series (University of Oklahoma Press) are comprehensive and have been most helpful. They are *Cochise: Chiricahua Apache Chief* (1991); *Mangas Coloradas: Chief of the Chiricahua Apaches* (1998); and *From Cochise to Geronimo: The Chiricahua Apaches, 1874–1886* (2010). Sweeney's work provides unrivaled context, detail, and understanding of the lives and worlds of Mangas Coloradas, Cochise, and Geronimo and their places in the American Southwest.

The writer and historian Robert M. Utley has for decades been a prolific contributor on many aspects of the Western frontier. We were fortunate that his terrific book *Geronimo* came out in late 2012. Although we disagree at times with Utley's assessments about Geronimo's character, Utley's scholarship and research are commendable and enviable and have aided our understanding of the chronology and events of Geronimo's life.

The Apache side of the story has been supported in no small part by the works of historian Eve Ball, who interviewed elderly survivors of the Apache Wars and produced the remarkable books *In The Days of Victorio: Recollections of a Warm Springs Apache* and *Indeh: An Apache Odyssey*.

In our minds the best and most readable popular narrative history of Geronimo and the Apache Wars is the phenomenal *Once They Moved Like the Wind* by David Roberts. Roberts approaches the subject matter with a novelist's sense of story and pacing—and it's one helluva read. It has been a dependable source.

Although the Geronimo story has been told cinematically in versions too many to list—for those wishing to watch the real deal look no further than the PBS documentary *We Shall Remain: The American Experience—Geronimo*. Narrated by Benjamin Bratt, featuring interviews with Chiricahua Apache descendants, scholars, and tribal elders, this is a moving and riveting documentary that is must-see viewing. The perspectives offered in this film have been influential in our interpretation of the Geronimo story.

NOTES

Sources for Cast of Characters

Sharon S. Magee, *Geronimo! Stories of an American Legend* (Arizona, 2002).
http://www.greatdreams.com/apache/apache-warriors.htm.
Dan L. Thrapp, *Encyclopedia of Frontier Biography* (Lincoln and Spokane, 1994).

Introduction

1. Greenville Goodwin, *Western Apache Raiding and Warfare* (Tucson, 1971), 16. On the name "the enemy," see Ross Santee, *Apache Land* (Lincoln, 1971), 31. David Roberts, *Once They Moved Like the Wind* (New York, 1993), 145.
2. http://www.myspace.com/greywolflimited.
3. Mike thinks they came from elsewhere. He likes the Thor Heyerdahl theory, so it's worth at least considering other options. Maybe they came from the south rather than the north. Mike likes that there are Indian people in Asia. He thinks the land bridge theory is absurd at every level. Why leave a warm climate to go freeze your asses off? Who knows, it might have been the other way around.
4. Vine Deloria Jr. *Red Earth, White Lies: Native Americans and the Myth of Scientific Fact* (Golden, 1997), 33–34.
5. Herbert E. Bolton, *Coronado, Knight of Pueblos and Plains* (Albuquerque, 1949), 245–47. Also see Edwin R. Sweeney, *From Cochise to Geronimo: The Chiricahua Apaches, 1874–1886* (Norman, 2010), 17.
6. Bolton, *Coronado*, 246.

Chapter One

1. Angie Debo, *Geronimo: The Man, His Time, His Place* (Norman, 1976), 13.
2. Barrett, S. M., *Geronimo, His Own Story* (New York, 1996), 59.
3. Ibid. On tepee types, see Opler, *An Apache Life-Way,* 385.
4. Morris Opler, *An Apache Life-Way* (Chicago, 1941), 45–46, 66–74.
5. Opler, *Apache Life-Way,* 48; Jason Betzinez, *I Fought with Geronimo* (Lincoln, 1959), 30.
6. John C. Cremony, *Life among the Apaches, 1850–1868* (New Mexico, 1868), 27–28.
7. Quoted in Opler, *Apache Life-Way,* 67.
8. Opler, *Apache Life-Way,* 72; Debo, *Geronimo,* 19.
9. Opler, *Apache Life-Way,* 73.
10. Ibid.
11. Roberts, *Once They Moved,* 149; Opler, *Apache Life-Way,* 340–41 (on poison).
12. Eve Ball, *Indeh: An Apache Odyssey* (Provo, 1980), 15; Opler, *Apache Life-Way,* 341.
13. Opler, *Apache Life-Way,* 341.
14. Roberts, *Once They Moved,* 149; Opler, *Apache Life-Way,* 340–42; Ralph Ogle, *Federal Control of the Western Apaches* (Albuquerque, 1970), 20–22.
15. Barrett, *His Own Story,* 71.
16. H. Henrietta Stockel, *Chiricahua Apache Women and Children: Safe-keepers of the Heritage* (College Station, TX, 2000), 10–12. Also see Thomas Mails, *The People Called Apache* (New Jersey, 1974), 87–88.
17. Barrett, *His Own Story,* 71.
18. Goodwin, *Western Apache Raiding,* 17.
19. Goodwin, *Western Apache Raiding,* 18; Opler, *Apache Life-Way,* 336.
20. Robert M. Utley, *Geronimo* (New Haven, 2012), 27. There is some discrepancy with this date. Conflicting sources include Geronimo (he's wrong, probably) and Mexican sources. Authors side with scholars Sweeney and Utley on this one, via Mexican source Carrasco.
21. Barrett, *His Own Story,* 77–78.

22. Ibid.

23. Ibid.

24. Debo, *Geronimo*, 38; Mary A. Stout, *Geronimo: A Biography* (Santa Barbara, 2009), 18. For more on Power, see Ball, *Indeh*, 9 and 60–65. Comments on Apache Power also in *The American Experience: We Shall Remain—Geronimo*.

25. Debo, *Geronimo*, 26; Opler, *Apache Life-Way*, 235–37; Jason Betzinez, *I Fought with Geronimo*, 8n. Also Ball, *Indeh*, 14.

Chapter Two

1. Opler, *Apache Life-Way*, 468–69; Debo, *Geronimo*, 38.

2. Barrett, *His Own Story*, 79; Debo, *Geronimo*, 38.

3. Roberts, *Once They Moved*, 92.

4. Dan L. Thrapp, *Juh: An Incredible Indian* (El Paso, 1973), 1.

5. Stout, *Geronimo*, 19–20.

6. Opler, *Apache Life-Way*, 344; Roberts, *Once They Moved*, 148–49.

7. Opler, *Apache Life-Way*, 260–61.

8. Barrett, *His Own Story*, 80; Roberts, *Once They Moved*, 148.

9. Ibid., 82.

10. Ibid.

11. Ibid., 83. The date of this battle is unclear, and there is some controversy about the events. Geronimo's memory might be faulty here. See Lance R. Blythe, *Chiricahua and Janos: Communities of Violence in the Southwest Borderlands, 1680–1880* (Lincoln, 2012). Also Utley, *Geronimo*, 24–27, and Sweeney, *Cochise to Geronimo*, 246.

12. Debo, *Geronimo*, 39; Woodworth Clum, *Apache Agent: The Story of John P. Clum* (Lincoln, 1936), 28–29; Roberts, *Once They Moved*, 111–13.

13. Debo, *Geronimo*, 63.

14. Barrett, *His Own Story*, 85; Debo, *Geronimo*, 48.

15. Barrett, *His Own Story*, 85.

16. Ibid. Also Peter Aleshire, *The Fox and the Whirlwind* (New York, 2000), 62–63.

17. Barrett, *His Own Story*, 86–87; Debo, *Geronimo*, 49; Roberts, *Once They Moved*, 117.

18. Barrett, *His Own Story*, 88.

19. Britton Davis, *The Truth about Geronimo* (Lincoln, 1929), 80. The bent finger must have been temporary, because it is not evident in pictures of Geronimo in later years. Also in Roberts, *Once They Moved*, 118–21; Barrett, *His Own Story*, 95–97.

20. Roberts, *Once They Moved*, 120–21.

21. John G. Bourke, *An Apache Campaign in the Sierra Madre* (New York, 1958), 102.

22. Britton Davis, quoted in Roberts, *Once They Moved*, 121 and 242.

Chapter Three

1. Barrett, *His Own Story*, 113.

2. Terry Mort, *The Wrath of Cochise* (New York, 2013), 10–11; Debo, *Geronimo*, 59–65.

3. Utley, *Geronimo*, 39. Also Debo, *Geronimo*, 62–63; Roberts, *Once They Moved*, 21–24.

4. Quoted in Roberts, *Once They Moved*, 23. Also see Utley, *Geronimo*, 38–43.

5. Utley, *Geronimo*, 40.

6. Barrett, *His Own Story*, 117. The entire episode is recorded in various places. Good ones include Mort, *Wrath of Cochise*, 3–17; Utley, *Geronimo*, 36–44; Roberts, *Once They Moved*, 23–25; and Debo, *Geronimo*, 62–63.

7. Quoted in Roberts, *Once They Moved*, 36; Ball, *Indeh*, 10, 15.

8. Ibid., 39.

9. Ibid., 40.

10. Edwin R. Sweeney, *Mangas Coloradas* (Norman, 1998), 453–60; Roberts, *Once They Moved*, 39–42; Debo, *Geronimo*, 69; Utley, *Geronimo*, 52–54; Ball, *Indeh*, 22–25.

11. Barrett, *His Own Story*, 118; Roberts, *Once They Moved*, 40–42; Utley, *Geronimo*, 51–53.

Chapter Four

1. Sweeney, *Mangas Coloradas*, 462; Ball, *Indeh*, 20.
2. Ibid.
3. Barrett, *His Own Story*, 163.
4. Utley, *Geronimo*, 55; Barrett, *His Own Story*, 119.
5. Stout, *Geronimo*, 39; Roberts, *Once They Moved*, 72–73.
6. Roberts, *Once They Moved*, 74; Stout, *Geronimo*, 39.
7. Sweeney, *Cochise to Geronimo*, 39.
8. Aleshire, *Fox and the Whirlwind*, 111; Edwin R. Sweeney, *Cochise: Chiricahua Apache Chief* (Norman, 1991), 318.
9. Quoted in Roberts, *Once They Moved*, 80. Also in John G. Bourke, *On the Border with Crook* (New Mexico, 1892), 112.
10. Ball, *Indeh*, 125–26. Crook gets called, alternately, "the Gray Wolf" and "the Gray Fox."
11. Sweeney, *Cochise to Geronimo*, 473.
12. Dan L. Thrapp, *Al Sieber: Chief of Scouts* (Norman, 1964), iii–v.
13. Debo, *Geronimo*, 88.
14. Sweeney, *Cochise*, 395–97; Roberts, *Once They Moved*, 141; Alexander B. Adams, *Geronimo: A Biography* (New York, 1971), 195–96; Ball, *Indeh*, 22–25.
15. Opler, *Apache Life-Way*, 474.
16. Sweeney, *Cochise*, 397; Betzinez, *I Fought with Geronimo*, 42.
17. Clum, *Apache Agent*, 136.
18. Odie Faulk, *The Geronimo Campaign* (New York, 1969), 17.
19. Clum, *Apache Agent*, 180.
20. Ibid.
21. Roberts, *Once They Moved*, 157; Ball, *Indeh*, 33.
22. Ball, *Indeh*, 37; Escape in Debo, *Geronimo*, 88; *The American Experience: We Shall Remain—Geronimo*.
23. Ibid.
24. Clum, *Apache Agent*, 193–94; Roberts, *Once They Moved*, 158.
25. Clum, *Apache Agent*, 185.

26. Eve Ball, *In the Days of Victorio: Recollections of a Warm Springs Apache* (Tucson, 1970), 51.

27. Clum, *Apache Agent*, 186.

28. Ibid., 194.

29. Ibid., 215; Roberts, *Once They Moved*, 162–65; http://www.ojospa.com.

30. Barrett, *His Own Story*, 126.

31. Clum, *Apache Agent*, 216–18. Also quoted in Roberts, *Once They Moved*, 164.

32. Clum, *Apache Agent*, 218.

33. *The American Experience: We Shall Remain—Geronimo*. Debo, *Geronimo*, 103–7; Stout, *Geronimo*, 47–49; Ball, *Indeh*, 38–40.

34. Barrett, *His Own Story*, 129.

Chapter Five

1. Quoted in Debo, *Geronimo*, 111; Ball, *Indeh*, 38–40.

2. Quoted in Sweeney, *Cochise to Geronimo*, 91.

3. Quoted in Roberts, *Once They Moved*, 171 (said by Woodworth Clum).

4. From the film *The American Experience, We Shall Remain—Geronimo*.

5. Britton Davis, *The Truth about Geronimo*, 31.

6. Quoted in Roberts, *Once They Moved*, 178. Also in Aleshire, *Fox and the Whirlwind*, 104–5. Also see Lozen in Henrietta Stockel, *Women of the Apache Nation* (Reno, 1991), 16, 29–30; Ball, *In the Days of Victorio*, 14–15.

7. Ball, *In the Days of Victorio*, 15; Roberts, *Once They Moved*, 178.

8. Ibid.

9. Ibid., 115–19. See Stockel, *Chiricahua Apache Women*, 65–76.

10. Dan L. Thrapp, *The Conquest of Apacheria* (Norman, 1967), 217; Aleshire, *Fox and the Whirlwind*, 162–63; Stout, *Geronimo*, 55–56, Sweeney, *Cochise to Geronimo*, 172.

11. For a good discussion of ghost dances see Louis S. Warren, *Buffalo Bill's America: William Cody and the Wild West Show* (New York, 2005), 358–89.

12. Stout, *Geronimo*, 56–58; Aleshire, *Fox and the Whirlwind*, 164–67; Roberts, *Once They Moved*, 198–200; Debo, *Geronimo*, 127–30.

Chapter Six

1. Barrett, *His Own Story*, 127–28.
2. Debo, *Geronimo*, 131.
3. Quoted in Utley, *Geronimo*, 110.
4. Barrett, *His Own Story*, 128.
5. Sweeney, *Cochise to Geronimo*, 182–85.
6. Ibid., 186. Also see Charles Collins, *The Great Escape: The Apache Outbreak of 1881* (Tucson, 1994), chapters 3–7.
7. Sweeney, *Cochise to Geronimo*, 185–86; Aleshire, *Fox and the Whirlwind*, 168–70.
8. Betzinez, *I Fought with Geronimo*, 58.
9. Sweeney, *Cochise to Geronimo*, 186–87; Collins, *Great Escape*, 62–63; Debo, *Geronimo*, 132.
10. Collins, *Great Escape*, 92; Sweeney, *Cochise to Geronimo*, 188–89.
11. Collins, *Great Escape*, 92–95, 101.
12. Quoted in Roberts, *Once They Moved*, 203. Nelson Miles quoted in Paul I. Wellman, *Death in the Desert* (Lincoln, 1987), 233.
13. Clum, *Apache Agent*, 265.
14. Ibid., 267; Collins, *Great Escape*, 138.
15. Ball, *In the Days of Victorio*, 22.
16. Ball, *Indeh*, 2.
17. Roberts, *Once They Moved*, 204–5; Utley, *Geronimo*, 112–13.
18. Barrett, *His Own Story*, 13; *The American Experience: We Shall Remain—Geronimo*; PBS—*The West: "Chief Joseph."* Also Aleshire, *Fox and the Whirlwind*, 217–21.

Chapter Seven

1. Ball, *In the Days of Victorio*, 128.
2. Ibid.
3. Ibid., 126.
4. *The American Experience: We Shall Remain—Geronimo*.
5. Ball, *Indeh*, 86.

6. Quoted in Debo, *Geronimo*, 72.

7. Ball, *Indeh*, 87.

8. Ball, *In the Days of Victorio*, 137–38.

9. There is some scholarly and Apache disagreement about whether or not Juh participated. But given the masterful conduct of the expedition, consistent with Juh's military tactics, there is enough to support his participation. See Debo, *Geronimo*, 138–39 and 139n.

10. Bud Shapard, *Chief Loco: Apache Peacemaker* (Norman, 2010), 148.

11. Sweeney, *Cochise to Geronimo*, 207; Debo, *Geronimo*, 138.

12. Shapard, *Chief Loco*, 152; Debo, *Geronimo*, 142; Sweeney, *Cochise to Geronimo*, 210.

13. Betzinez, *I Fought with Geronimo*, 56.

14. Ibid.

15. Ibid.

16. Shapard, *Chief Loco*, 155; Sweeney, *Cochise to Geronimo*, 211; Debo, *Geronimo*, 143; Aleshire, *Fox and the Whirlwind*, 176–77.

17. Shapard, *Chief Loco*, 155.

18. Betzinez, *I Fought with Geronimo*, 58.

19. Ibid.

20. Opler, *Apache Life-Way*, 395–96; Ball, *Indeh*, 116.

21. Betzinez, *I Fought with Geronimo*, 60.

22. Ibid., 60–61. Also see Opler, *Apache Life-Way*, 82–139, for a detailed description of the maturation process and rituals.

23. Betzinez, *I Fought with Geronimo*, 63.

24. Utley, *Geronimo*, 117; Roberts, *Once They Moved*, 211; Betzinez, *I Fought with Geronimo*, 63; Debo, *Geronimo*, 145.

25. Debo, *Geronimo*, 145; Utley, *Geronimo*, 117; Betzinez, *I Fought with Geronimo*, 65–66.

26. Utley, *Geronimo*, 118; Sweeney, *Cochise to Geronimo*, 216–18; Debo, *Geronimo*, 145–46; Shapard, *Chief Loco*, 162-64.

27. Opler, *Apache Life-Way*, 216; Stout, *Geronimo*, 66–67.

28. Sweeney, *Cochise to Geronimo*, 218; Utley, *Geronimo*, 118; Betzinez, *I Fought with Geronimo*, 66; Debo, *Geronimo*, 145–46; Shapard, *Chief*

Loco, 162–63; Sharon Magee, *Geronimo! Stories of an American Legend* (Phoenix, 2002), 54–65.

Chapter Eight

1. Dan L. Thrapp, *General Crook and the Sierra Madre Adventure* (Norman, 1972), 76–85; Thrapp, *Conquest of Apacheria*, 235–46; Shapard, *Chief Loco*, 163.

2. Roberts, *Once They Moved*, 210–11; Thrapp, *Conquest of Apacheria*, 237–38.

3. Quoted in Thrapp, *Conquest of Apacheria*, 237.

4. Sweeney, *Cochise to Geronimo*, 218–20; Betzinez, *I Fought with Geronimo*, 68; Shapard, *Chief Loco*, 166–67; Utley, *Geronimo*, 118; Debo, *Geronimo*, 147. There is disagreement about the man with the women at the mescal pit. Some sources (Sweeney) say he was Talbot Gooday, grandson of Mangas Coloradas. Others suggest that a man killed in the first volley was the son of Loco.

5. Betzinez, *I Fought with Geronimo*, 68–69; Utley, *Geronimo*, 119; Sweeney, *Cochise to Geronimo*, 220–21; Shapard, *Chief Loco*, 169–72.

6. The number of Apache dead varies between eight and fifteen, depending on the source. Sweeney, *Cochise to Geronimo*, 222; Utley, *Geronimo*, 119; Shapard, *Chief Loco*, 172; Debo, *Geronimo*, 149.

7. Betzinez, *I Fought with Geronimo*, 70.

8. Ibid., 69–70; Sweeney, *Cochise to Geronimo*, 222; Shapard, *Chief Loco*, 176; Utley, *Geronimo*, 119; Roberts, *Once They Moved*, 213.

9. Betzinez, *I Fought with Geronimo*, 70–71; Utley, *Geronimo*, 119.

10. Ibid., 75n. Also Sweeney, *Cochise to Geronimo*, 223. Sweeney says two hundred Mexican soldiers were involved in the ambush.

11. Betzinez, *I Fought with Geronimo*, 72.

12. Ball, *In the Days of Victorio*, 143. Sweeney argues that Lozen was not there—though he's outnumbered by other sources. See *Cochise to Geronimo*, 225 and 615, n75, in which he says that Lozen was at the stronghold with Juh at this time.

13. Quoted in Sweeney, *Cochise to Geronimo*, 225.

14. Betzinez, *I Fought with Geronimo*, 73; Roberts, *Once They Moved*, 212; Ball, *In the Days of Victorio*, 143; Shapard, *Chief Loco*, 179.

15. For a thorough assessment of Geronimo's participation at Alisos Creek, see Sweeney, *Cochise to Geronimo*, 227–28. Also in Debo, *Geronimo*, 150–55.

16. Betzinez, *I Fought with Geronimo*, 74–75.

17. Utley, *Geronimo*, 121; Sweeney, *Cochise to Geronimo*, 228.

18. Quoted in Roberts, *Once They Moved*, 213.

19. Utley, *Geronimo*, 121; Debo, *Geronimo*, 154–55; Betzinez, *I Fought with Geronimo*, 76.

20. Ball, *In the Days of Victorio*, 126.

Chapter Nine

1. Sweeney, *Cochise to Geronimo*, 283; Utley, *Geronimo*, 125.

2. John G. Bourke, "Distillation by Early American Indians," *American Anthropologist*, Vol. 7, No. 3 (July 1894), 297–99.

3. Barrett, *His Own Story*, 106.

4. Betzinez, *I Fought with Geronimo*, 78.

5. Sweeney, *Cochise to Geronimo*, 235.

6. Debo, *Geronimo*, 157; Sweeney, *Cochise to Geronimo*, 235.

7. Ibid., 159; Betzinez, *I Fought with Geronimo*, 81–92 (chapter 9). Roberts, *Once They Moved*, 214–16; Utley, *Geronimo*, 129–30.

8. Quoted in Sweeney, *Cochise to Geronimo*, 240; Betzinez, *I Fought with Geronimo*, 85.

9. Betzinez, *I Fought with Geronimo*, 90.

10. Ibid., 91.

11. Daklugie quoted in Ball, *Indeh*, 70.

12. Ibid., 72–73n; Roberts, *Once They Moved*, 214–15.

13. Juh's vision recounted by Aleshire, *Fox and the Whirlwind*, 233. Also Ball, *Indeh*, 76.

14. John G. Bourke, *On the Border with Crook* (New York, 1891), 452. Also

see Debo, *Geronimo*, 165–69; Utley, *Geronimo*, 133; Betzinez, *I Fought with Geronimo*, 99–101.

15.   Aleshire, *Fox and the Whirlwind*, 237.

Chapter Ten

1.   George Crook, edited by Martin F. Schmitt, *General George Crook: His Autobiography* (Norman, 1946), 187.

2.   Roberts, *Once They Moved*, 217; John Edward Weems, *Death Song: The Last of the Indian Wars* (New York, 1976), 211–13 and 218–19.

3.   Aleshire, *Fox and the Whirlwind*, 239; Roberts, *Once They Moved*, 217.

4.   Sweeney, *Cochise to Geronimo*, 294–95; Stout, *Geronimo*, 69; Thrapp, *Crook and the Sierra Madre*, 116; Debo, *Geronimo*, 167–68.

5.   Ball, *Indeh*, 51; Ball, *In the Days of Victorio*, 147.

6.   Betzinez, *I Fought with Geronimo*, 118.

7.   Bourke, *Apache Campaign*, 35; Utley, *Geronimo*, 136.

8.   Quoted in Thrapp, *Crook and the Sierra Madre*, 116–17. From LS346DA1883 Crook to Secretary of the Interior, Washington, D.C., March 26, 1883.

9.   Ben T. Traywick, *N'de, the People* (Tombstone, 2003).

10.   From Crook, Annual Report, U.S. Army Dept. of Arizona, Prescott, Arizona, 1883. Also quoted in Roberts, *Once They Moved*, 228.

11.   Davis, *Truth about Geronimo*, 31.

12.   Ibid., 32.

13.   Ibid., 58; Thrapp, *Conquest of Apacheria*, 272–73.

14.   Thrapp, *Al Sieber*, 276; Bourke, *On the Border with Crook*, 450–54.

15.   Thrapp, *Crook and the Sierra Madre*, vii. Also quoted in Roberts, *Once They Moved*, 227. Crook's force also in Aleshire, *Fox and the Whirlwind*, 245; Bourke, *Apache Campaign*, 56–57.

16.   Goodwin, *Western Apache Raiding*, 154.

17.   Bourke, *Apache Campaign*, 47, 64.

18.   Bourke, quoted in Aleshire, *Fox and the Whirlwind*, 247; Bourke, *Apache Campaign*, 76.

19. Crook, Annual Report, U.S. Army Dept. of Arizona.

20. Betzinez, *I Fought with Geronimo*, 113.

21. Ibid., 115.

22. Ibid.

23. Quoted in Thrapp, *Al Sieber*, 280. Also in Bourke, *Apache Campaign*, 103; Debo, *Geronimo*, 181–84.

24. Bourke, *Apache Campaign*, 111–12.

25. Sweeney, *Cochise to Geronimo*, 310–11; Debo, *Geronimo*, 188–89; Betzinez, *I Fought with Geronimo*, 121–22.

Chapter Eleven

1. Ball, *In the Days of Victorio*, 123; Geronimo's activities in Sweeney, *Cochise to Geronimo*, 329–30.

2. Roberts, *Once They Moved*, 205.

3. Juh's son Ace Daklugie related this information to Eve Ball during one of her interviews. In Sweeney, *Cochise to Geronimo*, 331.

4. Quoted in Sweeney, *Cochise to Geronimo*, 332. Juh's relatives insist he was not drunk.

5. Quoted in ibid., 335. Also in *Utley, Geronimo*, 145.

6. Quoted in Sweeney, *Cochise to Geronimo*, 336. See Utley, *Geronimo*, 298 n1 and n3 for list of sources. Most of the chiefs, as well as Geronimo, were interviewed on their return to San Carlos.

7. Quoted in Sweeney, *Cochise to Geronimo*, 336.

8. Sweeney, *Cochise to Geronimo*, 344.

9. Quoted in ibid., 347.

10. *Arizona Star*, June 17, 1883.

11. Quoted in Roberts, *Once They Moved*, 240.

12. Ibid.

13. Aleshire, *Fox and the Whirlwind*, 257.

14. Davis, *Truth about Geronimo*, 33.

15. Ibid., 145.

16. Ibid., 80.

17. Ibid., 82.

18. Ibid.
19. Ibid., 83.
20. Quoted in Roberts, *Once They Moved,* 242. Also in Sweeney, *Cochise to Geronimo,* 333–34. Also in an undated article in the *Deming Herald.* The description is from frontiersmen Wilson and Leroy, who said they made contact with Geronimo near Casas Grandes on a mission to locate Charley McComas.
21. Quoted in Sweeney, *Cochise to Geronimo,* 358.
22. Davis, *Truth about Geronimo,* 84–87. Also Aleshire, *Fox and the Whirlwind,* 260.
23. Davis, *Truth about Geronimo,* 87–88.
24. Ibid., 87.
25. Ibid., 90.
26. Quoted in Sweeney, *Cochise to Geronimo,* 357. Recounted in Davis, *Truth about Geronimo,* 91–100; Aleshire, *Fox and the Whirlwind,* 260–62; Roberts, *Once They Moved,* 244; Utley, 147–48; Debo, *Geronimo,* 198–201.
27. Barrett, *His Own Story,* 129.

Chapter Twelve

1. Quoted in Debo, *Geronimo,* 206.
2. Ibid., 207.
3. Ball, *In the Days of Victorio,* 156; Roberts, *Once They Moved,* 247.
4. Debo, *Geronimo,* 221–22.
5. Joseph C. Porter, *Paper Medicine Man: John Gregory Bourke and His American West* (Norman, 1986), 180.
6. Davis, *Truth about Geronimo,* 107; Sweeney, *Cochise to Geronimo,* 371; Utley, *Geronimo,* 153.
7. Ball, *In the Days of Victorio,* 168–74; Debo, *Geronimo,* 230. Also retold in Roberts, *Once They Moved,* 249.
8. Blythe, *Chiricahua and Janos,* 50–52, 173; Huera in Debo, *Geronimo,* 231.
9. Goodwin, *Western Apache Raiding,* 282–84.
10. Opler, *Apache Life-Way,* 363; also in Stout, *Geronimo,* 78.

11. Geronimo to Crook, Turkey Creek, May 8, 1884. Quoted in Porter, *Paper Medicine Man*, 165.

12. Ibid., 167.

13. Thrapp, *Conquest of Apacheria*, 303.

14. Davis, *Truth about Geronimo*, 128; Debo, *Geronimo*, 234–35.

15. Sweeney, *Cochise to Geronimo*, 376, 398.

16. Quoted in Ball, *Indeh*, 50.

17. Ibid.

18. Davis, *Truth about Geronimo*, 144. Quoted in Sweeney, *Cochise to Geronimo*, 398. Also in Utley, *Geronimo*, 157; also in Debo, *Geronimo*, 234–35.

19. Davis, *Truth about Geronimo*, 145. Also quoted in Sweeney, *Cochise to Geronimo*, 398.

20. Davis, *Truth about Geronimo*, 146.

21. Kraft, *Gatewood & Geronimo* (Albuquerque, 2000), 135–36. Thrapp, *Al Sieber*, 294; on throat-slitting see Debo, *Geronimo*, 231.

22. Norman Wood, *Lives of Famous Indian Chiefs* (Aurora, IL, 1906); also quoted in Sweeney, *Cochise to Geronimo*, 402.

23. Utley, *Geronimo*, 158; Roberts, *Once They Moved*, 236; Sweeney, *Cochise to Geronimo*, 402–3; Debo, *Geronimo*, 236. Roberts places Lozen there—through Ball, *In the Days of Victorio*, 119.

24. Ball, *In the Days of Victorio*, 177.

25. Davis, *Truth about Geronimo*, 149.

Chapter Thirteen

1. Ball, *Indeh*, 32.

2. Ibid., 250.

3. Kraft, *Gatewood & Geronimo*, 87–88; also in Roberts, *Once They Moved*, 256–57.

4. Davis, *Truth about Geronimo*, 151.

5. Sweeney, *Cochise to Geronimo*, 411.

6. Allan Radbourne, *Mickey Free: Apache Captive, Interpreter, and Scout* (Tucson, 2005), 155; Debo, *Geronimo*, 241; Thrapp, *Conquest of Apacheria*, 314–16; also in Roberts, *Once They Moved*, 257–58.

7. Kraft, *Gatewood & Geronimo*, 89; Utley, *Geronimo*, 161.

8. Debo, *Geronimo*, 241; also in Thrapp, *Conquest of Apacheria*, 318–27.

9. *Silver City Enterprise*, May 22, 1885. Quoted in Stout, *Geronimo*, 79.

10. Quoted in Roberts, *Once They Moved*, 259; also in Stout, *Geronimo*, 79.

11. Sam P. Carursi to President Grover Cleveland, June 15, 1885. Quoted also in Roberts, *Once They Moved*, 259.

12. James G. Warren, "Geronimo, the Wickedest Indian that Ever Lived, Crazed by Imprisonment," *New York World*, August 5, 1900.

13. Henry W. Daly, "The Capture of Geronimo," *American Legion Monthly*, June 1930, 42.

14. From Opler, *Apache Life-Way*, 348.

15. Ibid., 348.

16. Davis, *Truth about Geronimo*, 177–95; Roberts, *Once They Moved*, 262; Debo, *Geronimo*, 270.

17. Davis, *Truth about Geronimo*, 194–95; Utley, *Geronimo*, 172.

18. Ball, *In the Days of Victorio*, 179; Thrapp, *Conquest of Apacheria*, 339; Sweeney, *Cochise to Geronimo*, 480–83; Utley, *Geronimo*, 173–74; rescue of wife and child also in Roberts, *Once They Moved*, 262

19. *Silver City Enterprise*, quoted in Sweeney, *Cochise to Geronimo*, 483.

20. Dan L. Thrapp, *Dateline Fort Bowie: Charles Fletcher Lummis Reports on an Apache War* (Norman, 1979), 162–63; Utley, *Geronimo*, 175, 177, on the "Apache Problem."

21. Quoted in Debo, *Geronimo*, 252; Lozen parley in Ball, *In the Days of Victorio*, 182.

22. http://www.wser.org/records/ Western States 100 website.

23. Opler, *Apache Life-Way*, 74, and 318, 318n.

24. Ibid., 348; also see Ball, *In the Days of Victorio*, 17–18. Crawford's wounding and death see Thrapp, *Dateline Fort Bowie*, 162–181; Kraft, *Gatewood & Geronimo*, 114–15; Utley, *Geronimo*, 180.

Chapter Fourteen

1. Debo, *Geronimo*, 254–55; Bourke, *On the Border with Crook*, 473–74.

2. Bourke, *On the Border with Crook*, 113; Debo, *Geronimo*, 254–56.

3. Davis, *Truth about Geronimo*, 202–3.

4. Ibid., 202.

5. Ibid., 203.

6. Ibid., 202.

7. Ibid., 204–5.

8. Debo, *Geronimo*, 261; Stout, *Geronimo*, 83; Roberts, *Once They Moved*, 270.

9. Quoted in *Crook's Resume of Operations Against Apache Indians, 1882–1886* (London, 1971), 12.

10. Davis, *Truth about Geronimo*, 209.

11. S .C. Gwynne, *Empire of the Summer Moon* (New York, 2010), 57; Bourke, *On the Border with Crook*, 478.

12. Davis, *Truth about Geronimo*, 210.

13. Debo, *Geronimo*, 264; Stout, *Geronimo*, 84; Sweeney, *Cochise to Geronimo*, 524–25; Bourke, *On the Border with Crook*, 480.

14. Barrett, *His Own Story*, 132; Debo, *Geronimo*, 265.

15. Quoted in Thrapp, *Dateline Fort Bowie*, from Lummis's Special Dispatch to the *Times*, 20; Roberts, *Once They Moved*, 274–76.

16. *The American Experience: We Shall Remain—Geronimo.*

17. Quoted in *Crook's Resume of Operations*, 16; Roberts, *Once They Moved*, 275; Debo, *Geronimo*, 268–69.

18. Ibid., 17–18; Faulk, *Geronimo Campaign*, 94–95.

19. *Crook's Resume of Operations*, 19.

20. Newton F. Tolman, *The Search for General Miles* (New York, 1968), 23–25, 30; Nelson A. Miles, *Personal Recollections* (Chicago, 1897), 164–76.

21. Thrapp, *Dateline Fort Bowie*, 64.

22. Ibid., 65.

23. Eugene Chihuahua, quoted in Ball, *Indeh*, 100.

Chapter Fifteen

1. Stout, *Geronimo*, 85; Debo, *Geronimo*, 269.

2. Faulk, *Geronimo Campaign*, 102–3; Sweeney, *Cochise to Geronimo*, 535.

3. Paul I. Wellman, *Death in the Desert* (Lincoln, 1987), 49; Faulk, *Geronimo Campaign*, 190.

4. Barrett, *His Own Story*, 133.

5. *Silver City Enterprise* in Stout, *Geronimo*, 86; Sweeney, *Cochise to Geronimo*, 535–37.

6. Quoted in Debo, *Geronimo*, 270.

7. Ball, *Indeh*, 105.

8. Barrett, *His Own Story*, 133.

9. Goodwin, *Apache Warfare and Raiding*, 301.

10. Ball, *Indeh*, 102.

11. H. W. Lawton, "Report of Capt. Lawton," Typescript, *Arizona Historical Society*, 4–6. On the blood drinking, see Miles, *Recollections*, 491.

12. Roberts, *Once They Moved*, 280.

13. Sweeney, *Cochise to Geronimo*, 467–68.

14. Stout, *Geronimo*, 86.

15. Faulk, *Geronimo Campaign*, 203. They were never paid the three thousand dollars, but each was given a pension; Sweeney, *Cochise to Geronimo*, 556–57.

16. Debo, *Geronimo*, 280; Utley, *Geronimo*, 201; Stout, *Geronimo*, 87.

17. Curiously, it's spelled *Wrattan* with an *a* and *Wratten* with an *e* about equally, depending on the source. Mike likes the *e* spelling—for no particular reason.

18. Charles B. Gatewood, "An Account of the Surrender of Geronimo," Manuscript in Gatewood Collection, *Arizona Pioneers' Historical Society*, Tucson, 56–60. Also quoted in Debo, *Geronimo*, 282; Utley, *Geronimo*, 207.

19. Quoted in Debo, *Geronimo*, 283; from Opler, "Chiricahua Apache's Account," 375–77; *The American Experience: We Shall Remain—Geronimo*.

20. Ball, *Indeh*, 107.

21. Quoted in Debo, *Geronimo*, 283; from Senate Exec Doc. 117, 49 Cong., 2 sess., p. 4.

22. Quoted in Debo, *Geronimo*, 284; Kraft, *Gatewood & Geronimo*, 162–63.

23. Betzinez, *I Fought with Geronimo*, 138; Debo, *Geronimo*, 284–86.

24. Ibid.

25. Quoted in Debo, *Geronimo*, 291–92; from Miles, *Personal Recollections*, 520–21.

26. Quoted in Debo, *Geronimo*, 292.

27. Barrett, *His Own Story*, 136; Debo, *Geronimo*, 295.

28. Barrett, *His Own Story*, 136; final surrender in Faulk, *Geronimo Campaign*, 132–51.

29. Quoted in Roberts, *Once They Moved*, 56; Sweeney, *Cochise*, 251.

Chapter Sixteen

1. Faulk, *Geronimo Campaign*, 169.

2. Ball, *Indeh*, 131; Debo, *Geronimo*, 299–300.

3. Faulk, *Geronimo Campaign*, 164.

4. Ibid. Also Michael Lieder and Jake Page, *Wild Justice: The People of Geronimo vs. the United States* (New York, 1997), 28–29.

5. Faulk, *Geronimo Campaign*, 173; Debo, *Geronimo*, 321.

6. Quoted in Stout, *Geronimo*, 96. Also in Sharon Magee, "The Many Wives of Geronimo," *Arizona Highways* (March 2000), 20.

7. Lieder and Page, *Wild Justice*, 32.

8. Debo, *Geronimo*, 318–19; Betzinez, *I Fought with Geronimo*, 149–59.

9. Stout, *Geronimo*, 97; Magee, "Many Wives of Geronimo," 20. Sources say the young girl was named "Marion" for her birthplace at Fort Marion, but the historical records confirm that they called her "Lenna."

10. Barrett, *His Own Story*, 141.

11. Debo, *Geronimo*, 333.

12. Sherry Robinson, *Apache Voices* (Albuquerque, 2000), 12–13.

13. Schmidt, *Crook*, 292.

14. Ibid., 292–94.

15. Barrett, *His Own Story*, 132.

16. Roberts, *Once They Moved*, 306; *The American Experience: We Shall Remain—Geronimo*; Debo, *Geronimo*, 364; Stout, *Geronimo*, 107.

17. Debo, *Geronimo*, 339–40.

18. *The American Experience: We Shall Remain—Geronimo*.

19. Roberts, *Once They Moved*, 306. (The button and hat sales actually took

place in 1898, while on tour at the International Expo in Omaha. Debo, *Geronimo*, 400–1).

Chapter Seventeen

1.   Debo, *Geronimo*, 365; Leider and Page, *Wild Justice*, 40–41.
2.   Roberts, *Once They Moved*, 306. From Neil Goodwin, *Geronimo and the Apache Resistance* (Peace River Films, Cambridge, MA), 1998.
3.   Barrett, *His Own Story*, 143.
4.   Debo, *Geronimo*, 365. From Hugh Lennox Scott, *Some Memories of a Soldier* (New York, 1928), 182–84.
5.   Barrett, *His Own Story*, 136.
6.   Debo, *Geronimo*, 434; Opler, *Apache Life-Way*, 40–41 and 226.
7.   Debo, *Geronimo*, 443–44; Roberts, *Once They Moved*, 308.
8.   S. M. Barrett, *Geronimo's Story of His Life* (New York, 1907), 15–16. Also in Debo, *Geronimo*, 378.
9.   Marc Wortman, "The Skull—and the Bones," *Vanity Fair*, September 15, 2011. Numbers of Chiricahua are as of 2011.
10. Debo, *Geronimo*, 400; Stout, *Geronimo*, 109.
11. Quoted in Debo, *Geronimo*, 406.
12. Clum, *Apache Agent*, 290.
13. Ibid., 290–91; Debo, *Geronimo*, 406–7; Utley, *Geronimo*, 255–56.
14. Utley, *Geronimo*, 256; Debo, *Geronimo*, 407; Stout, *Geronimo*, 109–11.
15. Debo, *Geronimo*, 423–24; Roberts, *Once They Moved*, 309.
16. http://www.buybooksontheweb.com/peek.aspx?id=1988; Stout, *Geronimo*, 110–11.
17. Debo, *Geronimo*, 412.
18. Utley, *Geronimo*, 256. From *Guthrie* (OK) *Daily Leader*, June 20, 1904.
19. Barrett, *His Own Story*, 156.
20. Wood, *The Lives of Famous Indian Chiefs*, 50; Debo, *Geronimo*, 417.
21. http://blogs.smithsonianmag.com/aroundthemall/2013/01/photos-who-were-the-six-indian-chiefs-in-teddy-roosevelts-inaugural-parade/; Debo, *Geronimo*, 417–19; Stout, *Geronimo*, 111–12.
22. Gywnne, *Empire of the Summer Moon*, 283–87.

23. Clum, *Apache Agent*, 291; http://www.smithsonianmag.com/special sections/heritage/Indians-on-the-Inaugural-March.html?c=y&page=1#; Debo, *Geronimo*, 419; Stout, *Geronimo*, 111.

24. (Richmond, VA) *Times Dispatch*, March 5, 1905.

25. Wood, *Lives of Famous Indian Chiefs*, 556–59; also in *Alexandria* (VA) *Gazette*, March 9, 1905; and *New York Times*, March 10, 1905.

26. Ibid.

Epilogue

1. Barrett, *Geronimo's Story of His Life*; Debo, *Geronimo*, 388.

2. Barrett, *Geronimo's Story of His Life*, iii.

3. Ibid., v.

4. Debo, *Geronimo*, 388–90; Ball, *Indeh*, xiii, 12.

5. Barrett, *His Own Story*, 169–70.

6. Ibid., 144.

7. Ibid., 141.

8. Lieder and Page, *Wild Justice*, 44; Magee, *Geronimo!*, 130–34.

9. Barrett, *His Own Story*, 165.

10. Quoted in Roberts, *Once They Moved*, 314. See "Geronimo's Doleful Plaint," *Denver Times*, October 10, 1898, 3; *New York Tribune*, October 11, 1898.

11. E. A. Burbank, *Burbank among the Indians, as Told by Ernest Royce* (Idaho, 1946), 23, 30–31.

12. Debo, *Geronimo*, 439–42; Utley, *Geronimo*, 262; Magee, *Geronimo!*, 135.

13. Roberts, *Once They Moved*, 314; Debo, *Geronimo*, 443–44; Magee, *Geronimo!*, 136–38.

14. Barrett, *His Own Story*, 110.

15. Ball, *Indeh*, 77.

16. Lieder and Page, *Wild Justice*, 69–70; *The American Experience: We Shall Remain—Geronimo*.

17. Barrett, *His Own Story*, 110; *The American Experience: We Shall Remain—Geronimo*.

18. Frederick Turner, in *Barrett, His Own Story*, 19; *The American Experience: We Shall Remain—Geronimo.*

19. Barrett, *His Own Story*, 110.

20. Ball, *Indeh*, 81; *The American Experience: We Shall Remain—Geronimo;* Debo, *Geronimo*, 440–41; Magee, *Geronimo!*, 137–38.

SELECTED BIBLIOGRAPHY OF WORKS CITED AND CONSULTED

Books

Adams, Alexander B. *Geronimo: A Biography*. New York: G. P. Putnam's Sons, 1971.

Aleshire, Peter. *The Fox and the Whirlwind: General Crook and Geronimo, A Paired Biography*. New York: John Wiley & Sons, Inc., 2000.

Alonso, Ana Maria. *Thread of Blood: Colonialism, Revolution and Gender on Mexico's Northern Frontier*. Tucson: University of Arizona Press, 1995.

Arnold, Eliot. *Blood Brother*. New York: Duell Sloan and Pearce, 1947.

Ball, Eve. *In the Days of Victorio: Recollections of a Warm Springs Apache*. Tucson: University of Arizona Press, 1970.

Ball, Eve, with Noran Henn and Lynda Sanchez. *Indeh: An Apache Odyssey*. Provo, UT: Brigham Young University Press, 1980.

Barnes, Will C. *Apaches and Longhorns: Reminiscences of Will C. Barnes*. Tucson: University of Arizona Press, 1982.

Barrett, S. M. *Geronimo, His Own Story: The Autobiography of a Great Patriot Warrior*. New ed. Revised and edited by Frederick Turner. New York: Penguin, 1996.

———. *Geronimo's Story of His Life: Taken Down and Edited by S. M. Barrett, Superintendent of Education, Lawton, Oklahoma*. New York: Duffield and Company, 1907.

Basso, Keith H. *Western Apache Language and Culture: Essays in Linguistic Anthropology.* Tucson. University of Arizona Press, 1990.

———, ed. *Western Apache Raiding and Warfare, from the Notes of Grenville Goodwin.* Tucson: University of Arizona Press, 1971.

Basso, Keith H., and Morris E. Opler, eds. *Apachean Culture History and Ethnology.* Anthropological Papers of the University of Arizona 21. Tucson: University of Arizona Press, 1971.

Betzinez, Jason, with Wilbur Sturtevant Nye. *I Fought with Geronimo.* Lincoln: University of Nebraska Press, 1959.

Blyth, Lance R. *Chiricahua and Janos: Communities of Violence in the Southwestern Borderlands, 1680–1880.* Lincoln: The University of Nebraska Press, 2012.

Bolton, Herbert E. *Coronado, Knight of Pueblos and Plains.* Albuquerque: University of New Mexico Press, 1949.

Bourke, John G. *An Apache Campaign in the Sierra Madre: An Account of the Expedition in Pursuit of Hostile Chiricahua Apaches in the Spring of 1883.* New York: Charles Scribner's Sons, 1958.

———. *Apache Medicine Men.* New York: Dover Publishing Company, Inc., 1993.

———. *The Diaries of John Gregory Bourke.* Edited by Charles M. Robinson III. Vol 1, November 20, 1872–July 28, 1876. Denton: University of North Texas Press, 2003.

———. *On the Border with Crook.* New York: Charles Scribner's Sons, 1891.

Burbank, E. A. *Burbank among the Indians, as Told by Ernest Royce.* Caldwell, ID: Caxton Printers, LTD, 1946.

Catlin, George. *North American Indians.* Edited and with an introduction by Peter Matthiessen. New York: Penguin Books, 1989.

Clum, Woodworth. *Apache Agent: The Story of John P. Clum.* Lincoln: University of Nebraska Press, 1936. Reprint, Bison Books, 1978.

Coble, John C. *Life of Tom Horn: Government Scout and Interpreter, Written By Himself Together with His Letters and Statements by His Friends.* Denver: Louthan Book Company, 1904.

Collins, Charles. *Apache Nightmare: The Battle at Cibecue Creek.* Norman: University of Oklahoma Press, 1999.

————. *The Great Escape: The Apache Outbreak of 1881*. Tucson: Westernlore Press, 1994.

Cortes, Jose. *Views from the Apache Frontier: Report on the Northern Provinces of New Spain*. Edited by Elizabeth A. H. John. Translated by John Wheat. Norman: University of Oklahoma Press, 1989.

Cozzens, Peter. *Eyewitnesses to the Indian Wars*. Mechanicsburg, PA: Stackpole, 2002.

Cremony, John C. *Life among the Apaches, 1850–1868*. Glorietta, NM: Rio Grande Press, Inc., 1970.

Crook, George. *Annual Report, U.S. Army Dept. of Arizona*, Prescott, AZ, 1883.

————. *Crook's Resume of Operations against Apache Indians, 1882–1886*. Introduction and notes by Barry C. Johnson. London: Johnson-Taunton Military Press, 1971.

————. *General George Crook: His Autobiography*. Edited by Martin F. Schmitt. Norman: University of Oklahoma Press, 1946.

Cruse, Thomas. *Apache Days and After*. Caldwell, ID: Caxton Printers, LTD., 1941.

Davis, Britton. *The Truth about Geronimo*. Edited by M. M. Quaife, with a foreword by Robert M. Utley. Lincoln: University of Nebraska Press, 1976 (1929).

Debo, Angie. *Geronimo: The Man, His Time, His Place*. Norman: University of Oklahoma Press, 1976.

Deloria, Vine, Jr. *Red Earth, White Lies: Native Americans and the Myth of Scientific Fact*. Golden, CO: Fulcrum Publishing, 1997.

Derr, Mark. *A Dog's History of America: How Our Best Friend Explored, Conquered, and Settled a Continent*. New York: North Point Press, 2004.

Faulk, Odie B. *The Geronimo Campaign*. New York: Oxford University Press, 1969.

Gatewood, Charles B. *Lt. Charles B. Gatewood and His Apache Wars Memoir*. Edited and with additional text by Louis Kraft. Lincoln: University of Nebraska Press, 2005.

Goodwin, Greenville. *Western Apache Raiding and Warfare*. Tuscon: University of Arizona Press, 1971.

Green, Robert. *The 48 Laws of Power*. New York: Penguin, 2000.

Gwynne, S. C. *Empire of the Summer Moon: Quanah Parker and the Rise and Fall of the Comanches, the Most Powerful Indian Tribe in American History.* New York: Scribner, 2010.

Haley, James L. *Apaches: A History and Culture Portrait.* New York: Doubleday, 1981.

Kraft, Louis. *Gatewood & Geronimo.* Albuquerque: University of New Mexico Press, 2000.

Lamar, Howard R. *The New Encyclopedia of the American West.* New Haven, CT: Yale University Press, 1998.

Leider, Michael, and Jake Page. *Wild Justice: The People of Geronimo vs. the United States.* New York: Random House, 1997.

Levy, Buddy. *Conquistador: Hernan Cortes, King Montezuma, and the Last Stand of the Aztecs.* New York: Bantam, 2008.

———. *River of Darkness: Francisco Orellana's Legendary Voyage of Death and Discovery Down the Amazon.* New York: Bantam, 2011.

Lockwood, Frank C. *The Apache Indians.* Lincoln: University of Nebraska Press, 1938.

Magee, Sharon S. *Geronimo! Stories of an American Legend.* Phoenix: Arizona Highways Books, 2002.

Mails, Thomas E. *The People Called Apache.* Englewood Cliffs, New Jersey: Prentice Hall, 1974.

Miles, Nelson A. *Personal Recollections.* Chicago: Werner, 1897.

Mort, Terry. *The Wrath of Cochise.* New York: Pegasus Books, 2013.

Ogle, Ralph H. *Federal Control of the Western Apaches, 1848–1886.* Albuquerque: University of New Mexico Press, 1970.

Opler, Morris E. *An Apache Life-Way: The Economic, Social, and Religious Institutions of the Chiricahua Apache Indians.* Chicago: University of Chicago Press, 1941.

———. *Apache Odyssey: A Journey between Two Worlds.* New York: Holt, Rinehart, and Winston, 1969.

———. *Myths and Tales of the Chiricahua Apache Indians.* Memoirs of the American Folk-Lore Society Volume XXXVII, 1942.

Page, Jake. *In the Hands of the Great Spirit: The 20,000 Year History of American Indians.* New York: Free Press, 2003.

Porter, Joseph C. *Paper Medicine Man: John Gregory Bourke and His American West.* Norman: University of Oklahoma Press, 1986.

Radbourne, Allan. *Mickey Free: Apache Captive, Interpreter, and Indian Scout.* Tucson: Arizona Historical Society, 2005.

Roberts, David. *Once They Moved Like the Wind: Cochise, Geronimo, and the Apache Wars.* New York: Simon & Schuster, 1993.

Robinson, Sherry. *Apache Voices: Their Stories of Survival as Told to Eve Ball.* Albuquerque: University of New Mexico Press, 2000.

Santee, Ross. *Apache Land.* Lincoln: University of Nebraska Press, 1973.

Schwartz, Marion. *A History of Dogs in the Early Americas.* New Haven: Yale University Press, 1997.

Shapard, Bud. *Chief Loco: Apache Peacemaker.* Norman: University of Oklahoma Press, 2010.

Simmons, Marc. *Massacre on the Lordsburg Road: A Tragedy of the Apache Wars.* College Station: Texas A & M University Press, 2004.

———. *The Last Conquistador: Juan de Onate and the Settling of the Far Southwest.* Norman: University of Oklahoma Press, 1991.

Sonnichsen, C. L. *Geronimo and the End of the Apache Wars.* Lincoln: University of Nebraska Press, 1990.

Stout, Mary A. *Geronimo: A Biography.* Santa Barbara, CA: Greenwood Press, 2009.

Stockel, H. Henrietta. *Chiricahua Apache Women and Children: Safekeepers of the Heritage.* College Station: Texas A & M University Press, 2000.

———. *Women of the Apache Nation.* Foreword by Dan L. Thrapp. Reno: University of Nevada Press, 1991.

Sweeney, Edwin R. *Cochise: Chiricahua Apache Chief.* Norman: University of Oklahoma Press, 1991.

———. *From Cochise to Geronimo: The Chiricahua Apaches, 1874–1886.* Norman: University of Oklahoma Press, 2010.

———. *Mangas Coloradas: Chief of the Chiricahua Apaches.* Norman: University of Oklahoma Press, 1998.

Tate, Michael L. *The Frontier Army in the Settlement of the West.* Norman: University of Oklahoma Press, 1999.

Thrapp, Dan L. *Al Sieber, Chief of Scouts.* Norman: University of Oklahoma Press, 1995.

———. *The Conquest of Apacheria.* Norman: University of Oklahoma Press, 1967.

———. *Dateline Fort Bowie: Charles Fletcher Lummis Reports on an Apache War.* Edited, annotated, and with an introduction by Dan L. Thrapp. Norman: University of Oklahoma Press, 1979.

———. *Encyclopedia of Frontier Biography,* 3 vols. Lincoln and Spokane: University of Nebraska Press and the Arthur H. Clark Company, 1994.

———. *General Crook and the Sierra Madre Adventure.* Norman: University of Oklahoma Press, 1972.

———. *Juh: An Incredible Indian.* El Paso: Texas Western Press, 1973, 1992.

Tolman, Newton F. *The Search for General Miles.* New York: Putnam, 1968.

Traywick, Ben T. *N'de, the People.* Tombstone, AZ: Red Marie's, 2003.

Utley, Robert M. *Geronimo.* New Haven: Yale University Press, 2012.

Warren, Louis S. *Buffalo Bill's America: William Cody and the Wild West Show.* New York: Knopf, 2005.

Watt, Robert. *Apache Tactics 1830–86.* Oxford: Osprey, 2012.

Weems, John Edward. *Death Song: The Last of the Indian Wars.* New York: Doubleday & Company, Inc., 1976.

Wellman, Paul I. *Death in the Desert.* Lincoln: University of Nebraska Press, 1987(1935).

Wood, Norman B. *The Lives of Famous Indian Chiefs.* Aurora, IL: American Indian Historical Publication Company, 1906.

Articles, Films, and Other Sources

Adelman, Jeremy and Stephen Aron. "From Borderland to Borders: Empires, Nation States, and the Peoples in between in North American History." *The American Historical Review,* Vol. 104, No. 3 (June 1999), 814–41.

Alexandria (VA) Gazette, March 9, 1905.

American Experience: We Shall Remain—Geronimo. PBS (Film) 2009.

Ball, Eve, and Eustace Fatty. "Chiricahua Legends." *Western Folklore,* Vol. 15, No 2, (April 1956), 110–12.

————. "The Apache Scouts: A Chiricahua Appraisal." *Arizona and the West*, Vol. 7, No. 4 (Winter, 1965), 315–28.

Bass, Carole. "Apaches Sue to Recover Geronimo's Skull." *Yale Alumni Newsletter*, May/June 2009.

Bering Strait Land Bridge Theory. http://www.native-languages.org/bering .htm.

Bourke, John G. "Distillation by Early American Indians." *American Anthropologist*, Vol. 7, No. 3 (Jul. 1894), 297–99.

Elliot, Charles P. "An Indian Reservation Under General George Crook." *Military Affairs*, Vol 12, No. 2 (Summer 1948), 91–102.

Ellis, Richard N. "The Humanitarian Generals." *Western Historical Quarterly*, Vol. 3, No. 2 (April 1972), 169–78.

Forbes, Jack D. "The Appearance of Mounted Indian in Northern Mexico and the Southwest, to 1680." *Southwestern Journal of Anthropology*, Vol 15, No. 2 (Summer 1959), 189–212.

Geronimo: An American Legend. Columbia Pictures (Film) 1993.

Goodwin, Neil. *Geronimo and the Apache Resistance.* Cambridge, MA: Peace River Films, 1998.

Haes, Brenda L. *Incarceration of the Chiricahua Apaches, 1886–1994: A Portrait of Survival.* Thesis in History, Texas Tech University, 1997.

Jastrzembski, Joseph C. "Treacherous Towns in Mexico: Chiricahua Apache Personal Narratives of Horror." *Western Folklore*, Vol 54, No. 3 (July 1995), 169–96.

Lawton, H. W. "Report of Capt. Lawton." Typescript. *Arizona Historical Society*, 4–6.

Magee, Sharon S. "The Many Wives of Geronimo." *Arizona Highways* (March 2000), 20.

Native American Prisoners of War: Chiricahua Apaches 1886–1914. http:// www.chiricahua-apache.com/.

New York Times, March 10, 1905.

New York Tribune, October 11, 1898.

Norrell, Brenda. Smithsonian's Morbid Collection of Indian Skulls. http:// narcosphere.narconews.com/notebook/brenda-norrell/2011/06/smith sonians-morbid-collection-indian-skulls-0.

Oliva, Leo E. "The Army and the Indian." *Military Affairs*, Vol. 38, No. 3 (October 1974), 117–19.

Opler, Morris E. "Chiricahua Apache Material Related to Sorcery." *Primitive Man*, Vol 19, No. 3 / 4 (July–October 1946), 81–92.

———. "Humor and Wisdom of Some American Indian Tribes." *New Mexico Anthropologist*, Vol. 3, No. 1 (September–October 1938), 3–10.

———, and Harry Hoijer. "The Raid and War-Path Language of the Chiricahua Apache." *American Anthropologist*, New Series, Vol. 42, No 4, Part 1 (October–December 1940), 617–34.

PBS, *The West*. http://www.pbs.org/weta/thewest/people/index.htm.

Reitz, Stephanie. "Geronimo's Descendants Sue Yale's Skull and Bones over Remains." *The Huffington Post*, February 18, 2009.

(Richmond, VA) *Times Dispatch*, March 5, 1905.

Silver City Enterprise, May 22, 1885.

Smithsonian Magazine. http://blogs.smithsonianmag.com/aroundthemall/2013/01/photos-who-were-the-six-indian-chiefs-in-teddy-roosevelts-inaugural-parade/.

"The U.S. Cavalry." *History Magazine*. http://www.history-magazine.com/cavalry.html.

Truett, Samuel. "The Ghosts of Frontiers Past: Making and Unmaking Space in the Borderlands." *Journal of the Southwest*, Vol 46, No. 2, Scholarship from the William P. Clements Center for Southwest Studies (Summer 2004), 309–50.

Warren, James G. "Geronimo, the Wickedest Indian that Ever Lived, Crazed by Imprisonment." *New York World*, August 5, 1900.

"Wayfinders—Polynesian History and Origin." http://www.pbs.org/wayfinders/polynesian6.html.

Wortman, Marc. "The Skull—and the Bones." *Vanity Fair*, September 15, 2011.

Wrattan, Albert E. "George Wratten, Friend of the Apaches." *Journal of Arizona History* 27, No. 1 (Spring 1986), 91-124.

INDEX